Bard books by
Ishmael Reed

SHROVETIDE IN
OLD NEW ORLEANS

ISHMAEL REED

 A DISCUS BOOK/PUBLISHED BY AVON BOOKS

AVON BOOKS
A division of
The Hearst Corporation
959 Eighth Avenue
New York, New York 10019

Copyright © 1978 by Ishmael Reed
Published by arrangement with Doubleday and Company, Inc.
Library of Congress Catalog Card Number: 76-42386

ISBN: 0-380-42937-3

First Discus Printing, March, 1979

DISCUS TRADEMARK REG. U.S. PAT. OFF. AND IN
OTHER COUNTRIES, MARCA REGISTRADA, HECHO EN
U.S.A.

Printed in the U.S.A.

Grateful acknowledgment is made by the author to the editors of the following mazagines and newspapers, where many of these articles first appeared, for permission to reprint.

"The Liberal in Us All" first appeared in Spring/Summer 1976 issue of *Antaeus,* copyright © 1976 by Antaeus. Reprinted by permission; "Music: Black, White and Blue" in *Black World,* December 1972, "De Mayor of Harlem" in *Black World,* April 1972, "Before the War . . ." in *Black World,* February 1973, "The Song Turning Back Into Itself" in *Black World,* September 1972, "Ishmael Reed Self Interview" in *Black World,* June 1974. Copyright © 1972, 1973, 1974 by Black World. Reprinted by permission of Johnson Publishing Company, Incorporated; "The Old Music" first appeared in *City* magazine, January 1975, copyright 1975 by Ishmael Reed. Reprinted by permission of City Publishing Co.; "The Great Tenure Battle of 1977" (interview with Ishmael Reed by Jon Ewing) appeared in *The Daily Californian*'s Friday magazine, January 28, 1977; "Doyle Foreman" appeared in *Encore,* Spring 1972. Reprinted by permission; "Native Son Lives!" first appeared in *Literary Cavalcade,* Vol. 28, No. 2, November 1975. Copyright © 1975 by Ishmael Reed; "The Multi-Cultural Artist" first appeared in *Le Monde,* June 11, 1976, copyright © Ishmael Reed, 1976; "Born to Rebel" in the New York *Times,* April 25, 1971, "Gliberals" in the New York *Times,* March 31, 1973, "The Greatest, My Own Story" in the New York *Times Book Review,* November 30, 1975, "Harlem Renaissance Day" in the New York *Times,* August 29, 1976, "Remembering Josephine" in the New York *Times Book Review,* December 12, 1976, "The World Needs More Guys . . ." originally titled "Pee Wee's Wreath" in the New York *Times* (Op-Ed), December 16, 1976. All by Ishmael Reed. Copyright © 1971, 1973, 1975, 1976 by The New York Times Company. Reprinted by permission; "Image and Money" originally titled "Blacks Must Put 'Filthy' Money to Work" first appeared in December 26, 1974, issue of the Los Angeles *Times.* Reprinted by permission; "Shrovetide in Old New Orleans" originally appeared as "Voodoo in New Orleans" in *Oui* magazine, January 1977. Copyright © 1977 by Ishmael Reed. Reprinted by permission; "A Westward Movement" first appeared in San Francisco *Examiner Chronicle,* May 26, 1973. Reprinted by permission; "Letter to Roger W. Gaess . . ." appeared in *Small Press Review,* Vol. 6, No. 3, March 5, 1974. Reprinted by permission; "A Treasury of Afro-American Folklore" in Washington *Post,* August 6, 1976, "The Children of Ham" in Washington *Post,* April 11, 1976. Copyright © 1976 by The Washington Post. Reprinted by permission.

Contents

Contents

to the Reeds

SHROVETIDE IN
OLD NEW ORLEANS

Introduction

Writing. It has its ups and downs. Saturday night you're the host to a visiting Emperor; your toast contains two more lines than his. His Empress gives you the eye over her Japanese fan. Monday morning they got a crude wall-poster up and all of your business is in the streets. "Scoundrel . . . traitor . . . misogynist." "Renegade" is misspelled. As I write this it's Saturday night, but before it's all over it might end up Monday.

I am sitting in the Sitka Hotel, Sitka, Alaska. Through the window I can see the steeple of the Greek Orthodox Church, St. Michael's, whose architecture reminds one that Russians once occupied this territory. In the distance, I can see Arrowhead Mount Verstovia. Yesterday I walked down "lover's lane," near the Visitor Center of Sitka National Park, Alaska; walking among the Tlingit totems, totems of satire, often topped with Europeans wearing silly top hats. One of the faces was contorted with remorse. It was that of a Russian, who looked stylized, gloomy, and Neptune-like; he had violated a fishing agreement he made with the Tlingit. According to the ancient form of Tlingit satire, you take down your enemy's totem when he makes compensation for the wrong he committed against you. Apparently, this Russian never made compensation. Before I depart today from this strange land, I will walk through the forest with my hosts, pointing out the similarity between turtles, elephants, faces, and tree branches, as though Nature often attempts to become that which it admires.

Last night I sat talking with Eskimo artists Larry Ahva-kana and Joe Senungetuk, Aleut artist Fred Anderson, and Tlingit poet Andrew Hope, in the home of Andy's sister. Wayne Shorter's Brazilian music on his album "Native Dancer" was spinning. A framed black and white painting on the wall inspired a conversation about monsters. It showed a monster leaving a cabin in the woods. My hosts mention about six monsters which inhabit the area, the principal ones being "the Tlingit land otter," and "the Eskimo little men." I asked them had they heard of the underground continent Admiral Byrd was supposed to have discovered when he reached a mountain near the North Pole. No one up here thinks that this kind of conversation is crazy.

My writing has brought me here as guest of their Raven's Bones Foundation. We wish to include Raven's Bones in a large multicultural group, the Before Columbus Foundation, of which I am Chairman of the Board, and Bob Callahan, president of the Turtle Island Foundation, is Secretary.

It has been about two years since the raven appeared in my writing, led there by the Southwest coyote stories, introduced to me in 1974 by Leslie Silko, the novelist. And it's been about a year since Bob Callahan passed the word that Andrew Hope, descendant of the Tlingit warrior Katlian who, in 1802, led a fight on a Russian fort armed with only blacksmith's hammer and Raven's head, owned my books. (For his efforts Katlian has been described by historians as "surly" and "impertinent.") A correspondence began and shortly afterwards my house began filling up with Ravens. Raven books. Raven posters. Raven paraphernalia. As though my writing had conjured up the Raven.

I cannot express the uncanny feeling that came over me as I read Raven Quickskill's monologue, interior monologue, stream of consciousness, and narrative in *Flight to Canada's* first chapter while a movie screen Raven, provided for me by Andy, stared down at me. I read my work among the totems of the Tlingit museum. Outside I could hear the tides rolling in from the near Pacific. Sitka, in Tlingit, means "from-the-island-looking-out." One of the postcards had announced that the Tlingit culture was "vanishing" but Andrew Hope had, before I began, announced that the Raven's Bones Foundation was going to restore that which had been nearly destroyed by invaders. This is what my kind of writing is all about. It leads me to the places where I can see old cultures resurrected, and made contemporary. Time past is time present. This is why writing is good to me. It has made me a better man. It has put me in contact with those fleeting moments which prove the existence of soul. It gives me something to do. It keeps my body out of trouble. I mean, there isn't much else to do if you're sitting down typing away unless you know Rosemary Woods type Medicine Show stunts.

I guess I'm an old fashioned triadist at heart. My body has had a good time; my spirit has dined with the gods; but my mind—a parapsychologist, on television, said the other night that the mind might exist outside of the body; perhaps it exists outside of the spirit too, that would make sense; the body and the spirit are reported to look alike, the only difference being that one's solid and one isn't. While my body and my spirit are living it up my mind has suffered depression, anxiety, metaphysical guilt about the state of the world, the state of the nation, and for "personal problems" the only prescription seems to be writing in the essay form, which has received a bad reputation. When a critic—usually one with a political bent—wants to put your fiction down he calls it "essays" or "tracts" even though you use italics to indicate it's someone else's thoughts.

Perhaps, if nothing else, this book will show that I know the difference between an essay and a work of fiction, even though critics don't, and use a variety of techniques associated with both forms.

My body is a solid—except for a paunch that's a celebrity, having been written up in the Washington *Evening Star*, and is held by a big frame. Sit-ups are forcing the paunch back into its place. A middle-class complaint.

3

Could be a leper, or twisted, burnt or partially destroyed.

If my mind had a body it would be slight with birdlike bones. It would wear glasses and go live in a furnished room with strange pictures on the wall. It would play the flute and have women mamma it. It would haunt the coffee shops searching out conversation about Visionary Things. It would go to the library and say pardon me to everybody. My real body dwells in an on-the-make working-class neighborhood of campers, and friendly children, and huge dogs which howl at noon. "I thought you'd look like a ninety-eight-pound intellectual—serious," and well, you know. I lose more fans that way.

I lose fans and friends too because I'm blunt. A heathen, basically, I have cultivated as many enemies as friends, like the San Francisco cowboys who accuse me of being "arrogant" and "pompos [sic]." So, unlike many black writers who write autobiographies of the spirit, the body, or the mind, I don't love everybody. How many people do you know who use love as the old pitchmen used to use "Wizard Oil"? Because of questions like the last one these people who go around loving everybody say I write out of hurt. I do. Sometimes, maybe. I'm a heathen. A one-man heathen horde. When it hurts I say so and when it feels good I say so, too. Like sometimes I say ahhhhhhh, that feels good, usually during brilliant non-verbal moments.

Some of the following essays were written out of hurt, like "Pee Wee's Wreath," and some written from love like the review of "Remembering Josephine." I am human and don't devote my time to just one emotion. I'm not a flower child, (nor am I Hitler, who was probably, at heart, a flower child). I even get mad and jealous, emotions most people I know have gotten over, hear them tell it. I wouldn't part with any of these emotions. Jealousy and love are different perfumes from the same root. I live big, I eat big, love big, and when I die I'll die big.

Let me share with you a little demonic episode that, at an early age, showed me the power of writing. There was this creepy pre-Hitchcockian teacher character in

4

third-year English class who kept hassling me about "malapropisms." Her condition grew chronic and she began accusing me of ridiculing her when most of the time I was staring blankly out of the window. I had never heard of a "neurosis." When she assigned essay topics I chose "A Strange Profession," and wrote a fictional essay about an insane teacher who lived with her mother and indulged in bizarre practices with dogs and cats. Everybody else got their papers back; I was sent to the office. After a talk with the principal, who asked me did I know the meaning of all of those "big words," I said yes (I made a practice of carrying about a pocket dictionary). For the remainder of that semester I took English alone, in a room to myself. I thought it was punishment but at the end of that semester I received a B-plus. Later I learned that they didn't know whether to give me an A or to commit me; critics still have the problem with my work. I used to be a discipline problem, which caused me embarrassment until I realized that being a discipline problem in a racist society is sometimes an honor.

Later, while working as a stock clerk at a supermarket on Main Street, I saw that same teacher walking down the aisle. She introduced the older woman to me as "my mother." "A Strange Profession" was an early essay. Before that, while working in a drugstore stuffing my pockets with Mars bars and mixing myself milkshakes I wrote an essay in 1952 about how America was going to the dogs because Adlai Stevenson had lost to Eisenhower. About the same time I wrote a jazz column for the *Empire State Weekly* on Broadway across the street from St. Mary's Church. I wrote heads like "Sonny Stitt's It at the Copa Casino." After dropping out of college I returned to work for the newspaper and was staff correspondent under Joe Walker, who replaced my boss, A. J. Smitherman, a courtly, gentle, 1900s quality person who wrote light poetry. He used to work twenty-four hours a day to get his newspaper out and was constantly staving off creditors. When he died the Buffalo *Evening News* described him as "indefatigable." Joe Walker, now New York correspondent for *Muhammad Speaks,* was twenty-eight at the time, and I was twenty-two. Buffalo couldn't hold on to me and so I ended up in New York, green, country, and ready to write. I started writing visionary poetry and began to hang out with a group of writers called the Umbra Workshop. Some of them formed the aesthetic and intellectual wing of the Black Power movement. They didn't have any money and I used to support some of them in a house on East Fifth Street. While I worked they wrote great poems. Like this one fellow, whatever he calls himself, now accusing me of being in cahoots with capitalists, tyrants, and right-wingers, who told me that he was "a great poet" and "dying of cancer." I wrote my mother and said, "Look, Mom, I'm helping out this guy who's a great poet and dying of cancer." My mom said, "They're bums." I said, "No, Mom, they're great writers and great poets dying of cancer." If it were an election bet I would have ended up pushing a peanut up Main Street by the tip of my nose. Anyway, I was the first patron of the intellectual and aesthetic wing of the Black Power movement. I have helped more writers than Pound and Van Vechten put together. I've published writers I've had fistfights with. As long as they can write.

I returned to writing essays in 1964 at about the time a painter and I began the *East Village Other,* sometimes called, "The Mother" of underground newspapers. A "Black Power" article lost friends because I claimed that there were more black "Americans," than black "Nationalists." A racist cartoon the editor attached to the article didn't help.

The following essays form an autobiography of my mind starting in about 1970. Those printed shortly before have been printed as poetry and one is included in *Essaying Essays, Alternative Forms of Exposition,* an anthology compiled by Richard Kostelanetz. The essay he published, "The Neo-HooDoo Manifesto," came as close to a revelation as I'll ever come. It was sent from "spirit" land and written for HooDoos.

Most of the essays in this book were written for mass publication: newspapers and magazines.

I can't say which form, fiction, poetry, or the essay, requires the most discipline. Writing is hard work, don't let anybody fool you, all of yawl who call me up and say, "I'm a black writer; get me published." I'd say I get the most kicks out of writing poetry; fiction is the second most fun; the essay is the ditch-digging occupation of writing. I spend a lot of time running up and down the stairs for Facts!

Many people have called my fiction muddled, crazy, incoherent, because I've attempted in fiction the techniques and forms painters, dancers, film makers, musicians in the West have taken for granted for at least fifty years, and the artists of many other cultures, for thousands of years. Maybe I should hang my fiction in a gallery, or play it on the piano.

One thing common to my fiction, essays, and poetry; they don't claim to know all of the answers. They don't feel that life has to be a heavy Russian Dostoevskian din of intense pain as some of the junior existentialist Eisenhower Era critics from Harvard who own a closet full of trench coats and dangle their cigarettes like Camus, require black writers to believe. The crying towel doesn't show up in my writing; I feel a little uneasy crying the blues when my life is more comfortable than that of perhaps 70 percent of the people in the world and when I'm luckier than many of my enemies because I am able to work at projects which give me satisfaction.

I see life as mysterious, holy, profound, exciting, serious, and fun. The so-called "humor" which appears in my work is affirmative, positive. It teaches people, institutions, and me to be humble, not to take ourselves too seriously. This kind of humor has been a feature of multi-cultural art for thousands of years, like these totems in Sitka, the thousands of masks from Oceania, and the continent of Africa, the "little men" stories of the Celts, and the thousands of animal fables from all over the world. The fool stories which have taught generations of people how to be wise.

Maybe I should become a "stand-up" comedian as

some of my critics suggest—critics who would deny the artistic accomplishments of the American Medicine Shows, Newspapers, Vaudeville, Minstrelsy, the superior talents of Bert Williams, W. C. Fields, Lenny Bruce, Richard Pryor, Mark Twain, Jonathan Winters, and Bill Cosby. There these critics sit, poisoning the universities with their bewildering provincial attitudes.

Imagine me at Harrah's. A view of the lake. A French chef. I might even learn how to ski. I wouldn't have to worry about people keeping my books in some warehouse, presumably because they want them to be safe. I could hire someone to lock me in a velvet closet with candy apples and the complete works of Earl Hines, and Chester Himes when that fool pisces moon rolls around and the knave in me beckons to be let out.

Imagine me standing there, a black tuxedo, five thousand per night, David and Julie in the front row. But I always come back to my writing. It has brought me shelter from the winter and the wolves, both one-headed and two-headed—it has given a little quality to my act. It has introduced me to extreme depression, and jubilance. It has made me feel on top of the world. It's like an exotic woman I once knew. When she was away I was the meanest man in town, but when she was with me I was the easiest to get along with.

And so today—I feel honored to be a writer. In a few hours they will open the museum especially for me and Bob. Downstairs I'll have a lumberjack's breakfast. Although the rednecks operate the mills up here, they belong to the Japanese, and the Japanese count the change. Only in America. Rednecks fronting for Japanese. The Ravens haven't been around but now they're downstairs lined up like what the Russians used to call them, the North Archangel Police.

I expect this installment of an autobiography of my mind to receive the same kind of reception as my fiction and poetry. Controversial. Stir things up a bit. Wake America from its easy chair and can of beer. For example, the essay "An American Romance" was commissioned by the Los Angeles *Times,* which turned it down for fear of "repercussions"; it was then turned down by the Washington *Post* for being too short and by the New York *Times* for being too long.

I've also included "The Great Tenure Battle of 1977." You be the judge.

Ishmael Reed
Hotel Sitka
Sitka, Alaska
November 29, 1976

Shrovetide in Old New Orleans

Purists refer to it as Vodou or Vodoun, a word with Dahomean, and Togo, origins meaning "the unknown." In
the Americas, it has come to mean the fusion of dance,
drums, embroidery, herbal medicine, and cuisine of
many African nations whose people were brought to Haiti
during the slave trade. It is an element in many of the
syncretistic religions of South America (Pocomania, Umbanda, Santería), which, combined, claim more followers
than Christianity. There has been a religious war in Brazil
for years with the Vodoun cults now gaining the upper
hand. Vodoun has always had a remarkable ability to
blend with other religions, even those considered its rivals.
Edmund Wilson writes: "I was once in Haiti near Christmas and found that the Christmas cards, along with
'Joyeux Noel,' were sometimes decorated with a snake."
(The snake represented St. Patrick and was based upon
the symbol for Damballah, the oldest loa of the cults,
said to be a white python which appears every thousand
years.) Haitian Vodoun is said to be more "African" than
the "African" religions who've been influenced by the colonialists. The Haitians always kicked the rascals out, a feat
which struck dread in the hearts of southern slaveholders,
who felt that the spirit to revolt (Ogun, loa of iron, and
war) might be catching. Adalbert Volck, that genius
of Confederate cartoonists, the American Bosch, depicted
Lincoln as a satanic figure, signing the Emancipation
Proclamation, with grinning demons next to the ink bottle
and peering through the room's windows. Above Lincoln's
head, in a painting entitled "Santa Domingo, and Haiti,"

Negroes are seen putting the machete to the struggling whites. The Southerners felt that what happened to the colonial French would happen to them.

In the United States, Vodoun became "HooDoo," a word which appeared in about the 1890s, when Marie Laveau, the First, a HooDoo Queen, held power in New Orleans. Dimmed were the Haitian practices, which one scholar has described as "Baroque." The ceremonies were no longer secret and whites were invited, by Marie Laveau, the First, an extraordinary show woman, to attend the rites. HooDoo might be called Vodoun, streamlined. In New Orleans it's all over town, invisible to all but the trained eye. Faced with curious and sometimes comical suppression by the police, it never went underground; it merely put on a mask.

In New Orleans, one of the forms it took was what we call "Jazz," a music possibly performed in whorehouses whose madames were "HooDoo Queens" like Marie Laveau, and Mammy Pleasant of San Francisco, who catered to the local captains of industry and finance including officers of the Bank of California. A fearless abolitionist, she was active in the Underground Railroad, and was constantly pursued by the authorities until smuggled out of New Orleans by Marie Laveau.

Vodoun is based upon the belief that the African "gods," or loas, are present in the Americas and often use men and women as their mediums. Men and women of all races, and classes. Fifty per cent of the followers of American HooDoo have been white, including the masters and mistresses of some southern plantations where the "conjure man" or "HooDoo man" was the most powerful figure. Whites operate temples in some parts of South America, are possessed by African loas, and are, in some cases, loas themselves, for example Mademoiselle Charlotte, a French loa who possesses illiterate peasants to speak impeccable French. Augusta, a "tall, blond" woman, was Marie Laveau's assistant and was reported to have been quite good at orgies. The African loas, like the Greek, and Norse gods are very human in their behavior. They love, hate, get jealous, mess around, drink rum, and

12

cause mischief, injury, and even death, on the other hand they are healers, doctors, scientists, intellectuals, artists, warriors and counselors, and they are great dancers; they crawl up and down the side of trees dancing, as certain women do when possessed by Damballah.

They are also tough and persistent. In *All Men Are Mad*, by Philippe Thoby-Marcelin and Pierre Marcelin, a zealous young priest, unaware of the tacit agreement of tolerance between Catholicism and Vodoun, attempts to uproot the local Vodoun shrines. The peasants become possessed by Baron Samedi, the aristocrat of a family of loas known as guedes, and associated with the cemetery. Baron Samedi addresses the young priest through a host the loa has borrowed: "It's me, Baron Samedi, talking to you. What do you think you're doing, knocking down my cross? It's made of wood. You can burn it. But I, who am a loa from Guinea, you won't burn me. You won't chase me away from this country either."

Mardi Gras is also of ancient origins, when it was a celebration involving fornication, self-castration, human sacrifice, and flagellation with goatskin whips. Therefore, it's appropriate that it takes place in the South, where, in a former time, whipping was the chief entertainment. Mardi Gras is polytheistic, just as Vodoun is; it involves drumming and dancing as in Vodoun; both "religions" include ritual masking and costuming. Heathen and Christian rites blend. Mardi Gras is French for "Fat Tuesday," the Tuesday preceding Ash Wednesday. In Mardi Gras, there is a captain who stage-manages the ceremonies for each "krewe," or organization, or cult. In Haiti this role is taken by the Houngan (loosely translated "priest," a word of Fon origin) or Mambo (priestess). One of the big song hits of this Mardi Gras season was "Mardi Gras Mambo," by the Hawkettes.

Both Mardi Gras and Vodoun include secret societies equipped with flags, songs, and other rites unique to each.

On March 3, 1699, a few Frenchmen, with bread and fish, celebrated Mardi Gras at a place called "Pointe du Mardi Gras," or "Bayou du Mardi Gras." Over a century and a half later, in 1857, six young men, from Mobile,

Alabama (the only other American town where Mardi Gras is observed), of the Cowbellion de Rakin Society, organized the Mystick Krewe of Comus, which presented, on February 24, 1857, a New Orleans street parade. Its theme was "The Demon Actors in Milton's Paradise Lost," a Vodoun pageant if there ever was one, since Milton consigns African gods to hell.

Later came Rex, the carnival's elite krewe, which was hurriedly put together for the occasion of the visit to New Orleans of his Imperial Highness Alexis Romanoff Alexandrovitch, heir apparent to the Russian throne. A militant womanizer, the Prince, who had just hunted bison with Buffalo Bill, apparently followed an actress, Miss Lydia Thompson, to New Orleans. She was the star of the musical comedy called *Bluebeard;* according to contemporary accounts the Prince was a little too formal and "stiff" in the land of hospitality and the Colgate smile. He is remembered as being rude to his hosts and refusing to shake people's hands. The Rex song that year, dedicated to his Royalvitch, contained the lines: "If ever I cease to love, If ever I cease to love, May the Grand Duke ride a buffalo/in a Texas rodeo." Some historians claim that this song contributed to the Prince's irritable mood. The song, however, has endured.

Since those days, in the middle 1850s, many other krewes have been added, some formal and some outlaw, as this year's Krewe of Constipation, whose maskers dressed in boxes of Ex-Lax.

The history is interesting, but all but ignored by many of the Mardi Gras revelers. Vodoun interpretations vary from town to town, from family to family, and from individual to individual. Although the forms are similar, no two humfos (temples?) are alike.

"You get together with your friends to eat and drink," is the way San Francisco novelist Ernest Gaines defines Mardi Gras. The college girl, sitting in the aisle seat, on the Delta plane said: "It's like Halloween, I think."

I didn't know that if you planned to travel to New Orleans during the Mardi Gras season you had to book at least six months ahead of time. The motels are full within an eighty-five mile radius of New Orleans. I wound up in the Tamanaca Hotel on Tulane Avenue. It was like Alcatraz if Alcatraz were a ticky tack. I was down for a double but one of the beds had been removed to accommodate other Mardi Gras visitors. It was also a headquarters for some of the students who were attending Mardi Gras. Students are all over town; the place looks like Fort Lauderdale, or some other nesting place for students during the intercollegiate mating season. During the night they spent a lot of time knocking on each other's doors, asking for ice. "Got any ice?" "Hey, where's the ice?" I was feeling cranky. In my day we got our own ice.

Before the young girl and the businessman, who looked like a congressman, got on at Dallas, my companions were a middle-aged couple, which, though nice people, middle-aged is all I could remember about them. They looked like the handsome couple on the Geritol commercials tainted with forties sepia. They were discussing the Patty Hearst case. The front page of the San Francisco *Chronicle* said something about Patty Hearst being dehumanized. A modern word for "sacrificed." Months before I had written a piece, "An American Romance," about how the defense would concoct a story in which Cinque would be the sex-crazed Beast who shambled off with the society girl and traced the plot to Richard Wright's *Native Son,* and *Tarzan, The Ape Man,* both produced during the thirties. The Los Angeles *Times* couldn't handle it; the Washington *Post* said it was too short; the New York *Times,* too long.

I was reading this big book Steve Cannon lent to me, and the nice Geritol lady with the tinted-blue silver hair said, "Is that a heavy book?" I didn't know how to take the remark. The last time I went to New Orleans to visit the principal HooDoo shrine, Marie Laveau's tomb, two white men, who were de-planing at Dallas, noticed the book I was reading and said: "Niggers reading books. Educated niggers."

Besides, I was a little miffed because there was a fly in my coffee. Being a Negro in this society means reading motives in a complicated way. We write good detective novels. Was the stewardess deliberately putting insects into the coffee cups of Negroes? Was this an accident? It was an accident. The stewardess went to fetch me a hot cup of coffee. The lady sitting next to me wasn't the Texan in Dallas. She was genuinely interested in the book. It was a book with exciting and informative illustrations. I told her that I was going to New Orleans and was reading about Mardi Gras. The couple became so interested in Mardi Gras they decided to change their plans and go from Dallas to Mardi Gras. Everybody ended up laughing like integrated ads on television where black football players dash through airports on behalf of Hertz car rental.

An Older Man and a Flower Child got on the plane in Dallas. He is going to meet his family in New Orleans; she, her boyfriend. This is her first Mardi Gras. He is a Mardi Gras pro.

The plane is full of Mardi Gras visitors. There's a gay contingent. Mardi Gras is gay. Female impersonators. "Baby Dolls," as they are called, are everwhere in drag. These gays are dressed as cowboys. They wear turquoise and other jewelry in their belt buckles. They make ambiguous cracks to the male passengers and titillate the women. They pass out champagne and candy to the passengers. New Englanders considered the old Mardi Gras to be wicked. It does have a kind of Louis XIV light-opera decadence. "We bought twenty-two bottles of champagne and have drank twenty-three." In case anybody doesn't get it the man squeals it again.

"The men dress up like women, and do you know, some of them look better." The pro tells her. She's a freshman, eighteen, majoring in political science at the University of Arizona. I would hear this statement a few more times in the coming days. He was discussing Endymion, one of the krewes I'll catch later in the evening. The Older Man tells the Flower Child, "Mardi Gras is a big show, a freak show, which doesn't cost anything." He gave her something before they got off the plane. She clasped it in her hand and said, "I'll never forget you." I'm touched.

I headed from the Tamanaca to Canal Street, where the carnival suddenly came in upon me. One could see people, sitting on the curbs, watching the marchers and floats, all the way up to the Marriott Inn at Canal and Chartres streets. I caught images of corn hot dog vendors with Confederate flags waving from their carts, fried chicken, cotton candy, decorated lampposts, and electricity. The streets were lit up. People were sitting on deck chairs, or on the street curbs, watching. They were drinking beer, wine, and whiskey from thermos bottles.

It was the old populist crowd. Rednecks, country-western types in vans bearing spray-painted illustrations you could bar-b-cue from. Blacks. Not the urbane *New York Magazine* glossy "Superfly" or Negro Gatsby types but people who put on overalls and walk down the street holding their children's hands. This is the "field" division of Negro society. They're a taciturn hard-working bunch. "Their deepest dissent is silence," a slave master once said. They drink corn whiskey and dance at clubs with names like The Honey Hush and do their wash in the Splish Splash Washateria. Sometimes, they stand on the side of roads next to the old Buicks selling crayfish. Mardi Gras' past is not only scandalous and violent, but racist. The Irish of the 1860s used Mardi Gras as "Get Nigger Day," and amused themselves by invading Negro neighborhoods to murder and shoot up people. In the same decade, maskers dressed as apes delighted the crowds by chasing Negroes. Baron de Rothschild, a Jew, was denied entrance to Comus, and Proteus (elite balls formed in 1882). Even today, the floats carry caricatures of Indians with the kinds of faces on the old Cleveland Indians emblems.

For one day the establishment permits the old gods to parade up and down; gods it crushed, often mercilessly. The old gods of the Confederacy are people like Stonewall Jackson, Jefferson Davis, and Robert E. Lee, the last of whom generations of children have been taught was a kind of tragic Prince Valiant who led a noble but lost cause. The Confederate gods are those who tried to restore an imitation Middle Ages, a land of serfs, of Fair Ladies, and cruelty. During Mardi Gras, the old Romance is stirred, and floats bearing "colonels" and soldiers in those dreaded gray uniforms; I even caught a photo of a young man in full Confederate regalia, stranded in a Fiat, as yelping, hooting, "Black Indians" blocked traffic. He was wearing the Confederate battle flag as a head-rag.

The Stars and Bars, America's swastika, waved from everywhere. From balconies, from rooftops, from windows, from corndog carts of peddlers, right alongside the cotton candy. Designed by P. G. T. Beauregard, this symbol of that gothic anachronism, the old South, flies all over America these days. Waving on the lawn where President Ford greeted President Giscard, right alongside the Stars and Stripes; there it was, the morning after Jimmy Carter's Ohio win, on the left side of the future President. Is this harmless, or an omen? I'm thinking, like many other Negroes think when they see this hated flag. A reminder that when the North withdrew its troops, the old Confederate officers, through murder and terror continued slavery as usual, leading Henry Adams, a Louisiana freedman, to say, in 1877, "We lost all hopes. The whole South —every estate in the South—had got into the hands of the very men that held us slaves." Jefferson Davis died with a smile on his face, and down here they celebrate his birthday, and name freeways after him. A man who referred to Africans as a "weak" race, which shows how stoical and cool-headed Negroes are in the face of so much hurt. "Grudgeful hearted," as 133-year-old Charlie Smith would say. Grudgeful hearted politics. Busing! Busing! Busing! "The bus is us," as Jesse Jackson put it. Grudgeful hearted art. People can't even have fun without hurting or bullying somebody. What kind of fun is that?

The Mardi Gras loves Kings and Queens. Another ambition of the old Confederacy. A southern monarchy. Maybe that's why Huey Long tried to eliminate Mardi Gras, he must have seen through this attempt to revive the Confederate dream, old populist that the Kingfish was. The southern aristocrats paid Kingfish back by having their maskers satirize the Kingfish with a procession of marchers in robes and crowns who ridiculed his famous election promise. In the 1976 parade there was a float

18

honoring Huey Long with "Every Man a King" spelled out in flowers.

I am standing in this crowd, catching the tail end of Endymion Parade, Saturday night. The American Endymion is not only in a coma but dreams bellicose floats in his coma dreams. The theme of the parade is "Hail to the Chief." There was a "giant" of JFK and his PT boat. Other floats rolled by with giants of other Presidents; Truman, MacArthur in dark glasses with corncob pipe, Eisenhower, "who supported the anti-communists in Guatemala," and others are remembered for being tough, standing up to the Russians, refusing to bug out. Guns, and missiles roll by. In contrast, Alice Cooper, the rock person, is the grand marshall of this parade and somebody named Irving Wallace, the King. The black Southern University Bands march by doing K.C. and the Sunshine Band's "Get Down Tonight," and it goes on, Endymion, with a Nixon float even, with what appears to be a picture of John Ehrlichman on the side. After it was over I followed the Negroes who were heading towards Shakespeare Park because I figured they knew where something else was going on. There were hundreds of us moving uptown, walking towards the Promised Land for all I knew. It must have been this way when Negroes found out that "slavery," at least on paper, had ended and dropped what they were doing and started walking through the gates of the plantation. Hundreds of them. Walking. To Ohio, for all they knew. As if moving to freedom. From slavery to vagrancy. They got thrown in jail and were forced to work on plantations as punishment. Some of their descendants are in this bunch. Nobody writes about them as well as Ernest Gaines. "I spend time in the country and then, on Mardi Gras day I come into New Orleans," he said. The destination turned out to be the Greyhound bus station. I went into the bar and ordered a Budweiser, lest someone thought I was loitering about Greyhound bus stations these days in my leather jacket, and jeans. Barry Manilow was on the jukebox singing, "I write the songs . . ." The Negroes were boarding their buses, leaving

19

their white Mardi Gras, or "Caucasian" Mardi Gras, as my acquaintance Rudy Lombard, an architect, sneered.

Nobody in an ape's costume chased them this night. Mardi Gras had become civilized, far removed from its sordid past, when the New Orleans newspapers dismissed it as a gathering of rowdies. In fact, the next night, a leading Pan-Africanist intellectual, an independent man who publishes his own poetry, made a speech that could have been delivered by a Kiwanis. About how in a place like Russia he couldn't write his poems for fear of being censored. How America had made progress. This man was a dedicated and *serious* militant and he said, "Why, ten years ago, I wouldn't have been able to even stand here to watch Mardi Gras." I didn't know whether to faint or to salute. I did niether. There had been a lot of jargon, and political abstruseness about the politcal movement in the 1960s. I became cynical very early when I saw some of the militants picking up the habits of the oppressors. Like people who'd participated in Freedom Rides criticized our magazine, *Yardbird,* for printing an interview with George Schuyler, a brilliant political satirist and thinker from the Harlem Renaissance, a high point in American creativity. They wanted to suppress his free speech. They wanted to do to him what they accused white people of doing to them. The revolution had moved to the suburbs. The revolution had a carport.

When I got back to the Tamanaca from the bus station I went to my cave and watched some television. Yul Brynner, playing a Hollywood robot, was chasing some guy through sets from different periods of time. Finally Yul Brynner's cowboy face melted. I went to sleep and dreamed that a Mardi Gras of melting masks was chasing me.

The next morning I headed towards the French Quarter, where the HooDoo shrines are located, the principal one being Marie Laveau's tomb at St. Louis #1, though the name on the stone reads, "Glapion, the Widow Paris." The "VooDoo" museum is located at 1139 Rue Bourbon in New Orleans. It's dives like that give HooDoo a bad name, associating it with "Black Magic" and "Devil

Worship," when the Houngan (from the Fon) is known for his curing abilities, not hexes, and the "devil" does not exist in the Vodoun pantheon, this creation having to do with a Western quarrel—the conflict between the Christians and the old Pan cults, the cults of the "Golden Calf," and other horned gods. Inside was the cliché tourist display of dolls, and "hex" powders. No wonder HooDoo has received such an abominable reputation. Mr. Charles Gandolfo, the curator, unloading boxes. Though there was a "closed" sign on the door Mr. Gandolfo opened the door for me. "I don't usually do this," he said. He was unpacking a box shipped from Samuel Weiser's famous "occult" bookstore in New York City. A box of Tarot cards, a watered-down deck at that, with Camelot figures on it— a bogus deck since the Tarot originates in Africa. As phony as the old South. A black man entered the shop. It was the famous Prince Kyama, or "Chicken Man" as he is known, internationally. America's HooDoo Prince and, according to the Prince, the incarnation of Marie Laveau. "They coming next month to make a film on me," the Prince said. Tourists travel from Canada, and from all over the United States to see the Prince; they live in campers outside of town and send in emissaries to make contact with him.

"How about a photo for the folks in Detroit, Prince," said some collegiate-looking Negro kids as we walked down Bourbon Street. He makes a living "geeking," lying in caskets, handling rattlesnakes, and putting on shows for tourists who happen into the "VooDoo" museum. Some innocent-looking college girls entered the shop. He invited them to come on his "VooDoo Underground" tour. When they declined, he invited them to attend a concert, happening that night, in which he would perform with Doctor John. "He isn't the original Doctor John," I said. Prince Kyama was unacquainted with the original Doctor John. This should have deterred me from taking the "Underground" tour, but I decided that this was a case of consumer fraud which might be interesting. I had, a week before, paid fifty dollars to a plumber for sticking a pole down a stuffed toilet. A few weeks before I paid for the same automobile repair job twice and when I told the chief mechanic that I thought his operation was slippery he looked at me as though I was crazy.

The Prince was wearing beads made of turquoise and silver, fringed jacket, a bamboo hat shaped like a Stetson, a red and yellow checked jacket, and Bruce Lee T-shirt with Bruce Lee painted on it posing before a Dragon all done in snazzy graphics. He said that Bruce Lee was his student. The Prince had a lot of stories. He was born in Haiti, and had come to New Orleans only a few years before and now he had the whole scene. Oh, the police had busted him a few times for the chicken act, but outside of that he was well known and would star in a film. He told one fellow he owned 1,000 acres of land in Texas. For ten dollars he showed me Marie Laveau's tomb, a cottage reputed to have been invaded where the first black was said to have been hanged. I already knew about the tomb and the house.

Reluctantly and impatiently the Prince pointed out a beauty salon, on the reported location of one owned by Marie Laveau. It's very hard to separate the Laveau legend from fact. Were there two Marie Laveaus, or even three? Was it a title given HooDoo Queens after the death of the original Marie Laveau? There is evendence that there existed a Marie Laveau, born possibly in 1794 and died in 1881. Another "Marie Laveau" lived until the 1920s. So confusing are the accounts of the deeds of both that it's possible to speak of them as one person. For example, although thousands of pilgrims visit the St. Louis cemetery to pay homage to Marie Laveau, there is evidence that the daughter, not the mother, is buried there. The original Laveau is said to have disappeared from the earth without a trace. I shall speak of them as "Marie Laveau." There are accounts of the activities of a Marie Laveau in the nineteenth-century New Orleans *Picayune* newspaper. She was said to have conducted "ceremonies," which sound like orgies, attended by people of both races not excluding prominent men and women of New Orleans society. She has also been accused of murdering and driving her rivals out of town or even driving them mad. On the other hand, just as there are many aspects to the Haitian Venus-loa Erzulie, she has also been praised for her good deeds. The tomb of "Marie Glapion" (a lover's name) or "the Widow Paris" (a first husband?) reads in French: "She was a good mother." Erzulie of the Dahomean rites is often a virgin and child figure. Marie was a kind of patron saint of prostitution and was supposed to have performed a miracle which postponed the hanging of a prisoner. She operated a house of prostitution called The Maison Blanche, where "Negro Balls" took place, an astonishing name since no black males were admitted.

It was in these plush and opulent interiors that white men would rendezvous with Negro women called "quadroons," racially mixed women on whose beauty an Englishman commented: "[They resemble] the high-class Hindus; lovely countenances, full, dark, liquid eyes, lips of coral, teeth of pearl, sylphlike figures; their beautifully rounded limbs, exquisite gait, and ease of manner might furnish models for a Venus or Hebe."

"Marie's" chief rival in those days of "The Business" was Doctor John. Jean Montanet, Jean La Ficelle, or Jean Latanie, or Jean Racine, or Jean Grisgris, or Jean Macaque, or Jean Bayou, or VooDoo John, he went by many names but has come down to us as "Doctor John," reputed to have been a Bambara, from Senegal. Lafcadio Hearn, New Orleans writer known for his "jewel-like" words, and reputed to be one of Marie's lovers, described Doctor John as "a man of middle height, very strongly built, with broad shoulders, well-developed muscles, an inky black skin, retreating forehead, small bright eyes, a very flat nose, and a woolly beard. . . ." Hearn also says, "He had a resonant voice and a very authoritative manner." Doctor John was a wealthy man of expensive tastes and often received scorn from sections of New Orleans because of his adherence to the polygamistic ways of his Bambara tribe. He is said to have had an international harem of fifteen wives, in a Christian country, where only white men are allowed that many. He had knowledge of Obeah, the West Indian Vodoun, sometimes referred to as Pocomania. He knew botany, the knowledge belonging to only the high priests of Vodoun, the Houngans.

Marie's background, on the other hand, wasn't all that great. Daughter of a slave owner, and the slave woman he "raped," at least modern feminists would claim, she constantly vacillated between Catholicism and HooDoo and is said to have denounced HooDoo on her deathbed in favor of Catholicism. One can imagine the conflict between the two: Doctor John perhaps dismissing Marie I's HooDoo as humbug. He was "inky black," she was a quadroon. He knew the real thing, or at least the original thing. The HooDoo of the North Americans seems to be more muted, and faster: the phenomenon of Be-bop can be interpreted as a HooDoo loa.

There was also an altruistic side to Doctor John. He was supposed to have distributed "gombo," and "jimbalaya" to the poor. His career was brought to an end when somebody cut his throat. Marie Laveau went to jail for the crime until it was discovered that some female members of his cult did it. The conflict between Marie and John had been exacerbated over an incident concerning a slave girl named Pauline. It seems that a white man so fell in love with Pauline that he moved her in with his family. When he left town on a trip Pauline enslaved the family. When the authorities broke into the house they found his wife and children in a state of malnutrition. Doctor John was supposed to have provided Pauline with a charm to prevent her hanging. She was hanged anyway and so Doctor John was accused of bad gris-gris. A strange coincidence occurs when we find that the family's name was Rabbeneck, and Doctor John "The Nighttripper" spells his last name "Rabennack." Max Rabennack!

Like most of the tourists to New Orleans that week I had been "jacked up." It ain't all that free. They were even selling a Viva Mardi Gras lipstick on the radio. Now, if I were conducting a "VooDoo" tour I wouldn't have left out the church at 1229 Saint Philip Street. A most unusual church. I wouldn't have left out Congo Square, where African slaves fathered and performed ceremonies a few irrational observers have characterized as "stupid fetishism," I wouldn't have neglected the other shrines where slaves gathered and created such foment that the Spanish colonial Governor issued an edict against the importation of slaves from Santo Domingo and Haiti. "They are too much given to Voodooism and make the lives of the citizens unsafe," said the Guv. I couldn't understand why the Prince didn't point out the Pharmacy Museum at 514 Chartres Street, where HooDoo botany can be found. He left out the Quadroon Ballroom, located inside the Ramada Inn at 717 Orleans Street, where Marie set up quadroon "dates" for their fans who visited from all over the world for their favors. Royalty was into HooDoo! Queen Victoria was supposed to have consulted Marie Laveau.

I was getting hungry and the Prince recommended a place called the Vaucresson Cafe Creole, which was located at 624 Bourbon Street. Well, we went in and layed out five dollars for a scoop of something that looked like rice with some kind of red dye on it. The waiter, who looked "Latin," referred to the thing as jambalaya. He had on red jacket and black pants and came over to the table and made some motions about a bottle of wine. And so I said, "In Berkeley I buy this stuff around the corner at the Chinese-American Mom and Pop store at Cedar and California." There were these Belles at the next table with those white flop Belle hats. They were wearing white gloves. They broke up. The other man, a manager, gave me an angry look. He looked Creole. Creole originally was a derisive term created by the Spanish as a put-down of the French who seemed to enjoy fucking everything. The cockhounds of the colonialists. Maybe that's why the intellectual black cockhound's headquarters is Paris. Even some of those pushing "buy Black."

Nowadays, a Creole is someone who is of mixed white and black blood. It's kind of become confused with mulatto. There's a joke about New Orleans Creoles. Seems that during the freedom marches in New Orleans, an irate white person left her children with a Creole woman, saying: "Hold these children, we got to go down and do something with these niggers."

Well, after we'd eaten whatever it was, and drank a glass of wine and the Prince seemed as though he was real comfortable, I told him that I was writing about his "Voo-Doo" tour for a magazine. He just about fell out of the chair. He asked me did I want to meet Doctor John "The Nighttripper." Would I like to go rattlesnake hunting with him? Did I want to see him lie in a casket in broad daylight. All I wanted was a receipt. With trembling fingers he signed his name under "VooDoo tour." I smiled and shook his hand. I headed up Bourbon towards Canal Street. Gerald Jackson, Bob Thompson, Jack Levine or Ensor could paint this scene. The grotesque circus faces. Wine selling on the streets. More T-shirts than I'd ever seen. I felt like starting up a metaphysical bunko squad. America needs one. The hustling Charmers who give all the others a bad name. They say that most of the Vodoun ceremonies have been secret. Nobody hassling you at the airport with Swami books or knocking on your door all times of the day or telling you that you hate black people when you don't buy their paper. Senator Henry Jackson said: "Religion is private and personal." Scoop's finest moment!

The next night was spirit night. I attended Bacchus with two poets, Tom Dent, Kalamu Ya Salaam, and their wives. Each float was dedicated to a spirit. The "Spirit of Exploration," "The Spirit of '76," etc. Perry Como was Bacchus VIII, "the only outside King," a citizen who knows his Mardi Gras sneered. He seemed to be resting his feet on the shoulders of some old smiling "Uncle" dressed in a red suit. In one of the segments some Negro grooms led horses ridden by white Knights. There was the "giant" Bacchus, with the same blank, droll grin, clutching a goblet. The "Spirit of Courage" was a "giant" coonskin cap-wearing Daniel Boone clutching a revolver; it had the same sinister stare. The crowd cheered. Flashbulbs were going on and off like at a Muhammad Ali fight. Something cold hit the back of my neck and slid down under my sweater collar. It was a doubloon, Bacchus' doubloons were medallions with pictures of Bacchus on them. Somebody on one of the floats had thrown a doubloon and it landed in my collar? I was thinking of the odds for that. Others were hitting the deck for theirs. "Hitting the deck" is taken seriously at Mardi Gras; my friend dived for one only to have it trapped by some southern woman's foot. "Take a picture of this, Ishmael." I took a picture of it, but she wouldn't budge. She was staring straight ahead, determined to keep her foot on the doubloon. If looks could kill. I remembered this nice southern panel, at this nice university, in Winston-Salem. These southern ladies were saying that their plight was similar to that of the blacks and I asked did they know of a case where a man sent a bloodhound after a woman after she'd left him. "Race Issue Disrupts Panel." The Winston-Salem *Journal* said. "A "giant" black raven is before me. "The Spirit of Literature," and there were the names of Twain and Poe. On the side of the tableau was the typewriter next to which a Confederate soldier held forth a bayonet. Now, this float was trying to tell me something.

After the parade we went to Lu and Charlie's for pitchers of beer and hamburgers. On the walls were jackets of Tom Dent's *Magnolia Street*. Performing was the New Orleans French Market Band, a white Dixieland band. The leader, Barbara told me, was the city coroner. Anyway, they were keeping the old New Orleans spirits in shape.

I spent dead Monday, the day before Fat Tuesday, or Shrove Tuesday, with writers Toni Morrison (*Sula, The Bluest Eye*), Toni Cade (*Gorilla, My Love*), and Gloria Smart. At one point they asked me why I referred to them as the Seven Sisters. The Seven Sisters was a single conjure woman from Georgia. At least one of the Seven Sisters is a working Mambo. Root woman. Wrote dialect right up front in the New York *Times,* and who don't like it? I think I'd get along with them even if there were no feminist movement. I'd said some harsh things in the past about women intellectuals, now I only teased them. Maybe man should give up every "piggy" habit except the right to tease. Women, the right to blush. They can have everything else. They can have the millions of female maniacs who have custody of your children and all you get back is an endorsed check and the courts and the law go right along with the arrangement. They can have dying younger. They can have all the wrestling the dragons, walking the moon, entering, unharmed, the caves where rattlesnakes hibernate, and all the other things men do for, or over, or to impress, a woman. Like clawing and knifing each other to death. Have any of you brothers out there ever found yourself in some woman's bed, and her man is ringing the buzzer and she gets up and rings it 'for him to come up, and you only got sixty seconds to get your clothes on, and she's enjoying your anxiety? We do need a metaphysical bunko squad to explain that. I saw the face once of a woman over whom a man had been murdered. It was one of the most peaceful faces I've ever seen. Like a saint's face.

Was there ever a "Hal of Troy?" What man has ever had people go to war over him just because he was pretty? Men sweat, yearn, and risk great reputations to lie in the arms of a woman. The congressman took sleeping pills but the woman got $200,000 and a spread in the big magazines. Is it fair?

I think that's it. Chester Himes said it. He tried to be "fair." Like I've been clipping reviews by white male critics of novels, plays, and films by black women and you'd be astonished at the results of my research. People making love right in the paper!! They especially like this woman novelist who writes colored Norman Rockwell type stories about how Jesus was walking down the road with this old colored lady, and all about how Jesus had these "blue eyes," and "auburn hair"; the greatest American Romance has yet to be written. They hated the film *Mandingo* because *Mandingo* was accurate. Well, that day, we got along well. It was more than militant intellectual women and male chauvinist man but writer to writer. And when writers get together they talk about books. Their books, the competition's books.

We had lunch at a place called the Provencial. When I tasted the jambalaya I then could tell why it had achieved the status, through lore, of a holy food. It is better than Boston clams, Nathan's hot dogs, dinner at Wo Ping restaurant, Inc., on Pell Street, Prawns at Berkeley's Spenger's, Texas red at Schultz's in Austin, and Albuquerque's blue tacos. HooDoo food. Syncretic: Spanish, African, Native American, French—adaptable to all cultures. There was warm fellowship in this restaurant. The waiters and waitresses talked in a slow hum of good will. Not a drawl, but a hum. A hum that could put you to sleep. This was the sweet South of ambrosia, where people say yes mah'm and no mah'm, where there's always the best silver laid out, and places set in case somebody stops by hungry. Where the man sits at the head of the table and carves.

A land where the male leads are played by Clark Gable and Don Ameche, tipping their top hats, and escorting ladies to the ice cream parlor. And New Orleans is the thick cream of that sweet South. The South's vanilla. The city of po boy sandwiches, Frankie and Johnny, Louis Armstrong, the great Zulu, where the mayor's first name is Moon and every day a Frank Yerby novel. If you're a tourist they'll show you where Tennessee Williams lives and gossip about Clay Shaw. (Had whips in his closet!)

New Orleans like HooDoo is all over place and time. We walked from the French Quarter of the nineteenth century to the Spanish Cabildo of the Middle Ages. There were even jugglers performing in the courtyard. It's *so* nice. Almost makes you forget that other South which lies buried in the New South's soul to surface once a year as this pageant. The day when portraits of Robert E. Lee are dusted off and placed alongside the Audubon bird displays (Audubon was an Afro-American) in the windows of antique bookshops. The South where the Klan and the White League used to terrorize Negroes for having saved enough money to buy a house, or for raising uppity crops. For wanting to go to "Quality" schools. The same things they "lynch" Negroes for today. That's why I'm always a little uneasy in the South. I never know which one I'm going to run into. The elegance of Chapel Hill and Lexington, Virginia, or North Carolina's chicken coop: Winston-Salem. The difference between Jimmy Carter, smiling on his face's right side, the Stars and Stripes behind him, and Jimmy Carter, frowning on his face's left side, the Stars and Bars beside him. They thought they'd buried the old South before, only to have it rise, like Frankenstein, to pillage, terrorize, and plunder in the hooded robes of organizations whose charters refer to fraternity in the feminine gender. Perhaps the most important question the United States faces in the next ten years is: has the South finally got rid of its monster?

When we arrived at St. Louis # 1, the cemetery, the gates were locked. When I visited, the day before, in the company of Chicken Man, the tourists were white too. They were making wishes before Marie's tomb. People from all over the South—HooDoos—still come here. There are fresh flowers at her grave, and visitors are invited to make an X for good luck, on her tomb. The surface of the tomb is crowded with X's.

Toni Morrison mentioned a place called The Cabaret. Once there I was able to snap a photo to add to my Hoo-Doo altar, which consists of "evidence" and gifts from all over the world, including a Yemanja mask from some Argentineans. You see, above the bar, resting on a shelf, was a skull to each side of which were "bowling trophies" to the casual observer, but loas to the trained eye. Atop the skull's head lay a necklace beaded with snake vertebrae. It is what the Haitian Houngans call an Orret. There was a big butt woman standing at the bar. She had "kiss me" written all over her rump. Erzulie, no doubt.

Tom Dent and I are friends who spend a lot of time feuding with each other. Maybe it's "cultural differences." Like, Tom Dent eats lobster; I eat Kentucky Fried Chicken. He's a bourbon "black" as he once said to me, and his father runs a university. He's very "fair" looking, as they say. I'm brownish red. I left Toni Morrison, Toni Cade, and Gloria Smart at Tom's house because I didn't like the way Tom was "relating" to me, as they say. Plus he had this guest who was real boring. Real hung up on ideology. We couldn't even enjoy the Bacchus parade, he was spouting all of this uninteresting jargon I've heard, maybe a hundred thousand times. I made a joke. Something about tape recording everything he was saying from my Living History tape recorder bag where I had stuffed notebooks, evidence (menus, street maps, matchboxes, hundred-year-old postcards, doubloons, Kodak bulbs, Mardi Gras memorabilia), and other "junk" to go into the psychic vacuum cleaner. When I made the joke the dude took off like a hot-blooded rocket. WHOOOOO-SSSSSHHHHH. Berated me on the street. Called me names. He was louder than the drums of the marching bands. Raised a Methodist, I didn't like to get loud talked in public. Why do all of you talk so loud? a Third World person asked me once. We are an exuberant people, I explained. But there's a difference between being exuberant and a political basket case, like all of the shell-shocked who can't believe the revolution didn't come when even a glimpse of American history would have proven that Apocalypse is usually a false arrival. Anyway, Tom had joined us at the Gov. Nichols apartment, where the women were staying, and we all headed out to his house after about three hours of Tom pacing up and down the floor, cussing me out, signifying, attitudinizing. He wouldn't help me find the car. We had been out all day walking around New Orleans. It was night, and the streets had French names, and so I couldn't remember which French street I left it on. "If you parked it illegally I'll have to come down to the police station to help you look for it," he said. You can think any number of pleasant nostalgic thoughts about the South until somebody mentions The Police Station, a land where many Negroes have disappeared. I'm thinking of the movies of big-bellied Dixie police shooting into nigger cells for target practice and feeding them cockroach meat for breakfast. I didn't want to go into a southern police station for anything. I remembered the Auschwitz type diggings that had taken place in Arkansas a few years ago, where the bones of "lost" prisoners, killed by guards, were dug up. I was relieved when I found the car, and drove to Dent's house, triumphantly, stormed in, ate Barbara Dent's gumbo, and then told the women, "Let's go, I'll drive you home."

"Suppose we don't want to go," Toni Morrison said. I didn't want it to sound so crass, but then went on to make another M.C. remark. There was no way for me to win that night and so I huffed out, got into my car, and drove off: fast; loud; so everyone would know I was annoyed. So when I met everybody the next day for the trip to see "Black Indians," things were a bit tense.

The important parades on Fat Tuesday were Comus, Rex, and Zulu. This year's Rex is Frank Garden Strachan, a businessman. He looks like the couple on the Delta, a shipper who looks as though he probably has no problems with regularity. His consort is Miss Alma Marie Atkinson. Mr. Strachan wore royal golden robes. His sacrificial maiden is surrounded by maids, and jonquils, ribbons of purple, gold and green. Mardi Gras ladies wear laurel crowns. She wore a candy wool crepe suit. There's a "giant" ox. The Boeuf Gras, surrounded by huge berries and cocks. In the old days the oxen would have been slaughtered, a rite known as "burying the carnival." Interesting, when you realize carnival, loosely translated, means "farewell to meat." Other things, right out of the pages of the *Golden Bough:* wild men are all over town, carrying clubs, acting savage, black and white. I took a photo of one in a leopard skin outfit and club.

Mr. Strachan's favorite lines in the Rex poem, written by Ashton Phelps, were, "He dresses with care, never tatterdemalion/As becomes every proper Episcopalian." Anglicism, the church of the Confederacy. The theme was "Jazz—New Orleans' Heritage." The HooDoo shrines and the jazz shrines are in the same neighborhood, suggesting a possible connection. The "HooDoo" guide book says that "jazz" is based upon VooDoo ritual music. I'm thinking of all of the musicians called "Papa." It was the one ritual in which the "Papa" or the "King" told people when to stop playing. There are Ragtime floats and Muskrat Ramble floats and an "Oriental" "Chinatown My Chinatown" float. The bakery equivalent of this aesthetic is blueberry cheesecake. But if you think that's rich, in 1838 the Mardi Gras procession contained ". . . several carriages superbly ornamented—bands of music, horses richly caparisoned—personations of Knights, cavaliers, horses, demigods, chanticleers, punchinellos, &c, all mounted.

Many of them were dressed in female attire, and acted the lady with no small degree of grace." They knew how to put on the dog in those days. There seemed to have been more work put into the masks. Contemporary photos show the women of 1880, dressed in hoops, putting the masks together by hand.

Now, old-timers say that the Zulu Parade began as a response to Rex. Whereas Rex was white, mythical aristocratic, a Confederate pageant which once honored the daughter of Robert E. Lee, who was "took out" by Comus at the ball that 1870s night, the Zulu Parade involves an ancient Afro-American survival form. Adopting the oppressor's parody of themselves and evolving, from this, an art form with its own laws. I call this process loa-making.

If the whites had their King, Rex; we have our King, Zulu, a savage from the jungle like you say he is. While you're laughing at us we're laughing with you but the joke's on you. In the first Zulu Parade there was a jubilee quartet at each end of the parade. It was a proletariat parade of porters and laborers, who were put down by the Afro-American middle class, the colored six companies. What you put down you often join, someone once said, and so this year's Zulu King was Reverend Lawler P. Daniels of the great southern Negro industry death: preachers, insurance men, and undertakers, the millionaires of the race. His court included BigShot Soulful Warrior, and Witchdoctor. The social mobility of the Zulu Parade can be measured by comparing the style of this parade to that of earlier Zulu parades. King Peter Williams, the first Zulu King, wore a starched white suit, and for a scepter he carried a loaf of Italian bread. By 1914 the King could afford a buggy, and by 1922, the Zulus owned a yacht. This year's King wore turquoise vestments, and jeweled crown. He waved a feathered spear. His wife wore a trailing turquoise gown. The reminders of former times were those wearing animal skins, grass skirts, and Afro wigs. Coconuts are Zulu's doubloons.

Rudy Lombard is a handsome bearded architect who was dressed in SNNC denims! Chic. I told him that Lombard was the name of a family which appears in

Dante's *Inferno*. I'm always saying dumb shit like that. So when he said, "Yeah, I met him," after Toni Morrison introduced us, in that tone which sounded like a dismissal, I could understand where he was coming from. Well, he kind of made out that the Black Indians were a hermetic krewe, so secret that those who revealed them were not looked upon favorably. Jules Cahn, a film maker, has done a film on the Mardi Gras Indians, which was being shown at the Historic New Orleans Collection. Unkind remarks were made about his activities as we saw him walking down the street, during the Black Indian ceremonies. People have made so many billions of dollars from "The Black Experience," it ain't funny. And some wish to protect the last remaining secrets. I don't think the Black Indians are going to be so secret for long, if they ever were. I've seen them cited in a number of books concerning New Orleans and the carnival. Even Dick Cavett cited one book entitled Gumbo-Ya-Ya on nationwide television while touring the city in the company of Tennessee Williams.

I was told that they never cross Canal Street—"white zones"—but I followed them to Canal Street and beyond. But nobody had to tell me what to mention. In fact, some of the middle-class blacks with whom I visited somehow feel that New Orleans belongs to them and anyone interested in the city is an interloper into the New Orleans Nation. In her remarkable book *Black Dance,* Lynne Fauley Emery claims that none of the original HooDoo ceremonies has ever been witnessed. But the Black Indian ceremony was quite visible to blacks and whites.

The first thing I noticed at the black intersection, one of the stops for the Black Indians, was an old beat-up jalopy full of guedes. Guedes are statesmen, clowns, artists, known to "show each man his devil." In *Canapé-Vert,* by the Marcelin brothers, they are depicted as "Gay, rowdy, and a scandalous jester[s]." They are often proletariat gods who satirize government officials on their behalf, and are not afraid to mock the Houngan. Here they are on this New Orleans street, pouring beer into the water tank of the car. Six hours later, I saw them in the same car, making that car run on beer. There's a whole ritual of greeting, mock competition, Chief-saluting, and unintelligible, for me, lingo the Black Indians go through. There was a little boy named Spyboy who was into some heavy discourse with Wildman, crowned with a bull's horn.

The most extraordinary feature was the costumes, richly decorated, and fantastic. People work on them throughout the year. They carried on with this procession, wending their way through the neighborhoods, then heading uptown on St. Claiborne Street. This krewe had no police escorts and traffic, at some points, became jammed. Some of the inconvenienced were good natured, like the fellow in Confederate battle dress with the Stars and Bars wrapped around his head. Others menaced the blacks with their auto bumpers and the blacks yelping and whooping menaced back, waving their flowered axes about their heads. It was a "mock" race war. I was trying to identify the costumes. Though whites consider the Black Indians to be odd some claim that cohabitation between Blacks and Indians has produced a new race in America. One theory has it that the geometric designs (vé-vés) made by cornmeal, on the ground, used by Houngans to order "down" loas were a technique Haitians learned from the indigenous Indians of Haiti. They made the African gods meaner, they hated the Spanish so. Now, Bob Callahan, President of the Turtle Island Foundation, publisher of *Apalache* by Paul Metcalf, Melville's great-grandson, has a keen eye. We were sitting at the Golden Gate racetrack and from his seat he identified the golden grass—the original Spanish grass, behind the University of California's football stadium. I showed him the photos I made of the Black Indians, and he said the costumes were Caribbean. I left the Indians, they were invading "white" territory like some kind of prophecy was taking place before my eyes.

Since the major American holidays seem to induce anxiety and depression Mardi Gras is a bright moment on the American Death calendar. During Christmas, for example, everybody goes about with those airplane stewardess smiles in the winter when it's cold. The plot of Christmas was deliberately scripted to cause guilt, and the only Mardi Gras figure is Santa Claus, who is for kids. Mardi Gras is one of the few art forms in which the whole community can become immersed, just as in HooDoo, which not only Negroes but the Irish practiced in New Orleans.

It's a day of joy when people can act the fool and wild instead of acting that way for the whole year around. They ought to have a Mardi Gras in South Boston. There could be San Francisco, Chicago, Detroit, and New York Mardi Gras as well as Mardi Gras in Atlanta, Denver, and Philadelphia. Cults all over the community could organize their floats and participate in parades. This could become a land of a million krewes. A non-political holiday could continue through July, where the only thing we have is the Fourth, a day set aside to commemorate feudal slave owners whom tennis court historians would have us believe spent most of their time talking like Alistair Cooke and sitting, hands clasped, in a winged Chippendale, saying profound things. How many people do you know who live in places like Monticello and Mount Vernon? I'd like to see each town work together to put its local histories, legends, and gossip on wheel and foot. Why not a sexy day during the month when the whole earth is doing sexy things, getting swollen to stand erect like the Legba symbol you find both here and in Africa? Legba is a loa who would appreciate Mardi Gras.

Mardi Gras is the one American art I have witnessed in which the audience doesn't sit intimidated or wait for the critics to tell them what to see. The Mardi Gras audience talks back to the performers instead of sitting there like dummies, and can even participate in the action. Oscar Wilde said, "Why shouldn't the Fourth of July pageant in Atlanta be as fine as the Mardi Gras carnival in New Orleans? Indeed, the pageant is the most perfect school of art for the people." Wilde, an admirer of the Confederacy, said he "engaged in voodoo rites with Negroes."

Just think of what artists could do with Mardi Gras. There could be Romare Bearden floats, and Marisol floats, and Ruth Asawa could do a float for the San Francisco Mardi Gras. I'd like to see a Mardi Gras band performing Donald Byrd's music. Amiri Baraka could design a whole parade.

I'd also like to see Karin Bacon, who staged those multimedia spectaculars during the last golden days of New York, co-ordinate a coast-to-coast Mardi Gras by video hookup.

I for one had been over-floated with this Mardi Gras, I headed away from the Black Indians and took one last photo of an interracial motorcycle gang all leathered up and giving the carnival some existentialist stares. I saw the last Black Indian chief, who was wearing those robes I imagined Quetzalcoatl of African and South American lore would be dressed in.

Sitting next to me on the plane was a brother man, dressed in an outfit and with the features of what could only be described as Barry White Cavalier. He stirred when the stewardess shook him.

"Did you go to Mardi Gras?" I asked.

"Yeah," he said.

"What did you think of it? An obscene Confederate pageant?"

"I don't know nothin about that," he said. "Mardi Gras, to me, is gettin together with your friends and eatin and drinkin."

He dozed off leaving me to watch the Mardi Gras southwest sky, and sipping a burgundy. Robert Tallant wrote in his book *Mardi Gras,* "Mardi Gras is a spirit." HooDoo, too. Watch out Christmas!

Oui, January 1977

Gliberals

Berkeley, Calif.—A brilliant black woman once said to me, "Conservatives usually treat me as an individual." I thought of her comment recently when exchanging letters with Clark Whelton, a fine writer and decent man but whose columns about blacks remind me of the letters-to-the-editor Steve Allen used to mimic. I wrote and told him.

His reply dealt with the swing to the right by New York "liberals" (not the true right but the sort of intellectual depot where they are sheltered until it can be determined which way the winds of American opinion are blowing). "Mugger is now a liberal euphemism for blacks," he wrote.

This came as a surprise to me since I always thought that liberalism, classically, had something to do with the ability to reason, as well as "freedom from prejudice or bigotry," as the dictionary adds. Someone who sees all blacks as muggers certainly isn't seeing too clearly, a warped vision which, most likely, taints his perception of other events. To equate black with mugger because of the experience with one, two, or even a dozen is just as irrational as citing a few incidents in a novel to prove that all whites are bloodthirsty maniacs who harbor genocidal impulses—which isn't true although I'll bet I can find more of the second example than the first.

If these people who call themselves liberals, thereby degrading a noble word, aren't really liberals, then what are they? The word euphemism, in Whelton's letter, is the key. They are glib—gliberals.

Goldwater and Buckley, essentially, hold the same views they held ten years ago. The Stevensons, Kennedys, and Humphreys are able to flit from one position to another without the modifying transitions, because they say it so pretty. Honeyed words, swiftly delivered like cats scurrying up a wet fence; liberally seasoned with anecdotes, catchy syntax, biblical quotations, Shakespeare; writing techniques introduced by early political writers like Thomas Jefferson, the founding Gliberal, a slave owner who insisted that the Bill of Rights be added to the Constitution.

The heavyweight champeen gliberal, Norman Mailer, wrote in *Miami and the Siege of Chicago,* "I'm tired of Negroes and their rights," presumably because one black preacher didn't show up for a press conference on time, see? When we ain't mugging we preaching. Recently, Mr. Mailer announced the formation of a foundation with libertarian goals. That's a gliberal for you; play fiddle for the children in the morning, dine with the devil at night.

Because the communications industry is located in New York, gliberals root there. Whenever I read in San Francisco that someone has prophesied open warfare in the streets, I know that a gliberal has been here the day before, in this case, a black psychiatrist who's going about the country arguing that violence is healthy for the "oppressed" even if it kills them. Gliberal logic. Orwell's book was about what would happen to thought if gliberals took over.

Gliberals' influence in the communications industry is considerable; conservatives go into business. The welfare or mugger story makes page one of the gliberal press while the new black director of RCA, William J. Kennedy III, has to scuffle on the back pages for space. On San Francisco television, a story about the alleged inferiority of black genes was recently played side by side with one concerning a local anti-poverty scandal. All of these efforts can be interpreted as ways of setting up blacks as scapegoats for all that's happened to the United States in the last ten years, thereby taking the pressure off gliberals.

Of course, blacks could well argue that they didn't give

away any top government secrets nor did they prevent the Democrats from holding a successful convention in Chicago, 1968, even when prodded, but they won't; they're liberals, mostly, if political registration is a measure.

Propaganda against blacks isn't new in American history. A gifted black artist like Betye Saar is even able to invert this vilification; she has made some wonderful collages based upon early racist ads for items such as toothpaste and canned goods. Blacks will survive this latest campaign requiring them to wear a mugger's armband.

I wouldn't be too sure about the fate of gliberals though. The majority of Americans aren't as stupid as gliberals might think, and who knows? There may be more people west of the Hudson mad at them than at blacks.

New York *Times*
March 31, 1973

The "Liberal" in Us All

When European soldiers, their Christian front men, and "explorers" entered Africa, the African nations were divided and so they were conquered; when European soldiers, their Christian front men, and "explorers" entered South America, the Inca and Aztec nations were also divided; they too were conquered. When European soldiers, Christian front men, and "explorers" entered Asia, the Asian nations were divided and so they were conquered.

If by some miracle Cortez could be brought back to life and his soldiers, Christian front men, "explorers," and their ghostly crew were brought into this auditorium, this Third World conference would be conquered because we are all divided.

We are fighting each other. Fighting over who's the whitest; fighting over who can speak English the best. Who can say "How Now Brown Cow" without an accent. Fighting over who can cuss out the white man the best. Fighting over who can score the highest on the Europeans' IQ test, without realizing, as Shawn Wong says, that white racist love is just as invidious as white racist hate.

We're fighting over who's going to head the ethnic studies department, or who is the most "civilized," or who's the most "militant."

In Berkeley Third World people are arguing and are about to kill each other over some arts money which amounts to chump change. In San Francisco the same thing is happening.

In the 1960s it was very popular to malign the "liberal."

He was the guy who always put his foot in his mouth when attempting to relate to Third World people. To him, we all looked alike, or had rhythm, or were crazy about hot tamales. We were the noble cigar store Indian yearning for his profile to appear on the nickel. If we were Asian-American it was, "Why can't you speak Chinese?" or, "Why aren't you wearing jade?" or "Why aren't you preserving your culture?"

We all had a good laugh on the liberal until we discovered the liberal in us all. That we often relate to each other as liberals relate to us. Some of us even relate to each other the way crackers used to relate to us. "Have you ever made it with a southern belle?" the cracker used to ask the Negro hitchhiker in the 1940s films about Mississippi.

Last week we gave a poetry reading for the publication of *Yardbird* 3, our annual Reader, which includes prose, poetry, and graphics. The reading was held at the Rainbow Sign, a black club on Grove Street.

While Shawn Wong, an Asian-American novelist, was reading from his work, a black woman approached to tell him that she wanted to give him better lighting. She called him Frank Chin. The Asian-Americans were amused by this incident. I was too, because that afternoon in the Food Cooperative's parking lot, on Shattuck Avenue, a famous Chicano novelist addressed me as Al Young, an Afro-American novelist.

In May of 1974, while attending a conference in Ellensburg, Washington, a Chicano advised me that Aretha Franklin was on, and asked why wasn't I dancing. That's okay because I'm always calling a Puerto Rican friend Jose, when that's not his name.

After a rehearsal for the radio version of Frank Chin's *Chicken-coop Chinaman,* I asked the Asian-Americans, assembled in my living room, wouldn't it be nice if we adjourned to the "swell Chinese restaurant around the corner?" I deserved the chilling silence that followed, because it was similar to a white liberal inviting me to sample this "nice soul food" restaurant which featured Uncle Ben's rice. We ended up in a Chinese restaurant anyway, because the Italian restaurant, Giovanni's, they wanted to go to had no room.

In contrast to this attitude there is evidence that our ancestors engaged in trade and cultural exchange. African vases which predate Columbus were discovered just a few weeks ago in the Virgin Islands. The Olmec Negro people were in South America at least three thousand years ago.

The Chinese Emperors used to send emissaries all over the world, including to East Africa, to invite other nations to the great celebration in Peking. Our religions contain gods which have similar characteristics. Our myths and legends also run parallel, and often our art forms merge, creating syncretic forms. In Ragtime's heyday there was a form known as the "Oriental" Rag.

In South America, Afro-Americans accept Native American gods, and rituals, and Native Americans have accepted Afro-American gods and rituals.

The art forms, gods, and myths seem to go together, nicely, even though the nations from which these art forms arose may be treating each other the way their conquerors treated them.

We've become Christianized and Europeanized and whitenized; still praying to the banner of the cross and obeying the "requirement."

The Puerto Ricans are now debating whether they should accept their Spanish or African heritage.

Puerto Ricans say that Chicanos reject them because Chicanos claim they lack African blood, even though Africans have been in Mexico for hundreds of years. The Mexican Governor of California, Pio Pico, 1845 to 1846, was a Negro, and the name California is derived from Califia, a Negro Queen who appears in a novel written in 1510 by Garcia Ornodes de Montalvo.

Even in the so-called "Black Community" there is a color caste whose segments have been engaged in a cold war for three hundred years, so much so that in some nineteenth-century writing, brown, black, and yellow are treated as different races.

The whole thing is a mess because all of us have similar

45

problems living in a country whose cultural and political leadership views it as an extension of Europe.

These divisions are exploited by third- and fourth-generation Knights and Knightesses, or Knightpersons, dedicated to maintaining the Judeo-Christian domination of our cultural affairs. When the Irving Howe clique did a "West Coast issue" of *Harper's Bookletter,* writer Suzanne Mantell sought to compare writing by Afro-Americans unfavorably with that of Asian-Americans when she wrote: "Surprisingly, the pieces in *Aiiieeeee!* don't read like a minority literature. Anger, frustration, confusion there may be, but they have been annexed in every case to well-crafted sensitivity via memoir, story or play."

"Minority," in case you didn't read between the lines, means "black." Suzanne Mantell was using the same Colonialist's techniques to pit native against native in the same manner that the billionaire's son promoted head-hunting between the New Guineans to increase his museum collection. She separated the polished item from the primitive one.

A Third World organization can expose these Colonialist intruders, selling us praise which merely turns out to be ammunition we use against each other; foolish, when you consider that they've armed both sides.

What a powerful political tool a Third World coalition would be. If blacks stopped drinking Thunderbird wine the Gallo empire would be collapsed tomorrow.

I didn't come here to make a passionate speech. Our nations have always produced great orators. Speeches by blacks, Asians, and Native Americans contain such elegance and passion that even our enemies are influenced by our oral poetry and prose.

George Wallace borrowed "We must keep on keepin' on" from Martin Luther King, Jr.

There has been a lot of orating in recent years. We have orated and orated and speechified and speechified, but in the old country church, at the end of a fire and brimstone sermon, the collection plate is passed, and so I say it is time to pass the collection plate, brothers and sisters.

In the panels and readings during this conference great passionate speeches will be made and lofty abstract questions will be ingeniously debated—but we should never forget the collection plate. We must think of concrete, practical proposals that will emerge from this conference or it will merely be a collection of papers piled so high that they will be as tall as the Transamerica building in San Francisco.

This is a cultural conference.

In the field of American culture we are still being short-changed; we are still receiving a black eye.

On television we are still oppressed by "Kung Fu," "Khan," and "Charlie Chan." Norman Lear and his Jewish writers are still rulers of television's Afro-American experience. If I'd really write the Al Jolson story they'd call me an anti-Semite.

Whole Native American tribes are still being exterminated, on the tube, by one virile white man toting a six-shooter.

In big publishing we are still viewed as fads dredged up, periodically, titillating a white readership, and then remaindered when that titillation has ejaculated.

Big-time publishing is still a white sport. Our books are not promoted and often the salesman, distributors, and booksellers are hostile to them. "Why do you want to order that book?" a salesman asked the owner of a bookstore after she ordered a book written by an Afro-American novelist published by the salesman's company.

Tax-supported public museums, reluctantly, exhibit paintings by Third World artists and the big-time galleries exploit them.

Last week I attended an Asian-American writers' conference, and one of the young writers asked why I hadn't attended some of the earlier sessions. "I thought maybe you wanted to be alone," I replied.

I didn't mean that flippantly. Blacks have been in the agitation business for two hundred years, and so we know how it is. Sometimes you want to be left alone. You don't want nobody peeping thru the keyhole at your business.

47

Amiri Baraka, formerly LeRoi Jones, recently said in connection with his switch from black nationalism to Marxist Leninism, and his rejection of racism as irrational and ineffective, that it was necessary in the 1960s to call the white man a devil because many of us grew up thinking he was god.

Nationalism is healthy! Go through it! Just don't go through it for ten years, or go through it over and over again. Learn from the black movement, which has inspired many movements in modern times, so much so that even in Ireland, the minorities sing "We Shall Overcome."

Studying the black movement will lead you to shortcuts.

In 1964, at Town Hall in New York, the black and white intellectuals engaged in a dialogue.

People shouted at each other and there was much name-calling. Nobody won the debate and so they went out into the streets to fight it out. Nobody won that either and so they retreated into their separate nations for years, and some of the major issues became hairstyle, cosmetics, diet, name changing, and dating game. They became the political equivalents of the cultural "drop out" movement.

Recently, the whites and blacks have been sending out peace feelers and talking about forming an alliance again. Dr. Alvin Poussaint, who came on real "black" at a National Black Writers' conference, November of 1974, had just a few weeks before called for an alliance between the blacks and the Jews.

I hope that Third World people will not have to go through a similar ordeal. How can the debilitating disaster that occurred between blacks and whites be prevented from happening between reds, yellows, and browns?

We will have to begin by stopping pretending that everything is peaches and cream. We will have to learn more about each other. We will have to admit that some of us are flattered when the Colonialists, like the one from the Irving Howe circle, tell us that we have better "craft" than the Chicanos, or that we have more balls than Asians.

We all know the names James Baldwin, Ralph Ellison,

but how many of us know John Okada, Jim Welch, Leslie Silko; learning about each other will take time and homework so that when we come together in a future conference we won't relate to each other the way liberals and crackers relate to us.

We can do more to promote multi-culturalism in California.

In the East, the power of the arts has been recognized for some time. In New York, there is a full-time arts commissioner. Mayor Beame has appropriated millions of dollars for the arts. The arts attract industry, and tourism. In California, a piddling amount of money has been devoted to the arts—this in a state whose multi-cultural resources are unequaled in the United States, even though World War II San Francisco columnists, who can't see beyond their cigarette holders, pretend as though only white people do art in the San Francisco Bay Area.

You have to start somewhere, and so Third World people must agitate so that the new arts development council does not continue the policies of the old arts commission, which meted out money to white elite groups: the Opera and the Ballet.

Maybe it's premature to begin a political coalition, we have enough troubles. But we can certainly construct a Third World arts lobby from this conference. We could see to it that Third World people receive their fair share of the money taxpayers have set aside for the arts.

This is a modest beginning. But it's one way of influencing arts legislation on national, state, and local levels. It would also serve as an experiment on how a future coalition, which would cover broader issues, would work.

We should proceed cautiously, scientifically and rationally so that the sorry debacle which happened to the white liberal black liberal dialogue doesn't happen to us.

Santayana said: "Those who do not learn from the mistakes of history are condemned to repeat them."

Antaeus, Summer 1976

Native Son Lives!

Richard Wright wasn't simply a "major" writer; he challenged the sacred irrational taboos of both blacks and whites and so he did more than "master" his craft; Richard Wright risked his neck.

His creation, Bigger Thomas, loomed over the late thirties like the mugger-rapist in the editorial cartoon, towering over urban skyscrapers: a Frankenstein with no tradition and no future, "born dead" and "whipped" before he started; a raw sexual superman who stumbled from murder to senseless murder.

Wright's problem was to place Bigger, described by a member of one of the novel's mobs as a "black ape," in an intimate situation with a rich white girl, daughter of a powerful slum-lord family whose philanthropy was motivated by the same kind of clumsy Christian guilt that places orphans on defective airplanes. This was at a time when any public personal contact with blacks was considered anathema. Much is made in both the novel and play about Bigger, Jan Erlone, and Mary Dalton eating and sitting together.

The possibility that Mary Dalton was victim of a "sex crime" is played up by the novel's sensationalistic media more than the manner of her death, suffocation, and the gruesome manner of the body's disposal: beheading and cremation. For their intimacy both Bigger and Mary are burned.

Bigger Thomas and his crime meant different things to different people. In his introduction to the novel Wright compared him with the traditional southern "bad nigger" who defied the Jim Crow laws; for the author, he is also the "superman"—both a 1930s philosophical and "pop" idea which, simply put, argues that some people are superior to others and the moralities which apply to most people don't apply to them.

Wright carefully worked out imagery dealing with transcendence in writing about Bigger's murder of Mary Dalton. It is compared with Charles Lindbergh flying across the Atlantic. The author also invokes ideas relating to Behaviorist psychology: Bigger "conditioned" by a society "blind" to him, this blindness conveyed through the blindness of Mrs. Dalton, Mary's mother, and the "blindness" of his girl friend, Bessie—blindness is used as a metaphor throughout the novel.

Orson Welles, who directed the play, had a similar notion of Bigger: an individual trapped by socio-economic forces beyond his control. Bigger's defense lawyer Max saw him as part of a class whose plight is no different from that of The Worker while Jan Erlone saw him as a potential revolutionary.

Paul Green, Wright's personal choice as collaborator on the play, viewed Bigger as a militant Christ and so the play version contains substantially more Christian symbolism than the novel. In the play, Bigger compares Jan and Mary with Christ: "His po' face like the face of Jesus hanging off the wall—like her face." Mary is a martyr who "suffered" to expiate the crimes of the Daltons, a feminist Christ who crossed the line between civilization and savagery and was destroyed by her altruism.

In the novel, the author's, and Bigger's, contempt for Christianity is clear. "Take your Jesus and go," Bigger says to Reverend Hammond, a buffoon given lines like "Ef his sins be as scarlet, lawd, wash 'em white as snow." At one point Bigger says, "The white folks like for us to be religious then they can do what they want to with us."

Bigger's motives, like Bigger, are malleable, shaped by characters, the author, director, and the collaborator. Even Bigger is confused about his motives for killing Mary Dalton. Was it revenge? Did society make him do it, the bloody culmination of a life which began with Bigger watching his father being lynched, a Freudian view?

Evidence in the novel suggests that Mary Dalton's was an accidental death; Bigger killed her because he didn't want to be found in the bedroom with a white girl. "They kill us for women like her," Bigger says in the novel. "He knew that sex relations between blacks and whites were repulsive to most white men," comments the narrator. Bigger resents Mary and Jan because their liberal familiarity with him puts his life in jeopardy and risks his ostracism by the blacks who saw them eating together in Ernie's Kitchen Shack.

In these days of permissiveness, explicit interracial sexual relationships in books, movies, and television barely raise an eyebrow, but for Wright's time it was a national nightmare. Even in the nineteenth century Northerners were warned that black migration would mean competition for jobs; the demagogues also warned about what would happen in the bedroom. Even Lincoln raised the sexual question,* but unlike Wright he was concerned with intimacy between white men and black women. It could be argued that Wright had Bigger kill the girl rather than make love to her because, to his contemporaries, interracial violence was more acceptable than interracial intimacy.

The novel was written for a sophisticated literary public, and though it's been labeled a "realistic" novel Wright uses mixed forms: ". . . clinging filmy spider webs that came thick onto his lips"; or "There were many empty buildings like skeletons standing with snow on their bones in the winter winds," are lines which do not belong to the naturalistic tradition.

How does one transfer to the stage the incredible third-person psychological and physical details of Bigger in the narrative; the intricate symbolism of the furnace which Bigger tends like an executioner in a sacrificial rite; the details of the implements of murder arranged on the court-room table like items in a still life painting. Wright was deeply interested in psychological as well as social forces

* Herbert Mitgang, *The Fiery Trial* (N.Y.: Viking, 1974).

and didn't feel that the human psyche should be tapped only by the political madmen of the time.

The aesthetic possibilities of the novel have been "hindered" by circumscribed criticism which demeans the author's vision. *Native Son* is symbolist, realistic, expressionistic, satirical (the devastating satire of newspaper sensationalism; Reverend Hammond's portrait), psychological, philosophical, political, sociological, even anthropological—the newspaper descriptions of Bigger as primitive man. It was, in short, a prodigious accomplishment. Gertrude Stein wrote: "Dear Richard . . . you and I are the only two geniuses of this era."

He saw Orson Welles as a "human locomotive" and according to Michel Fabre, "consented to all the changes Welles suggested."

Directed by Orson Welles and John Houseman, the play opened on March 25, 1941, at the St. James Theater in New York. It ran two hours without intermission.

The critical response was mixed. According to some reviews, it was an artistic success, but it was condemned by others. Just as the masses of blacks enjoyed Bert Williams' characterizations while the intelligentsia disapproved of them as "stereotypes," average blacks enjoyed the play while some contemporary black intellectuals objected to the character of Bigger. One group threatened to picket.

It moved from the St. James to other theaters in New York, including the Apollo, and to New Jersey, Pennsylvania, Massachusetts, Illinois, and elsewhere.

October 23, 1942, saw the play back on Broadway, where it was attacked by censorship committees including the Catholic Movement for the Theater. It closed January 2, 1943.

There's a disadvantage in writing about a play one hasn't seen. The staging of *Native Son* by Welles, Jean Rosenthal, and James Morcom was apparently brilliant: the lighting, the one-minute scene changes, and the sets suspended above the stage. However, reading the play and the novel one realizes that there were significant changes made—changes which, to my mind, would lessen the impact of Wright's powerful novel.

Richard Wright's Bigger was a brute but a cunning brute who constructed a kidnapping plot so clever that the newspapers asserted that the Negro mind was incapable of such a plot. The play's Bigger is just that, a brute. Played by Canada Lee, the role of Bigger was given such directions as (*"with a piteous child-like cry"*).

In the original book, Mary Dalton behaves no differently from the standard rich dilettante female; the "penitent rich" who attempts to appease her liberal guilt (the Hearst papers didn't like the play). She's a liberal and likes to cavort among the darkies, which has been a sport among the rich and bohemian for over 300 years. She gets drunk, engages in some heavy petting with her date and has to be carried to her room.

In the play version she is someone who likes to have her breakfast in bed and comes onto the scene "lips rouged heavily," perhaps done so you won't feel so bad when she gets killed and burned. After all, she deserves it, trying to come on so black: "Oh, I wish I was black—honest I do—black like you," Mary says in the play; a line or motive which doesn't exist in the novel. Black (primitivism, sexual excess, drums beating real loud, heathenism!).

Bessie, Bigger Thomas' girl friend, whose rape and death is often ignored by critics, becomes Clara in the play version. Most of the time she speaks like an upwardly mobile secretary instead of the illiterate, hopeless slum girl whose lines and descriptions are some of the most poignant in the novel. With the reduction of Wright's character Jan Erlone the essential Communist theme is diminished and the audience is denied Wright's white-who-is-not-like-the-rest-of-them, a recurrent figure in black writing. In the novel he is the idealized (positive?) Communist worker to whom Bigger says, "You make me feel something could happen. Something good maybe."

Richard Wright's novel *Native Son,* like Bigger, Mary (an object sacred to the Daltons), Bessie (mere "evidence" to be introduced at a trial), become "property" to be interpreted in ways the creator may not have had in mind. Significantly, Wright wrote the play in former slave quarters not too far from Chapel Hill, North Carolina; it could be read as a fugitive narrative since it abounds in metaphors having to do with the individual under wraps, restricted; Bigger is "hindered"; the narrator says, ". . . they had shunted him off into a corner of the city to rot and die." Bigger, the slave who obtains his freedom through murder of something precious to the owner of the plantation; Dalton's home is referred to as "the Big House"; one section of the novel is called "Flight."

The world of *Native Son* is similar to our own. Americans are still attempting to Christianize and Americanize Asia; millions of blacks still live in one-room apartments full of discord, rats, and humiliated men and desperate women. Black victims of black crime are still ignored since the Colonial Office sees ethnic-on-ethnic crimes as a cheap way of exterminating the native population, of no use since it's been replaced by machines; "the only good Injun is a dead Injun," is a saying in the old West. Mockeries of justice still exist where men in high places get off easy while the poor and the black fill the jails; the sensational news media still serve as a vehicle for promoting racial strife as if their true business was that of raising lynch mobs against non-white people; the entire non-white community is still held responsible for the actions of any one non-white psychopath, a situation similar to that which exists in a state of war, where there are reprisals against the enemy population for the murder of any single ally. Welfare still exists, that arsenic of the milk of liberal kindness which has probably contributed more to the destruction of Afro-American culture than any other institution, which makes me believe that Hitler was innocent, the social workers did it.

Some blacks viewed as revolutionary by naïve whites are still in actuality thieves and murderers among Afro-Americans who, like Bigger, rob black businessmen, bully and extort black people. Terrorize and murder them (Mary's death is accidental; Bessie's, deliberate). Bigger permits whites to slap and shove him around while he threatens to cut out the belly buttons of his black comrades. Some black critics still insist that black characters in a black novel be too-good-to-be-true. Even the play's ghetto sets could have been the sets of a dozen black plays written over the last ten years.

The similarities do not end here. Scott Joplin was judged "paranoid" because he "imagined" that someone was stealing his Rags (they was); similarly Bill Gunn's recent play *Black Picture Show* was criticized because it suggested that Hollywood is a ruthless industry which exploits black talent.

Of the film rights to *Native Son* Orson Welles received 33⅓ per cent, Green, 35 per cent, while Wright shared less than 32 per cent with his agent. Wright received a total of three thousand dollars from the film, which was "cut" and "mutilated" by those who had other interpretations of his "property."

Were Paul Green and Orson Welles Wright's Jan Erlones?

Scholastic Teacher, November 1975

An American Romance

In Richard Wright's *Native Son*, published in 1940, a black chauffeur accidentally murders the rich socialist-leaning daughter of a philanthropic slum-lord. The book shocked America in those pre-"Shaft" days.

In the course of the book the narrator and the characters ridicule Jim Crow laws, the economic gulf between the classes, the American judicial system, and racial inequality; but the most devastating satire was saved for the press's treatment of the crime—a treatment characterized by smut-yellow journalism, and exotic soap-opera sensationalism.

Judging from the coverage of the Hearst kidnapping case, electronic journalism of the 1970s is about where the lewd tabloids were in the late 1930s.

In Northern California, two female reporters were the first to offer that the SLA's "Cinque" (Donald DeFreeze) became Patty Hearst's lover before his dastardly deed had even cooled. It was revealed later that the real object of her affections was one Willie Wolf.

Were these women reporters permitting their fantasies to hang in public, or were they merely giving the "Public what *it* wants!"—as media bigwigs in the Board Rooms say as they review the fall lineup of video bilge.

On the day the famous "affidavit" was revealed, it was illustrated in color on both local stations and national television networks in a series of realistic drawings.

With the means available to the defense, it's surprising that the background wasn't provided by the San Francisco

Symphony; perhaps a little Debussy mixed with the sound track from *Jaws*.

In the first picture we saw Ms. Hearst attired only in a white slip, bound and gagged, in the trunk of the kidnap car. Second, we saw her in the same helpless position and attire, stuffed in a closet. When the audio got to the part about Ms. Hearst being threatened with "execution" there appeared on the screen an old photo of Ms. Hearst in all of her debutante innocence. Next, they cut to a photo of "Cinque" taken by a photographer who apparently permitted racism to influence the lenses of his mug shot camera. I wouldn't be surprised if there existed a Heisenberg principle of police photography. It was the kind of profile you see mounted in the Museum of Natural History with the physical characteristics that Richard Wright's fictional press ascribed to Bigger Thomas.

The public was asked to sympathize with Patty Hearst, a veritable campfire girl, pawed over by a "gorilla" as the "white-hope" Heavyweight Champion is fond of calling his opponents who are endowed with classical Negroid features, and are darker than he is. The kind of face that "art collectors" cram their mansions with. You know. "Primitive" art.

The "affidavit" backfired, I'd like to think, because of the public's growing sophistication. Most likely, it failed because the story line was stale. We see "ape-men" carrying off half-clad women in the 1930s reruns: *King Kong* and *Tarzan, The Ape Man* appeared in the same decade as Wright's novel.

I wonder who thought up this defense.

Perhaps, one of those endearing World War II-minded San Francisco cowboys who talk loud at Trader Vic's.

Fiction didn't die as some authors of the 1970s warned it would; fiction obtained a press card and joined Actors Equity.

One of the most interesting fictions to arise from the Hearst kidnapping case concerns the derivation of Donald DeFreeze's adopted name "Cinque."

Some writers have asserted that the original Cinque, Joseph Cinque, an African, who in 1839 rose against his enslavers, and was acquitted of a murder charge, through the legal efforts of John Quincy Adams, returned to Sierra Leone to become a slaver himself.

Warren Hinckle, who knew "Eldridge," and conducted guerrilla warfare from a suite in the Algonquin Hotel, was the latest writer to repeat this bold-faced falsehood.

There is no historical evidence to support the conclusion that Cinque became a slave trader.

Finally, it turns out, Ms. Hearst wasn't the author of the "affidavit" after all; it was based upon information provided by an "anonymous woman."

Image and Money

The most powerful symbol in America today is the dollar. Coins were invented to make communcation between tradesmen less difficult, therefore they serve a useful purpose. Coins are not in themselves filthy. Some of them lie behind glass cases in museums. It's the purposes to which they are put that are filthy. For example, Hollywood. The reason for the crisis in the American character is that dollars rule images instead of serving them. Here is a dollar. Go and produce *Under the Yum Yum Tree,* which will bring in dollars to produce *Son of Under the Yum Yum Tree*. The traditional dilemma of American intellectuals is that they believe that they can combat their dollar-supported ideas—images—with images which have no resources behind them. They believe in politics when anyone can tell you that the best way to capture a congressman's imagination is to send him a vicuna coat, a stereo, or a belly dancer.

Another characteristic of American intellectuals as well as other talented, gifted individuals is that they disdain money. They disdain material things even though they may live on Long Island or in Georgetown. They have swallowed the myth that business and art do not mix, even though Charles Ives, one of this country's great composers, retired in 1929 a multimillionaire from his insurance companies.

Free enterprise is not a bad idea and has produced art. The horseless carriage was a work of art. At one time there were three thousand automobile companies in the

United States, producing a variety of images. So going on a Sunday drive in 1910 was an aesthetic experience.

What happened to free enterprise was that a few selfish men, not even connected to the process of invention —through cunning were able to accumulate more and more of the available technology, expanding their interest to other fields, and stifling the competition, sometimes through brute force. Their descendants manage conglomerates which are beyond nations, beyond politics, sometimes supporting the left and the right of the same country. (The recent example of a major American oil company supporting the Communist Party in Italy.) They weren't too bright, either. They bought Europe's junk and put it on the walls of their estates while Europe snickered behind their backs. There are currently eight thousand works signed "Rembrandt" in the United States— Rembrandt only created three thousand.

Without competition they became smug. Craftsmanship suffered. New ideas were suppressed and new images. They came to rely more on administration than imagination. More on style than on substance and endurance.

Faceless executives were shipped from place to place and so the vice-president of MacDonald's hamburger chain could possibly become the vice-president of MGM. They weren't really interested in fresh images, but only ones proven to sell. Dollars ruled images instead of being the servants of ideas.

Meanwhile all the good, intelligent, talented, and gifted people kept preaching their disgust with material things. With money, with business. We knew they were intelligent. You could read the mind-splitting jargon in the publications they wrote for. They talked about economics when most of them had never filled out an invoice.

I imagine the motivation behind the call for this conference to be that some people are dissatisfied with the way Afro-Americans are depicted in film, plays, and books and to discuss ways by which this can be corrected.

One way would be to have the writers submit their characterizations, dialogues, plots, and descriptions to a committee which would decide which ones are acceptable and which aren't. This wouldn't work because there isn't enough manpower to do the job adequately, besides, from my reading and my experience I would suggest that Afro-Americans would not tolerate a committee deciding on which images they should perceive, as anyone who has tried to push some pet structure upon them has found out. Afro-Americans constantly produce fresh images and will not tolerate a situation where abstract painters are hosed down; beaten by a regime under which books considered "poison weeds" by the leadership are burned, while those considered to be flowers (the leadership's books) remain on shelves.

Another way would be to create enough financial resources, enough dollars, that would guarantee the free flow of a variety of images in a way that would have the dollar serving fresh and original images as well as sustaining classical ones. (Like, who was responsible for the revival of Scott Joplin?) This is what used to be called Free Enterprise, before David, Laurance, the Butcher of Attica, and their ilk got ahold of it.

Where do you usually get money? From a bank. Which bank? Well, it takes $250,000 to begin a bank. Why not borrow an idea from a Negro who gets overlooked by historians who crave action, who don't realize that a great deal of history is boring and not shoot-outs or sword fights. I'm thinking of Alexander Hamilton. I am proposing an Afro-American Cultural Bank with initial assets of a few billion dollars to finance the Afro-American's strongest industry—culture. The top business run by Afro-Americans is a cultural business—Johnson Publishing Co., Inc. There is money in culture. Mayor Beame of New York wants to put $102 million into culture because culture attracts industry and dollars, not because he has some interest in art. The first thing he did when he moved to Gracie Mansion was to remove the modern art left by the Lindsay administration.

The national income of Afro-Americans is between $30 and $40 billion. Surely there is enough left over after essentials to put dollars into a common bank. A bank that would make loans, investments, and begin foundations so that someone can buy radio, television, and newspaper space to inform people of their right to eat or to inform them of where to obtain food, for example. (During the Hearst food giveaway episode in San Francisco, it was learned that there were at least twenty-five centers in San Francisco where people could obtain free food every day.)

Another way to raise revenue with which to begin a Cultural Bank with branches spread throughout the country would also be a way to test the "International Solidarity" with the Afro-American *struggle* at home. Since many Afro-Americans are adopting ways and customs associated with the religion of Islam, perhaps representatives of these groups would approach governments whose rulers follow the religion of the prophet Mohammed. (The prophet Mohammed I'm talking about was born in A.D. 570.) We might approach these people who follow this religion. It might be argued that just as the government of the United States owes reparations to Afro-Americans for previous atrocities, that Islamic governments may owe reparations too. Seeing as how the followers of the prophet Mohammed participated in the uprooting of the African people and selling them into the slave industry. Would it be too much to ask Arab governments to make a long-term, low-interest loan to Afro-Americans for the purpose of beginning a Cultural Bank so that they can finance their own industries as well as buy out existing machinery and to buy stock in existing corporations, a method which Dr. Carlton Goodlett, editor of the San Francisco *Sun-Reporter,* has found to be quite useful in changing the policies of corporations.

The Shah of Iran, a Muslim, recently lent two billion dollars to France. Surely, His Excellency can lend that much money to people in the United States who share his beliefs. Arab interests have already bought businesses in many areas of American life. Perhaps they would put Afro-Americans in charge of these businesses as a token gesture of regret for the pain and suffering perpetrated upon our ancestors by the followers of Islam. And as a precedent, the German Government is still paying millions of dollars to the Jewish people for the atrocities committed upon Jewish people by their German grandfathers.

Another way would be for those intellectuals, like Angela Davis, who believe that the Soviet Union is the ideal worker's paradise, to approach that government concerning the six billion dollars in lend-lease money with the stipulation that it be used to set up industries in the Afro-American Community, and this would be an ideal way for them to show solidarity with the Afro-Americans that they write about in *Pravda* all the time.

The best way to accomplish something is on your own. Billions of Afro-American dollars are passed back and forth through illegal lotteries carried on in Afro-American communities throughout the nation. Some of the money remains in the community and the rest ends up in Long Island, Las Vegas, Buffalo, San Francisco, and Miami. How does one take these chance lotteries and channel funds towards constructive ends like a Cultural Bank whose board of directors would be drawn from various cultural segments in the Afro-American Community?

The Catholic Church raises billions of dollars through legal gambling and the Catholic Church is a pretty venerable institution. How do you get these millions of dollars, made through illegal lotteries, and put them to where they can do some good? I don't know. Some good lawyers could come up with something—it's something technical for someone with legal skills to work on.

Recently, in New York State it was proposed that the numbers be legalized. But instead of the proceeds going to the state, some way should be worked out where the proceeds would go into a cultural bank that would support worthwhile projects for people with good ideas—films, television, theater, writing, etc.

Another way of raising revenue so that a variety of images regarding Afro-American life could be made available is to go through existing channels. Afro-Americans have deposited billions of dollars in banks across the country even though when you enter the bank to do business the bank guard starts to fiddle around with his gun holster. These billions of dollars go to support white businesses mostly. How many people do you know who have gone to apply for a business loan? Most of the dollars handed out by the Small Business Administration went to whites and some have a sneaking suspicion that many of the Afro-American businesses supported by officials of SBA were those the SBA knew would self-destruct.

Maybe instead of sitting in on lunch counters in the 1950s for some abstract goal like "dignity," it would have been better to sit in on loan departments of these banks. In this connection I would like to recommend a book called *Where the Money Is and How To Get It*. There's not a wasted word of rhetoric in this book. It sticks right to the facts. This is a good book. You try this book out; you can understand it.

A lot of people say that my writing is a lot of mumbo jumbo but I'll tell you I'm a hell of a lot clearer than Marx. This book was written by Ted Nicholas and it's published right near here—Enterprise Publishing Co., Inc., 1000 Oakfield Lane, Wilmington, Delaware 19810.

It lists all the foundations in your state, all ways to raise capital, and you'll find that some states subsidize businesses.

So I'm saying that trade has taken place between nations for thousands of years; they've found African vases in South America and Chinese objects in Africa. When the Spanish first encountered the Incas, the Incas were into trade. They were on a boat and they had all this stuff they were going to trade somewhere—including something the Spanish author calls "Moorish" colored clothes. So trade has been going on a long time and the reason that trade has gotten such a rotten name—names like "capitalism"—is that dollars rule images, instead of the other way around.

So it's time for the artists and intellectuals and other creative people who have traditionally rejected trade to get into the field and give the rascals a run for their money. Don't worry if you can't add—like me—I can't add—there are plenty of electronic calculators on the market. They're cheap.

The lesson of our common folklore all the way back before Aesop is that you don't go out there and slug it out with a bear or try to jump up all in his chest and try to maul him. Our heroes are outwitters; rabbits not bears; brains not brawn. Seeing as how the model railroad train, including the locomotive smokestack, the railroad signal, the switching device for railroads cars, water closets for railroad cars, train alarm system, electronic railroad trolleys, were invented by Afro-Americans—you can go check the patents—I'm suggesting that maybe John Henry should have begun a rival Railroad Company.

Finally, a good deal of discussion in the last years has been clogged up with pseudo-Marxist nit-picking; abstract thought. Marx recognized man's material needs, but he didn't recognize man's psychic needs. That's why the people come up with a Nixon from time to time—'cause Nixon knows more about the people than Marx did; and I suggest that just because Marx spent twenty years in the library, doesn't mean he's all that smart. I used to work in a library, and a lot of people just came in to get warm.

The socialist countries are now trying to outcapitalize capitalism, and they tolerate a private sector which rides around in limousines and stocks the best vodka in their villas. People of Havana want parts for their Detroit road hogs. If you think it can work I suggest that you set up a commune or start a co-operative and see if it isn't true that the work falls on the shoulders of individuals. Everybody will not sweep when it's time to sweep.

So in conclusion I think that a Cultural Bank is very feasible and very practical and that there's the energy available to set it up. For those of you who think that merely an attitude of love is effective, I say that there's a song on the radio which says, "Love don't love no one." And for those of you think an attitude like hate is effective, I say that hate causes asthma. And for those of you who think that a variety of fresh images can get across without money dollars backing them up, I quote

another song—"Nothing from Nothing leaves Nothing."
Thank you.

National Conference of Afro-American Writers
Howard University, Washington, D.C.
November 9, 1974

Letter to Roger W. Gaess Concerning the Literary Achievements of Walter Lowenfels

Roger W. Gaess
Box D
S. I., N.Y. 10301

Dear Roger W. Gaess:

Forgive me for not sending in the Lowenfels piece on the day I promised but you know it's hard to write about Walter. Do you write about Lowenfels the poet whose poetry is superior to his politics? Do you write about Walter Lowenfels the gourmet raconteur, classical music connoisseur, John Coltrane admirer before it was Fashionable, butter scion, or Walter Lowenfels Poetry's hustler who flies all over the East in her name (at his age, tsk tsk!); or what about the Lowenfels who is our Special Prosecutor with carefully prepared indictments of The White Literary Mob?

What do you say about this man whose poem *For Lillian* ("I love you/even though all I say is/'please pass the soap.'"), to Lillian is a love poem so wonderful, so warm, so fine that it makes you want love to come back in these days when men and women are spitting blood at each other and calling it poetry.

Right now as I type this I am glancing at the 5,000 or so words I am writing about Walter Lowenfels—pages full of my bad typing with green and light penciled notes running around the margins like crazy. I became so entangled in trying to write about Walter Lowenfels that the papers piled up into a heap of babbling mass. I put it aside and I wrote some poems; I wrote an essay; I wrote a letter to the president of CBS about this bedeviled, corny, Daly City priest out here who's blaming the problems of his church on VooDoo ("ensnaring people to the devil"), a beautiful art form of tapestry, desire, song, dance, good food, healthful herbs, when the Catholic Church invented the devil and they are full of it and he is full of them: the chief killers at Attica were mainline Catholics and so was the prison chaplain who called the murdered men ANIMALS!!!

CBS, which is supposed to be so much for free expression in the political sphere, wouldn't permit me to debate this man who smeared the art forms of my people.

I even had time to write some ad copy for Yardbird Publishing Company and do a press release on Alison Mills' novel, *Francisco,* which Reed, Cannon & Johnson Company is publishing.

Then I went back to the pages of material I had written on Walter Lowenfels and found that I was sounding long-winded in my old age and pompous.

I was sounding like the neo-classical orator who preceded Lincoln on the lectern the day Lincoln delivered the Gettysburg Address, which, like Whitman's introduction to *Leaves of Grass,* is an awkward primitive strident, in the American tradition (the clenched fist is introduced early in American painting, see David Gilmore Blythe's [1815–65] "Trial Scene"; also Paine's prose—slavery and Indian oratory) masterpiece of American rhythms—good old folk art prose. (Lowenfels the Whitman scholar.)

According to the 1863 edition of the *Herald Tribune,* the Latinate clown made the day but Lincoln made the ages.

I don't want to be remembered as a pompous ass and so let me just say this about Walter Lowenfels.

He is a good man and a great poet and he is living and devoting his life to the betterment of his fellow man and sometimes nearly convinces me that they deserve it.

His intellect is as clear as the Hudson River 100 years ago.

Even though *Herrenvolk* apologists like Allen De Loach try to say it differently the *Umbra* writers were right in turning out the Metro in 1964—a little racist den where poetry readings were patrolled by men with guns.

Walter Lowenfels was one of the white poets who saw through this poetry cover just as Kurt Schwitters used to spit on Hitler's portrait right in front of plainclothes Gestapo agents. (Paul Blackburn, gods bless him, saw too.)

While the new missionaries say that Third World people wouldn't be writing had it not been for Whitman and Williams (they're ignorant and see all black poetry as one individual poet—they can't stand but one at a time) Lowenfels stands up and says that Whitman was influenced by American Indian poets and publishes anthologies which prove that Third World people are writing out of their own traditions (like my Neo-Hoo-Dooism)—anthologies which are ignored by people who cry crocodile tears over Solzhenitsyn when they've been practicing censorship, by neglecting subversive cultural ideas and promoting acceptable ones.

Behind his back after a few drinks at their parties on the Upper West Side, the lit. mob must ask, "What kind of white man is he?" just as their crude klansman at Attica, New York, asked Tom Wicker, "What kind of white man are you?" for daring to suggest that prisoners were human beings and had rights.

They don't like Lowenfels' politics either, I understand. They like Pound's politics, you know, Jew hating and nigger baiting. There's a lot they don't like about him but the man just won't go away. He has been talking about dying for forty years, leading me to believe that in order to live to 130 you have to talk about dying all the time.

Lowenfels must be conning his cells, which are contrary things anyway and if you send down information all the time that you're dying they do just the reverse, so Lowenfels is doomed to be like my friend Charlie Smith, who runs a tobacco store in Bartlow, Florida, and tells

Tall Tales about events that happened 100 years or so ago. Some doom.

At the age of ninety he will be streaking through the New York lit. rooms like a thirty-year-old jogger, telling everybody they're full of shit like he cussed out Yevtushenko about Vietnam when the publisher told all of the guests not to say anything about Vietnam, West Twelfth Street, 1966.

Well, Roger Gaess, that's about all I have to say about Walter Lowenfels—his good manners belie the fact that he's on the Left. He has a terrific wife, a great proofreader and copy editor (Nan), four good-looking daughters and twelve handsome grandchildren, and has already received accolades as one of the great American poets. A poet who gave his contemporaries a handicap by quitting for a number of years, but yet coming back stronger like the Long Distance Runner he is.

Next time you go up to Peekskill have a drink with Walter on me. Tell him that one of the best moments of my writing career was the day I introduced *Where's Vietnam?* to Doubleday and they decided to publish it. Tell him he is one of the greatest discoveries I've ever made.

Tell this old fox that I want him with us on that day of an old-fashioned bar-b-cue, banjos, guitars, Injun drums, nigger dancing, jigs, reels, hoedowns, cakewalks—on that day the curse will have been lifted from our beloved land whose traditions extend back at least 10,000 years when our real "founding fathers" left records of themselves on mounds, rock, on skins, and in gold, jade, and wood, and lived here peacefully until that first priggish, uptight, little boat of dreadful Monotheists landed at Plymouth Rock. The Monotheists who tried to make everything gray, somber, boring, and bland like them: running through the land, destroying people's art forms and then setting up missions trying to make the "Injun" and "nigger" "civilized"; this from people who destroyed cultures in South America, Africa, and Europe. (It took them 1,500 years to wipe out pagan resistance in Europe. The casualties were in the millions since Monotheism has to have a "devil" and feeds off blood and the broken arts of other people.)

We'll all be there on that day when the 500-year-old curse is lifted from the land and the American Dream picks up the pieces and continues its poly-theistic, poly-artistic, and poly-cultural course. They say that Lowenfels is dead. This essay finds such an idea preposterous.

March 5, 1974
Berkeley, California

The Old Music

The great migration of Afro-Americans which took place in the 1940s changed their culture and politics.

North became the immigrant's "streets paved with gold," while the South became their "Old Country." Somebody from that neck of the woods became your "homeboy." "Country" became a word of disparagement meaning a backward, innocent way of life. Relatives wrote relatives "down home," about how wonderful it was in Detroit, Chicago, and New York. They were often lying and writing these letters in a furnished room with only the blues to keep them warm. The best novel about the results of this migration is Richard Wright's *Native Son*.

The intellectuals came in contact with nihilistic philosophies and heard utopian ideas from immigrant "radicals." The artists became "avant-garde," not the true "avant-garde" which, as in VooDoo, treats "tradition as a contemporary function," but an "avant garde" which viewed the past as "reactionary."

Jelly Roll Morton got a cold reception when he went to New York, which he referred to as "bitter"; he returned to Los Angeles to die. The Northeastern "avant garde" dismissed Louis Armstrong as a "Tom."

This school of thought has dominated Afro-American culture until recently.

One who realizes his tradition recognizes Jelly Roll Morton, a HooDoo believer, as the guardian of spirit rhythms and Louis Armstrong as the King Zulu, the New Orleans Houngan, worthy of the respect due to his office:

"Strong-armed bodyguards and shiny black limousines, rented from the Geddes and Moss Undertakers, always accompany him to the Royal Barge at the New Basin Canal and South Carollton Avenue. Cannons are fired, automobile horns blast, throats grow hoarse acclaiming him."

A riot nearly developed when Louis Armstrong was not accorded the King Zulu's funeral. He was buried in Queens and not New Orleans.

By rejecting their traditional music, this "avant-garde" rejected the one medium next to dance which acted as the preserver of their ancient art forms, for there are parallels between the coherent confusion one finds in New Orleans music (what Ortiz Walton terms "Classical Afro-American" music, what Creole Tom Dent of New Orleans, a HooDoo worker, ethnographer, archivist, refers to as "Old Music," and what is commonly called "Dixieland") and VooDoo rites, the art form with origins in Africa whose simplified American version is called Hoo-Doo.

The instruments in the old music substitute for the spirits who possess the human hosts in a ceremony; in old music the instruments sound like "voices." Early New Orleans music even bore HooDoo titles such as "Up Jumped LaBas," most likely Creoles trying to say Legba, protector of the Holy Gates and Guardian of the Crossroads; Stackalee's real love was a HooDoo Queen in New Orleans.

It can be argued that the majordomo who precedes the mourners in the funeral parade where the "second line"* occurs is a symbol of Baron Samedi, lord of the cemetery. The majordomo wears the costume of Baron Samedi, and uses his whistle to summon the loas (spirits) and his baton is the symbol of Ghede, a New World loa of satire with no European and African antecedent according to Zora

---

* "Once the band starts, everybody starts swaying from one side of the street to the other, especially those who drop in and follow the ones who have been to the funeral. These people are known as 'the second line' and they may be anyone passing along the street who wants to hear the music. The spirit hits them and they follow." (Louis Armstrong)

Neale Hurston. A loa which came about through an ancient process—a process which probably gave rise to forms like "Rags" and "Blues"; the "Blues" is often treated as a loa: "Good Morning, blues/blues, how do you do," from "Jailhouse Blues," the Houngan greeting a loa.

The performers of the old music weren't interested in knowing esoteric scales or rhythms or even "reading" music though their inventions often startled professors. Being a virtuoso at the instrument didn't become an end in itself, which you could prove by playing real fast. They weren't ashamed of the banjo, an Afro-American invention, and played the tuba like a bass. They had a sense of humor and wit and didn't turn their backs on the audience, what Kropotkin called showing your behind to the bourgeoisie. In fact, they encouraged audience participation and played for HooDoo holidays, parades, marriages, and funerals.

The "avant-garde" played professor music—music you couldn't dance to. Music played to impress a new breed of critics who had developed a whole industry of pedantic newspeak criticism; loaded down with bibliographies; dwelling upon minutiae about who played with so-and-so on what date at which studio in what town and what-not. The new Monks. For years they ruled and often misappropriated Afro-American music in order to further their political ends. Their reign is coming to an end.

The kids of Martin Luther King Junior High School who are now listening to Ohio Players, Little Beaver, Rufus, Earth Wind and Fire, and the Miracles will soon be asking their parents to buy them Jelly Roll Morton, King Oliver, Bunk Johnson, Kid Ory, The Preservation Hall Band, The Eureka Marching Band, and the King HooDoo Zulu Louis Armstrong as well.

City magazine
January 1975

Born to Rebel

At the conclusion of his autobiography *Born to Rebel,*
Dr. Benjamin Mays lists his degrees both earned and honorary. I have often wondered why blacks are so degree
conscious. A critic recently chided a black magazine for
listing more degrees than the average scholarly magazine.
He counted fifty footnotes accompanying one article. Before the advent of ethnic studies, degrees displayed that
the recipient had successfully become initiated into Western intellectual mysteries.

In the song "Express Yourself" the 103rd Street Watts
Band advises, "Whatever you do, do it good." Dr. Benjamin Mays is of this tradition, for whatever he did he did
it good. Excellence. Ralph Ellison's "Long Oklahoma
Eye," Satchel Paige's "Hesitation Pitch," the legendary
black man who built a whole town with five million handmade bricks; Garvey's tenacity. Product of a home in
which his industrious sharecropper father owned his own
property, he worked his way through schools, became
Dean of Howard University, and has served as President
of Morehouse College for thirty years—a college whose
alumni list reads like a Who's Who of black America's
recent intellectual, cultural, and political history. Dr. Mays
directs his message to a younger generation of Americans.
What he seems to be saying is, "You're not the first to
come along with black pride and a quest for dignity. My
generation possessed all of these qualities and what is
more we had it worse than you!"

Dr. Mays's generation strove for first-rate accommoda-
tions, services, and the right to be addressed by their titles

instead of "John," "Charlie," "boy," "Jane," "Sallie," "girl," "Uncle," "Aunt," and "nigger," which were the traditional ways of greeting blacks by whites no matter what the blacks' ages. He contends that things have changed because now, for instance, black dentists and doctors are permitted to play golf in Atlanta, Georgia, and blacks receive courteous treatment at the department stores. After reading Dr. Mays's book I would agree that some things have changed; but would propose that some haven't.

There aren't the frequent white mobs roaming through the streets as they did during the Phoenix Riot or the Atlanta Riot of the kind who would drag a black college official from a train and administer a severe beating to him. No. The mob has gone indoors, where they await the pollster who conveys their grunts to the spineless robots referred to as "political leaders." Nowadays the lynchings come in the form of Omnibus Crime bills. The whites don't stare "daggers" at the "uppity" nigger who rides Pullman coach, but watch them glare at the black passenger riding first-class Jumbo Jet. Black passengers are also more likely to be searched before boarding a plane than whites. Formerly, Dr. Mays contends, the white male was allowed to use the black female any way he desired while the few intimate contacts between black males and white females were inflated into a De Mille spectacular (Gelen in the clutches of the sinister Moor of Summerland), and used as an excuse for lynchings. One only has to view the "craw-tickling" publicity accompanying Howard Sackler's poorly researched travesty on Jack Johnson's life to see that things really haven't changed; or read a white male editor's 1970 introduction to a "black anthology" in which all he could discover in his black female contributors' complex works was that ". . . Black women are not likely to join the women's liberation movement."

Dr. Mays suggests that his generation had no control over what they were called or how they were viewed. Warner Brothers hired Erich Segal, not Ed White or Ed Bullins, to write the film script for the movie concerning "Railroad Bill," a black cowboy, and next time you tune in the television show "Julia" notice the director's name. It certainly isn't Toni Morrison, Julia Fields, or Jayne Cortez.

Dr. Mays mentions the penalties aimed by whites and blacks at the "uppity nigger," "the cute nigger," "the 'hincty' nigger," the nigger who was trying to show out, meaning: step out of his place.

Lost in the controversy concerning Muhammad Ali's difficulties with the Army was the fact that originally he flunked the induction test! It was after the mob was stirred that he was ordered to return for a second test; sort of like a peasant's vision becoming papal dogma. Adam Clayton Powell accomplished one of the most formidable legislative records of this century and if one believes that Washington is chaste may I recommend Drew Pearson's novel *The Senator*, which contains a scene in which a drunken southern senator pursues a young woman down a hotel corridor crying for "poontang." Girl friends? Junketing? Ridiculous; more like a "nigger trying to look too good." When Dr. Mays mentioned the punishment black soldiers received at the hands of white mobs who wanted to keep them in their place—"Take off those uniforms and act like a nigger should"—I thought of the young soldier who received sixty days for wearing an Afro. Even the techniques for survival have remained about the same.

Dr. Mays asked 118 people who were born about the same time as he was (1894) "How their parents taught them to behave towards White people." The answers were "outsmart them," "be submissive," "stay in your place," "be bitter," "think of them as treacherous," "show respect," "fight whoever attacked you," and some were told to "avoid White people," etc. It took the sociologists, lawyers, and politicians to transform these tribal masks into integration, separation, and other confusing names for contemporary strategies.

One can go on listing the similarities between the problems confronted by Mays's generation and a new generation of blacks. The goals of the Atlanta Commission on Interracial Cooperation formed in 1921 could be those of a modern organization's multiple-pointed program: "Legal justice, educational equality, sanitation and housing, economic opportunity, the prevention of lynching, adequate travel and recreational facilities, and child welfare." What has changed?

Reading *Born to Rebel* one is struck by the abundance of classical and Christian references the author employs to get his story across. His generation of scholars was one firmly grounded in the Western tradition. He quotes lines by Countee Cullen: "Make plain the reason tortured Tantalus/is baited by the fickle fruit; declare/if merely brute caprice dooms Sisyphus." In his eulogy to Martin Luther King, Jr., perhaps the last of the great Christian leaders of Afro-America, Browning is quoted; St. Paul, Galileo, Copernicus, and Shelley are invoked. Even the author of "If We Must Die" was not immune to Western influences. Claude McKay owns to a Victorian poet's influence upon his poetry. It seems that Dr. Mays's generation of Greek-speaking Phi Beta Kappas never questioned the reading list! But merely passed all the "tests" of Western scholarship and achieved "degrees." The younger generation in many ways has modified the reading list or in some cases thrown it out altogether and substituted their own. Compare W. E. B. Du Bois' *The Quest of the Silver Fleece* to young Larry Neal's forthcoming *HooDoo Bebop Galloping Ghost* and the careful reader who is not simply seeking "story" or "what it's all about" can readily discern the revolution in consciousness and aesthetics that has occurred. Askia Muhammad Toure's use of Islamic aesthetics, Baraka's experiments with African and black urban languages; N. H. Pritchard's bold neo-lithic solar rock markings (a black poet not reluctant to term his work "primitive"); Mike Harper's anchoring his poetry in the music of John Coltrane; David Henderson's use of Zen, Yoga, Rock and Roll; Al Young's writing the word doodleysquat without the apologetic quote marks; Clarence Major, the best of the dozens writers; and Steve Cannon's erotic New Orleans (not English!) fantasies—all of this work indicates an unparalled experimentation towards overcoming the consciousness barrier erected by an alliance of eastern-based black pseudo-Nationalists and white mundanists who in the 1960s sought to dominate Afro-American intellectual thought with their social realist position papers and promoting those works that made them "feel better" or on the basis of critical standards vaguer even than that. While the classical-Christian generation prided itself in its competence in Western languages, William Melvin Kelley learned French in order to talk to French-speaking blacks in many parts of the world. The result is the marvelous and underrated *Dunfords Travels Everywheres*. The new generation seems to have decided that self-determination begins with the head.

Certainly there were always those unashamed to employ "vernacular" language and music: Chester Himes, Langston Hughes, and Scott Joplin, the great Zora Neale Hurston among them—brave souls who risked the condemnation of their contemporary racist white and elite club-oriented blacks posing as critics; but never before has it been so widespread, with creative ferment on East and West coasts, North and South.

Dr. Mays has written a valuable book. There are interesting portraits of his acquaintances: Presidents, educators, people like Martin Luther King, Jr., Mahatma Gandhi, and the author demonstrates that even ultra-pragmatist Booker T. Washington possessed a sense of humor. He once said: "The only thing wrong with tainted money is that it taint enough."

In the 1960s the younger generation of Afro-Americans was told by this eastern-based alliance of black and white mundanists that they were the first generation to fight back. Many artists and intellectuals who disagreed with their official line were given their spiritual Siberias and villas on the Black Sea; ironically by some of the same people who sanctimoniously oppose the Soviet censorship of Soviet writers. Prior generations of Afro-Americans were depicted as fawning, cringing, and shuffling darkies. Even Nat Turner's revolt was open to an inadequate Freudian interpretation. This censorship by neglect of "cultural independents" resulted in a generation who viewed their ancestors with contempt. Hopefully, Dr. Mays's *Born to Rebel* will convince them that the "black experience" is a galaxy and not the slave-pen many whites and blacks seem to desire it to be. Count Basie and Duke Ellington have unique styles. Claude Brown does not write like Cecil Brown. Dr. Benjamin Mays's experience is as valid as that of someone salivating "right on" at the drop of a hat, or someone confusing a mindless attack on Whitney Young with poetry, or those who characterize an ancient people living in America as "untogether," or those weird mulatto poets who overuse the word "nigger" with the telltale cracker intonation. Perhaps Dr. Benjamin Mays's *Born to Rebel* will be promoted as vigorously as the latter.

New York *Times*
April 25, 1971

De Mayor of Harlem

In the early 1960s, three writers—Calvin Hernton, David Henderson, and Tom Dent—began the *Umbra* magazine writing workshop on Manhattan's Lower East Side; some critics have traced the current proliferation of Afro-American poetry to this event. David Henderson was about nineteen then, and was called, affectionately, by his admirers "the boy genius." His first book, *Felix of the Silent Forest*, was published by Poets' Press and now E. P. Dutton has published his second volume, *De Mayor of Harlem*.

I have not seen reviews of this book in publications controlled by what I call the Axis: that tacit alignment between "black nationalists," "black revolutionaries," "white radicals," and "white liberals" which views the Afro-American writer as a kind of recruiter for their rather dubious political programs. This neglect by the Axis is perhaps a tribute to Henderson's independence. He is a poet who writes about his nomadic wanderings (he calls himself "a foot soldier, front man, messenger, journey-man") through Harlem, Columbia Heights, from the Lower East Side to Chelsea, and occasionally he takes a plane to Berkeley or Omaha only to discover that in the United States every town is a neighborhood of another town; New Orleans is 125½ Street.

The city poems are as tabloidy as the *Daily News:*

> "Pope Arrives in New York City"
> "Broadway Hustlers Go Wild"

Headlines, Theodore Bernstein claims, are an American invention and they aren't the only American invention Henderson uses in his art. His classic poem concerning the Harlem Riots of 1964, *Keep on Pushin'*, was inspired by Curtis Mayfield and the Impressions, a rock and roll group.

Henderson's Harlem isn't the exotic Harlem of the 1920s handbill, but the Harlem of Malcolm X and the Apollo Theater; a Harlem where the treaties are not likely to be composed in the language of Ellsworth Bunker:

brother/you my boy/if anybody fuck with you/they got to fuck with me/we are down together/if they get you/they got to get me/too

But are binding just the same.

Henderson also uses an aesthetic currently employed by other contemporary Afro-American artists, I would call Neo-HooDooism; HooDooism being an ancient North American version of VooDoo rites involving dance, poetry, music, and possession which originated in West Africa, underwent modifications in South America, and continued to go through changes when brought to North America by slaves. Practices associated with HooDoo varied from Louisiana, where it commingled with Catholicism, to Georgia and Alabama (an early map of the state denotes the southeast as "Conjure Country"), where it thrived alongside Protestantism.

Always subversive (Billy Graham recently warned of "VooDoo priests taking people away from God" as if the first amendment didn't exist), it was from the beginning an underground movement, and although associated in the popular mind with "evil" (Webster's *New World Dictionary* defines it as "bad luck") it was used to heal both body and mind; Ernest Gaines's characters consult HooDoo to work both "good" and "bad" deeds.

HooDoo artists serve the community as "soothsayers, exorcisers, organizers of public entertainment, and choirmasters." They did not lead people in "Holy Wars" or administer "absolution"—that's Christian. They made conjure, gris-gris, spells (HooDoos call these elements "The Work"), and when one reads early HooDoo tales one is struck by the free use of what professors call "the vernacular," the lack of division between the natural and the supernatural, animism, the discontinuous sense of time, the listing of rites, and the talking of that talk (talking in codes; among HooDoos of New Orleans of the 1850s it was said that a message could be sent from one end of the city to the other in a single day without being detected by a single white!).

The fact that David Henderson—along with Joe Overstreet (who designed the cover for *De Mayor of Harlem*) in painting, Wes Robinson in theater, Ortiz Walton and Marcus Gordon in music, Doyle Foreman in sculpture, Glenn Myles in graphics—uses this tradition in his work has baffled certain establishment critics like the one in the *Saturday Review of Literature* whose mystification, however, didn't prevent him from plunging ahead anyway with a trite ("incoherent," he said) dismissal of the book because he didn't possess the necessary scholarship to analyze Henderson's book.

Consciously or unconsciously, Afro-American writers have continued the HooDoo tradition. The listing of rites? Ralph Ellison compiled *The Big Wormy Apple, The Chicago Get Away, The Shoo Fly Rub,* and *The Slow Drag.* One of Calvin Hernton's major poems is entitled *Jitterbugging in the Streets,* and the invocation of Al Young's book of poems *Dancing* is, "Do you love me/now that I can dance?" from a song popularized by the rock and roll group known as the Contours. Henderson writes of "Karate Bougaloo," and "bojangling children in the streets." Talking that talk? What do you make of John A. Williams' "sleptis joon cut from the moon"? or Paul Lofty's "Jody Grinder" or David Henderson's "blues & fish of jesus frying across the boardwalk/snake dancers walk mojo [black cat bones used as charms] along the wide boulevard."

Even the malice and vengeance side of HooDoo finds its place in contemporary Afro-American writing. No mainstream writer or existentialist (it's considered hip in New York to express no emotion when your mother dies) is likely to curse "the Governor" as the writer Redd Foxx does in his work *The Prayer,* which, incidentally, has sold more than 100,000 copies among Afro-Americans but is never mentioned when *Time, Newsweek,* and other organs are busily nominating their "dominant figure in black literature today"—they all have candidates; John Lahr of the *Village Voice* even has two.

Afro-American writers still summon the loas (sermons) or prophesy, and signify, which I have defined as taking off the slave master's head and making him think you're giving him candy. While most Afro-American writers are HooDoos in principle—each HooDoo priest was allowed to bring his own improvisations to the rites because Hoo-Doo is elastic enough to incorporate any number of loas (spirits)—David Henderson is a HooDoo poet in substance as well.

Included in *De Mayor of Harlem* are a series of poems concerning New Orleans, or New O., early capital of American HooDoo. One concerns Marie Laveau (who was promoted by her writer-lover, Lafcadio Hearn, as "The Queen of VooDoo" when there existed those who were more original than she, and were not belabored by her Catholic influences). Another poem is entitled *Sprinkle Goofer Dust,* goofer dust being the earth gathered at a grave site and used in "The Work." In his poem *Pentecostal Sunday/Song of Power,* Henderson knows that in the original Church St. Expedite is a VooDoo loa (Baron Samedi) concealing his identity in Christian garb as expertly as Chester Himes's nuns do. Henderson even draws altar pictures as in *Ruckus Poem,* and performs a spell as in *Kenny Clark Blues or Jamboree.*

The last poem in Henderson's book is a song. An actual Blues that can be sung. Many Afro-American poets are writing songs these days, perhaps pointing the way to a collaboration involving writers and musicians.

Though David Henderson's HooDoo book is fully appreciated when viewed within the tradition I have sought briefly to describe, I have a few gripes about *De Mayor of Harlem.* I would like to know more about the loa Shango than merely his association with the color red; many things are "psychedelic," and in some cases this works but in other instances it doesn't; we know that certain sections of New York are pervaded by "ennui," and "malaise," but we don't have to know it over and over again; the poem for Langston Hughes is a little heavy in undertaker's cosmetics.

This might be considered an esoteric book for eastern critics still carrying the torch for "Modernism" or Europe, a disaster in intellectual values that has kept Americans unaware of their own traditions, and still at this late date, a few years before the anniversary of the United States' founding, wandering about confused in a land still strange to most of them. But for those of us who know "The Work," *De Mayor of Harlem* is truly a delight. I'm from Tennessee and my grandmother used to speak of some of the things David Henderson writes about.

Black World
April 1972

Chester Himes: Writer

*It was simply that I've always had a tendency
to view all situations from a writer's point of view.*
                                        Chester Himes

On November 4, 1974, in the New York *Times*'s "The
Last Word" column, John A. Leonard, in an extraordinary admission for the editor of a newspaper whose arts
sections have carried some of the meanest remarks concerning the creative abilities of blacks, wrote: "The White
man is stealing [black writers'] material."* He wasn't
specific but he could have had Saul Bellow, Bernard
Malamud, John Updike, Shane Stevens, and even
Richard Nixon in mind. ("And so as the young people
say—'right on.'") To this list you could add poets from
the New York school (one of them swiped an A. B. Spell-
man poem almost word for word), and Norman Mailer,
who sought to structure his *Why Are We in Vietnam?*
along the lines of Be-bop terminology; he failed. The
black influence is not limited to the writing arts. Anna
Halprin's dance troupe, the majority of whose New York
performers were blacks, was described by critic Clive
Barnes as "Blacker than Alvin Ailey."

On November 28, in the same "Last Word" slot, Mel
Watkins in an incredible statement for someone who edits
the *Black Review,* said: "Despite its vaunted richness and

* "Then, tired but smiling broadly, the Governor stepped to a
battery of microphones on the airport apron and, using a phrase
borrowed from the Rev. Dr. Martin Luther King, Jr., he told his
greeters, 'We're going to keep on'" (from the description of a
speech made by Governor George Wallace on the eve of the Wis-
consin primary in 1972 as reported by the New York *Times*).

depth, alas [in the mid-sixties], black culture was exhausted and eclipsed." A few months later, in Quincy Troupe's *Confrontation* magazine, in a negative review which pitted black writers against black musicians, black critic Eugene Redmond wrote "Little wonder, then, that whites are imitating our Bluesists and not our writers. Whites apparently know the source and location of the concentrated depth of Black creativity—even if many Black writers don't!" Another leading black critic had said that the black novel is "lagging behind," and still another, described by *The Nation* as the "leading spokesman for black revolution," made the comment that "no black writer has done for black people what Isaac Bashevis Singer had done for Jewish people." In contrast, in its winter issue, *The Virginia Quarterly* said: "[Chester Himes] has long been unjustly ignored," while the publication of a Ford-Rockefeller-sponsored black theater group termed Himes "a black Mickey Spillane." (Of course, Himes was publishing "crime stories" [1934] long before Spillane [1947]; one wonders why these blackopaths wouldn't call Spillane a white Chester Himes. Well, you know why, don't you?) There have been many instances, recently, where white critics have been willing to admit the effect of black writing, dancing, music, and painting upon mainstream arts while those critics who proclaim their fondness of blackness have denied the abilities of black creative artists. What gives? "Blackness is being used to save Western Civilization," a very thoughtful woman told me the other day; and maybe there is more to that remark than mere rhetoric, for what else would explain why some of the more spiteful, frivolous comments on black writing would come from those who claim to be its champions? Some of the academics among them write as if they haven't read a book since passing their orals.

Have issues surrounding black culture always been this confusing? How does one find out? Harold Cruse's *The Crisis of the Negro Intellectual,* although inadequate as a critical survey of the painting, writing, and music of the period it covered, was invaluable because it was a narrative by someone who participated in that period—someone with an astute eye. With Cruse's book we were rewarded with the witness of a skillful political scientist; with Chester Himes's *The Quality of Hurt,* Vol. I, we have a writer's viewpoint of a similar period:

> No matter what I did, or where I was, or how I lived, I had considered myself a writer ever since I'd published my first story in *Esquire* when I was still in prison in 1932. Foremost a writer. Above all else a writer. It was my salvation, and is. The world can deny me all other employment, and stone me as an exconvict, as a nigger, as a disagreeable and unpleasant person. But as long as I write, whether it is published or not, I'm a writer, and no one can take that away. "A fighter fights, a writer writes," so I must have done my writing.

Who else, but a writer, when faced with extermination by a "long barreled .38," would notice the gunman's attire: "blue sneakers, denims, and a bright-red silk shirt."

Himes chose his title *The Quality of Hurt* from Shakespeare's, "The quality of mercy is not strain'd/ It droppeth as the gentle rain from heaven." And the chapters and Books are connected to each other by "hurts" Himes endured in a long History of Hurts. He was hurt by his mother, a strong-willed, highly intelligent woman who could handle a pistol so well, she "beat anybody to the draw." She taught Himes and his brothers so expertly that when they entered school they were ahead of their classes, but she also "squeezed the bridges of our noses to keep them from becoming flat." He was hurt by the reception of his writing, especially *Lonely Crusade* (1947), the adverse criticism of which was one of the major factors leading to his exile. He was hurt by accidents so unbelievable as to lead one to compare the plight of the Himes family to the fictional Gothic ones, laboring under a curse. A chemistry accident almost totally blinded his brother, Joseph; the tormented relationship between his mother and father led to their divorce. He was hurt by a judge who sentenced him to twenty to twenty-five years for armed robbery, and he was hurt by his inability to support his black wife, Jean.

> Up to the age of 31 I had been hurt emotionally, spiritually, and physically as much as 31 years can bear: I had lived in the South, I had fallen down an elevator shaft, I had been kicked out of college, I had served seven and one half years in prison, I had survived the humiliating last five years of the Depression in Cleveland; and still I was entire, complete, functional; my mind was sharp, my reflexes were good, and I was not bitter.

And this is one of the remarkable things about *The Quality of Hurt,* Vol. I, the absence of rancor and self-pity. After being hurt by relative, friends, institutions, cities, even world events, Himes never fails to mention how he hurt his wife, his relatives, and others. Pistol-whipping and punching women, taking such foolish risks with the law after criminal feats of genius capacity that one has the feeling he craved capture, and it is significant that he sees the seven and a half years he served in Ohio State Penitentiary (he survived a fire there, one of the worst penal disasters before Attica) as a period free from hurt. "The seven and a half years I actually served did not seem to hurt me at all." Himes enters some interesting remarks at this point concerning the violent careers of sons who aren't disciplined by their fathers (they become criminals or writers).

Chester Himes, gambler, tuft-hunter, busboy, caretaker, porter, cat burglar (jewels were involved), blueprint reader, but mostly writer, was born on July 29, 1909, in Jefferson City, Missouri, one of three sons of an "octoroon" mother and a father (". . . short black man . . . bowed legs . . . ellipsoidal skull") who taught blacksmithing and wheelwrighting as the head of the mechanical department at Lincoln Institute. Some of his relatives were fair enough to "pass" and pursued careers associated with the economic middle class. Nothing demonstrates the difference between his father's and mother's mentalities more than their suggestions about how to collect, one month after Himes incurred injuries in an elevator accident. His father persuaded him to sign all waivers to all rights for additional money after the Wade Park Manor, his employer, awarded him a pension. His mother felt he should have rejected the pension for the purposes of winning a suit for more money. It turns out that his mother had the best advice. Himes writes,

> My father was born and raised in the tradition of the Southern Uncle Tom; that tradition derived from an inherited slave mentality which accepts the premise that white people know best, that blacks should accept what whites offer and be thankful . . .

On the other hand,

> My mother, who looked white and felt that she should have been white, was the complete opposite . . . She was a tiny woman who hated all manner of condescension from white people and hated all black people who accepted it . . .

Much of the Himes family history has been fictionalized in *The Third Generation* (1954).

As a student at Ohio State University, he is the well-heeled Alpha Phi Alpha fraternity man equipped with "coonskin coat . . . knickerbocker suit, and Model T Ford roadster." He is admired by black students and envied by the white ones. For taking some college students to a brothel Himes knows in the Cleveland ghetto, he is suspended from school. After this incident he drifts into trouble. He meets a buddy from his busboy days at the Wade Park Manor and begins to hang out. They begin frequenting Bunch Boys, a rough gambling club on Cleveland's Cedar Avenue near Ninety-fifth Street. He steals a car, cashes a bogus check, and pulls off a near perfect crime. (The fence turns him in; there is a fiction account of this episode in *Cast the First Stone* [1952].)

For the latter, an armed robbery, he receives a stiff prison sentence. Noteworthy is the fact that his mother seems to offer the authorities an apology. "She blamed my father for not disciplining me and she felt that his indifferent attitude toward my behavior was the root of all my troubles."

In these times of the black convict as "political prisoner," what Himes has to say about his prison experience is pertinent. Himes writes:

I found the convicts like idiot children, like the idiot giant of Steinbeck's *Of Mice and Men,* intensely grateful for small favors and incomprehensibly dangerous from small slights. . . .

When I read this I thought of the brilliant young prisoner who was being primed for "revolutionary spokesman" by the usual crew. He told an interviewer, "I'll be your friend for a cigarette." (One wonders whose friend he would be for a pack!) Himes continues:

Convicts stabbed, cut, slashed, brained, maimed, and killed each other almost every day for the most nonsensical reasons. Two black convicts cut each other to death over a dispute as to whether Paris was in France or France in Paris.

Himes's literacy protects him from these outrages: "The black convict had both an instinctive respect for and fear of a person who could sit down at a typewriter and write. . . ." It is in prison that Himes "grew to manhood," and where he begins to write. He sells his first short story, "Crazy in the Stir," to *Esquire* magazine in 1934. At the end of seven and a half years in prison Himes emerges with an insight that remained with him. "The only effect it had on me was to convince me that people will do anything—white people, black people, all people."

Cast the First Stone is the novelistic account of Himes's prison experience. Published in 1952, it contains the expression "down with the pig."

After release he marries an old sweetheart, Jean: " . . . An extremely beautiful brown-skinned girl." He works again in a country club as waiter and bellhop but doesn't abandon his writing, selling stories to *Esquire* and *Coronet*. For the Works Progress Administration (WPA) he works as "a laborer, digging sewers and dredging creeks . . . and then as a research assistant in the Cleveland Public Library." The Jeliffes, a white couple who ran Karamu Settlement House, come to his assistance and get him a job at Louis Bromfield's Malabar Farm in Pleasant Valley, Ohio.

It doesn't work out. "I had thought that Malabar Farm might soothe the tensions that were overwhelming me from my new experience of the horror of racial prejudice. But I soon discovered that I was merely hiding."

Himes, with his wife, Jean, travels Greyhoud bus to Los Angeles and he writes his first novel, *If He Hollers Let Him Go* (1945). It is a hard novel. The characters talk hard, love hard, and eat hard: "On the way home I stopped at a greasy spoon and had a couple of fried pork chops, some French fries and baked beans." The novel's style is jive with characters talking out of the corners of their mouths. " 'Don't hand me that hockey,' she said, leaning one hand on the bar and looking at me. 'That is the saddest jive; that is pitiful puleeze bulieve me!' "

Expressions like ". . . the hot licking lilt of James' trumpet," abound. The Zoot Suit riots are remembered. The dream which begins chapter 9, and events following a "blinding explosion" it recalls (chapter 4), anticipates a major sequence in *Invisible Man* (chapter 11). The opening of chapter 18 is a movie. The love bouts between the plant leaderman, Bob Jones, and Madge, the white trashy Texas broad, forecast the one involving Rufus and Leona in James Baldwin's *Another Country* (1962).

If He Hollers Let Him Go is about the Depression generation. The Depression was mean and the people who came out of it, impatient with heart-throbbing. (The acting styles of Moses Gunn and John Garfield.) The novel is youthful, insulting, risky, brash, bad-assed, revolutionary, violent, and struts about as if to say, here come cocky Chester Himes, you litterateurs, and I hope you don't like it. A cousin's wife, Molly Moon, influences the Julius Rosenwald Foundation to award Himes a fellowship, and he travels to New York City for its publication by Doubleday, Doran and Company.

His comments about this New York trip are revealing. "New York hurt me in a different way—by accepting me. That sounds like a contradiction but it's the truth. I knew that, as much as I had been hurt by then, I was sick. But New York accepted me as normal, and that made me sicker."

New York is the American breeding ground of fads, fashion, slogans, trinkets, and rhetoric. When Himes went there, the fascination of the moment was Roosevelt. Himes writes that everything was used to "garner" votes for him, ". . . sex, white women, black women, married women, single women; money, eloquence, and intrigue." Events surrounding "the New Deal" provide a setting for Himes's satirical novel *Pinktoes* (1961), which lampoons the phoney 1940s New York cultural and political world of forty-year-old "young poets," lecherous preachers, society dames, and philanthropists with unconventional sex habits. (It is the book with the best tall rat story in the business.)

New York is not for Himes, the prolific writer, and so he returns to California and begins his most controversial novel, *Lonely Crusade* (1947). Upon publication of *Lonely Crusade,* Himes becomes a target of a campaign of vilification experienced by few American writers. "The left hated it, the right hated it, Jews hated it, blacks hated it." The *New Masses,* the *Daily Worker,* the *People's Voice, Ebony* magazine, *Atlantic Monthly,* and *Commentary* attacked it. Christian novelist James Baldwin wrote an unfavorable review in the *New Leader.*

Lonely Crusade was bound to rankle, for no group, race or system is spared Himes's scathing, thoughtful rebukes: the cult of the worker, Jews, blacks, whites, Ideology. The hero, Lee Gordon, possesses elements of

Himes's personality. He is sardonic, often cynical and in-dividualistic:

Lee Gordon reached a conclusion sitting there: that the one rigid rule in human behavior was to be for yourself and to hell with everyone else; that within all human beings, himself included, were propensi-ties for every evil, each waiting its moment of ful-fillment; that honor never was and never would be for the Negro, and integrity was only for a fool; that from then on he would believe in the almighty dol-lar, the cowardice of Negroes, and the hypocrisy of whites, and he would never go wrong.

Himes's comments about white workers seem relevant to these days of hard hats:

He could see the hostile faces on the white workers, their hot, hating stares; he could feel their antago-nisms hard as a physical blow; hear their vile asides and abusive epithets with a reality that cut like a knife.

In the dialogue, Himes is able to put Lee Gordon's bitter, skeptical viewpoint to good usage.

"Enough culture for one day, my Caliban," she [Mollie] said, then lifted her glass. "To F.D.R."
"To Joe Stalin," Luther said.
"To the three component parts of Marxism," Lee said slyly. He caught the quick glances exchanged between Mollie and Luther and grinned to himself.

When I read, in *Lonely Crusade*, of the attempt by Jewish people to get white people to evict Lee Gordon, and his wife, Ruth, from a neighborhood, I thought of the current bilious effluvia emanating from the works of some Jewish playwrights, cartoonists, film makers, novel-ists, magazine editors, and television writers which depict blacks in such an unfavorable light as if to say to whites,

"We'll supply the effigy, you bring the torch." (Spiro Agnew didn't create Archie Bunker; a Jewish writer did.) I thought of recent remarks by Nathan Glazer telling blacks to slow down in their quest for long overdue rights, and the recent front-page picture of rabbis meeting with Senator James Buckley on how to keep blacks out of Forest Hills. I thought of David Susskind, teased silver hairdo, plastic-surgery face, defending the troopers' actions at Attica; I could see the phantom of Hitler in the wings during the "Dick Cavett Show" saying to Susskind, "My son! my son!"

Lee Gordon says in *Lonely Crusade,*

With Jews being slaughtered in Europe by the hundreds of thousands, brutalized beyond comprehension, you Jews here in America are more prejudiced against Negroes than the gentiles.

Himes was also critical of blacks:

For like many other white people whom Lee had met, Smitty mistook the mugging of a Negro for integrity. And if he, Lee Gordon, had any sense, Lee said to himself, he should have learned, as had the great Negro leaders who always mugged, that white people preferred the mugging to the honesty.

Pop nationalists were likely to be distressed by some passages too:

The *Negro!* How many times had he, Lee Gordon, used the term *"The Negro"* with that pompous posturing of ignorance to describe the individual emotions and reactions, appearances and mentalities, the character and souls of 15 million people.

Both Richard Wright in *The God That Failed* (1950) and the first person in Ellison's *Invisible Man* (1952) reach a conclusion similar to the one Lee Gordon makes in *Lonely Crusade.*

And yet there were times such as this when he was more Negro than Communist, and his American instincts were diametrically opposed to the ruthless nonconformity of revolutionary maneuvering; when the long list of his acts as an executive of the Communist Party judged themselves in the light of Christian reason; when the voice of his Baptist mother could be heard in the night of his soul; when virtues such as honesty, loyalty, courage, and kindness, charity, and fair play had meaning and value; when his mind rebelled and could not follow the merciless contradictions of reality. . . .

In *Lonely Crusade* Himes is on no one's team, and then as now, when people seek to use the black writer as a human mimeograph machine, grinding out their notions, however ridiculous, Himes had to decide whether he was going to remain in the United States and call them the way he saw them or go into exile:

Of all the hurts which I had suffered before—my brother's accident, my own accident, being kicked out of college, my parents' divorce, my term in prison, my racial hell on the West Coast—and which I have suffered since, the rejection of *Lonely Crusade* hurt me most.

And he derives a moral from the experience that all contemporary black writers and those of the future might heed:

I had tried to be fair. It is the one single thing no one will forgive you for, neither the communists nor the fascists, the rightists nor the leftists, the white racists nor the black racists . . . One will make more enemies by trying to be fair (marked by impartiality and honesty) than by trying to tell the truth—no one believes it possible to tell the truth anyway— but it is just possible that you might be fair.

A campaign was waged to interfere with promotion and distribution of *Lonely Crusade* and other processes by which the writer's book gets from publisher's press to reader. Communists and others so quick to call people "facist pigs" harassed booksellers. Public appearances were mysteriously canceled. One of Himes's few consolations was a caustic remark made by his father, who said, "Remember, son, New York is not the only city that has skyscrapers. We have one on the new Union Station in Cleveland." After the fiasco surrounding the publication of *Lonely Crusade,* Himes travels to Yazoo College at the behest of his old friend Horace Cayton, where he reads a paper called "The Dilemma of the Negro Writer."

The audience's reception is chilly, if not hostile, and he spends the duration of his stay drunk. After some more menial jobs and an incident in Connecticut where he receives a bum rap on a traffic violation which was the other driver's fault, a drunken but respectable and influential old woman, Himes travels to New York, where he meets Richard Wright. Before leaving the United States he is reunited with his brother, Joseph, a distinguished sociologist, who invites him to North Carolina College to conduct a seminar on writing. Finally, he returns to New York, where he resumes an affair with a white woman, Vandi Haygood, the woman he almost murders. His last night in the United States is spent in the Albert Hotel, hating her.

Book II begins in April 1953 on the boat to Europe. Himes meets Mrs. Alva Trent Van Olden Barneveldt, a Philadelphia aristocrat who later joins him in Paris. In Paris he is introduced to cafe society and meets many Afro-American cultural intellectual luminaries (E. Franklin Frazier is remembered as "an extraordinary *raconteur*"). He becomes acquainted with the famous Leroy and Gaby Haynes bar-b-cue restaurant and jazz clubs like the Blue Note.

After an amusingly lustful incident involving Vandi Haygood, who formerly was associated with the Rosenwald Foundation, Himes becomes a very much sought after bed partner.

One thing you notice about many of the black writers who began writing in the middle thirties, forties, and fifties. They could write well (especially the ability for scrupulously reporting reality in detail: see Himes's description of Luther, the Communist dupe, in *Lonely Crusade*, page 28, A. Knopf hardcover), they could shoot well (in the course of *The Quality of Hurt,* Vol. I, Himes handles a variety of rifles and pistols; the book also reports a day Himes spends with Ralph Ellison hunting "cottontails"); and they were (and are) not reluctant to accommodate the amorous yearnings of beautiful women. Although Himes calls himself "a puritan" he was in and out of as many beds as Legba. Truly robust, virile men they were and are. Richard Wright had more than a routine interest in the matter, Himes reports, and Himes believes that had he lived he might have written a book on "odd couples." But on his more raunchy side, Himes quotes Wright as saying: "Chester, when it gets warm these American girls go down the street, flinging open their arms, and cry, 'Take me! Take me! I'm young and good in bed.' "

Many black writers have been scolded by critics, both black and white, not only for the candid descriptions of sex in their books but the manner in which sex plays a part in their private lives.

It seems plain why white ones object; white writers create NBC's Geraldine; but more One-Step-Beyond is why black critics, especially those who claim they love black history so much, would join in these attacks.

Dahomean myths certainly aren't for the sexually squeamish, and the ancient Egyptians were expelled from Rome at one point because their theater was so sexually frank. (They did worship the cat, you know.) Both were ancient African cultures. So why would certain black critics term these writings "decadent?" (A European style of art, incidentally.)

One has the feeling that critical elements of the blackness movement (one of them recently termed women "garbage") fear the heterosexual black writer, and Himes's description of the generation of writers I have mentioned lends substantiation to claims made by Calvin Hernton and others regarding the white literary—and factions of the black literary—establishment's fascination with the epicene, small-boned, slight, and delicate black writer. Perhaps this explains why these heterosexual writers haven't received the critical acclaim due the quality of their output. Oh, they claim to love Richard Wright so much, one suspects, because they like the last few chapters in *Native Son*. (Nowadays, instead of employing Bigger Thomas as a chauffeur, Mary Dalton and her boyfriend Jan would begin a "radical" magazine and give Bigger a column.) It took Gertrude Stein to hail Richard Wright as the best American writer of his time; it will be a long time before white male-dominated eastern book reviews will own up to this.

Steve Cannon's book *Groove, Bang and Jive Around* has sold 150,000 copies without a single ad or review, and if one did a market poll of this lascivious HooDoo book's readership it would turn out to be the same "brother-on-the-street" these black critics claim they champion. One imagines these critics as similar to the man who walks to the edge of the cliff and shouts, "Blackness." The echo bounces back Jesus; Marx peeping over the "Saviour's" shoulder.

The Quality of Hurt, Vol. I contains many interesting accounts of Himes's first trip to Paris, including the famous encounter between Richard Wright and young James Baldwin.

Wright considered Baldwin ungrateful because of his "scurrilous" attacks on Wright after Wright helped launch Baldwin's career by obtaining for him an award from Harper and Brothers. Baldwin's defense has become famous: "The sons must slay their fathers." (After Baldwin's previous attacks on Countee Cullen, when alive, and on Chester Himes, one might legitimately ask, "How many fathers does one son need?")

Himes makes a keen observation about this incident. "All of the women and the majority of men, including the artists, took Baldwin's side, chiefly, I think, because he looked so small and intense and vulnerable and Dick appeared so secure and condescending and cruel."

Mrs. Barneveldt arrives in Paris to join Himes. Wright's treatment of her seemed to cool an already tenuous relationship between the two writers.

He had decided he didn't like Alva. He thought that if she was going to leave her husband and children to come and live with me there was no reason why she shouldn't live like other American tramps in the Latin Quarter, in a cheap hotel room, and take public baths. He resented my considering her something special.

When Himes leaves for Arcachon, France, the men aren't on the best of terms. His departure to Arcachon takes place at about the same time that Wright leaves for Ghana to write a book on nationalism, and Nkrumah.

Himes reveals Richard Wright as a hard-working, disciplined writer; big-hearted but given to occasional pettiness and vindictiveness; a devoted family man and a lover. "As all of his friends knew," Himes writes, "Dick had an excitable temperament and was given to such self-indulgent exaggeration that the buzzing of a blowfly could rage like a typhoon in his imagination."

Himes is not kind to many of the "soul brothers" he encounters during this Parisian sojourn. In one scene, Wright takes him to a cafe in search of some fellow black American expatriates.

Dick expected a gathering of our soul brother compatriots, all of whom knew I was to arrive the night before, but not one of them appeared, an eccentricity which I was later to learn was the natural reaction of the envious and jealous American blacks who lived in Paris—or anywhere else in Europe, for that matter. They did not want any arriving brother to get the idea they thought he was important.

When Himes and Mrs. Barneveldt leave Arcachon, the fishing village (". . . noted for oysters"), they travel to London, where, on the first night, they have a frightening experience with a psychopath. After London, they voyage to Mallorca, Spain, and are introduced to, among others, Robert Graves. (He asks Himes, "What instrument do you play?" Himes replies, "The radio.") Due to a dispute with a Mallorcan landlord, they have a harrowing escape from the landlord's friends, a local mob. But despite the unpleasantness, Himes is able to complete *The End of the Primitive* (published, *The Primitive*), the book which on a superficial level is about an interracial love affair. *The Quality of Hurt,* Vol. I, ends with Himes taking Mrs. Barneveldt to France, where she departs for America. When I read the ending I imagined rolling movie cameras stationed strategically to record the scene, because it would make a great love story:

> I went across to a bar on rue Saint-Lazare and had a couple of Cognacs. Suddenly I found myself crying like a baby. Tears streamed down my cheeks. French-men at the bar turned to stare at me. I wiped my eyes and tried to pull myself together. I'm just too emo-tional, I upbraided myself. My feelings are too in-tense. I hate too bitterly, I love too exaltingly, I pity too extravagantly, I hurt too painfully. We American blacks call that "soul," I thought deprecatingly.

And then, superimposed upon this is the rust-colored film used to invoke nostalgia. The scene from *Lonely Crusade;* Lee Gordon's wife, Ruth, is mixing drinks, and the narra-tive reads:

> *For a long time—ever since she had first learned a little of the fear inside of him—she had expected Lee to be hurt, dreading it and yet convinced that it would happen, because she did not see how Lee Gordon could live in the society of America and es-cape being hurt. And she had feared that when it*

*happened, there would be nothing she could do; that
he would be hurt and that he would be alone with it.*

The Quality of Hurt, Vol. I, is retrospective Himesiana.
It is a love story, sometimes amusing, sometimes sorrowful;
it's a cops and robbers story as gory as Peckinpah; it's a
story about the tragedies that shatter a proud, noble, and
gifted family.

One would think that in a Book of Hurts there would be
a lot of sniveling self-pity that has become associated with
black autobiographies. As for his capacity to narrate these
Hurts calmly without cloying, Himes writes, "I hate ex-
hibiting my wounds."

Volume I of the Himes *Lonely Crusade* is told coolly
and objectively, Himes utilizing his considerable novelistic
gifts, one of the major qualities of which is a fantastic
memory. His descriptions of Los Angeles, Cleveland, and
New York geography read like street maps. He and writers
like Albert Murray are scholars of Harlem's topography
as well as of its innards. He seems to recall everything he
and others ever ate, wore, every landscape he ever saw,
everything anybody ever said and how they said it. (Edward Margolies made a big thing about Hime's placing
"railroad tracks on West 10th Street in the Village," a
picayune point. Herntonians will notice that Margolies, in
Native Sons, dwells almost exclusively upon male-female
relationships in Himes's works as if the books contain no
writing! Margolies and others like him who moonlight
"criticizing" black writing are like the passenger examining
a great train instead of a skilled train engineer. All the
passenger can bring to the train is his own baggage.)

An avid moviegoer in his youth, Himes's memory of
musicals starring Ethel Waters and Josephine Baker (*Running Wild*) is utilized in *All Shot Up* (1960) to create a
kind of Harlem "camp." He is able to relate to the black
American experience even while in Spain. In *Blind Man
with a Pistol* (1969), he invokes the clichés, slogans, and
fads of the 1960s. He keeps in touch; on the back jacket
photo of *The Quality of Hurt,* Vol. I, a copy of *Jet* can
be seen on Himes's desk. (Of course when black Ameri-

can writers write about America without being here they are criticized for being away from the front. When Jules Verne, Shakespeare (who never traveled to Italy), Stendhal, and Stephen Crane write about events they never "experienced," they are saluted for their great imaginative abilities. This comes under the heading of aesthetic racism.)

Himes's powers of imagination have been underrated. Reading *The Quality of Hurt,* Vol. I, one gets the feeling that incidents in the detective novels didn't take place in Harlem exclusively, but are assemblages of experiences Himes had in Cleveland, Oakland, and Los Angeles, as well as in New York, and some of the situations in those novels might be based upon stories Himes heard while in the Ohio State Penitentiary. This makes Himes's Harlem a kind of every ghetto, as the professors might say.

Himes has been criticized for his frank portrayals of ghetto life, especially its glamorous hustling side, by those who apparently don't know the difference between a Bucket of Blood and an East Fifties restaurant where five waiters bring you the pepper.

Himes knows what he's talking about, too (see knifing scene, page 318, Knopf's *Lonely Crusade*):

Warren Street was a microcosm of all the slum streets in the world; it was drab, dreary, dirty, depraved and repulsive. Its facades were grimy or unpainted; its pavements full of loose streetcar tracks and deep potholes; its sidewalks crammed with black Christians, black workers, black drunks, black whores, black thieves, black cripples. Its ugliness was an afffront.

This is Columbus, Ohio, but it could have just as well been Akron, Cincinnati, or Youngstown. So you see, Himes didn't come to the material in his detective novels by reading *Lenin,* 8 Volumes, or taking a course in "Existentialism As a Way of Saying Nothing"; he was there, dealing the cards. (While in Ohio State Pen, Himes was chief black gambler and played poker, blackjack, and the georgia skin. He utilizes this skill in his novels; see crap game in the early pages of *If He Hollers Let Him Go,* the incident which gives the plot its send-off.)

In these days of professors' controversy about "The Black Aesthetic," it can be seen how Himes consistently uses this aesthetic in his *writing.*

No mainstream writer is likely to exploit the metaphor of the chicken as effectively as Himes does in chapter 13 of *The Crazy Kill* (1959), so that the cock almost begins to materialize within the text like a West African fetish.

But being raised multi-regionally and multi-culturally, Himes is eclectic, as in "Headlights glowed yellow in the gray gloom, and from the flanking murk a drab panorama of one-storied, stuccoed buildings unfolded in monotonous repetition" (*Lonely Crusade*), or "The gold-plated Swiss clock on the nightstand whirred softly, curling the silence of the small dark room" (written twice in *The Primitive*). Although the first example is a little busy they both stand as superior lines of English prose.

When talking about craftsmanship it is necessary to be specific. We could write about Himes the poet (test for creative writing class: remove the rhymes from *The Primitive* [1956], *Blind Man with a Pistol* [1969], and *Pinktoes* [1961] and see if they stand alone; they do), Himes the folklorist (see the "Signifying Monkey" in *Lonely Crusade*), and Himes the critic (his remarks concerning Faulkner and Hemingway in *Amistad I* are so cunning as to have only been made by a master reader and writer). So Himes is a careful reader of English and French writing; we find that he reads Faulkner, Lawrence, Ford Madox Ford, and Rimbaud, among others.

The Quality of Hurt, Vol. I, reveals how early occupations actually intensified his writing skills, as if the man was destined to write. His experience as a busboy and waiter (one of his brothers, Edward, is a master waiter), probably accounts for the variety and detail of his characters' menus. (See what Mamie Mason eats in "Harlem U.S.A.—Cooking with Lass," first page of a section in *Pinktoes;* the author doesn't even have to tell us she's a glutton, and furthermore an ugly and stupid glutton.) This ability makes *The Primitive* more than a routine thriller about interracial love but a parable on people who consume and are consumed.

His early experience as a successful street hustler taught him fashion: ". . . I bought very expensive suits, shirts, ties, shoes and coats—stylish but not outlandish. I never went for any of the wayout fashions like peg tops, zoot suits, bell-bottoms, box-backs, etc. I like tweeds, Cheviots and worsteds. I remember my most daring venture was a pair of square-toed yellow pigskin bluchers by Florsheim, which today in Paris would be the height of fashion." This haberdasher's eye for clothing enables him to relate his characters' actions to what they wear.

His job as research assistant at the Cleveland Library enabled him to take his mother's notes on the Himes family genealogy and fashion *The Third Generation*. Reading blueprints taught him how to lay out accurate rooms, as in the description of the prison (page 8, *Cast the First Stone*, Signet paper).

Not only is Himes a great writer but his story lines and plots are masterful too. *All Shot Up* (1960) has a plot that when rendered geometrically resembles intersecting circles.

Of course a writer who has sweated over millions of words is bound to make some bloopers and Himes has his share of ouches, and flops, repetitions, speechiness, plots that start out strong and fizzle; that's probably why some people call it quits after two books. But Himes wouldn't be Himes if he didn't continue striking.

In the course of *The Quality of Hurt*, Vol. I, many institutions come under fire, but none as much as the cultural institutions. In Himes's book it is the publishing industry but it could just as well be the tax-supported museums whose racist curators hate black painters, therefore have none in their collections; or it could be the symphony orchestra which disdains black musicians and composers. "There are so few American composers," said the conductor of the San Francisco Symphony, which just received $300,000 from the National Endowment for the Arts. (He's Japanese. If you think that racism towards blacks is limited to whites, come to California!)

The fact that after two excellent novels Chester Himes was compelled to work as a porter and caretaker, and after four novels, pawn his jewelry, tape recorder, and typewriter is an ignominy in an industry that prides itself as standard-bearer of all that is idealistic and good about Western civilization. The piddling advances, the racist distribution and promotional policies, the sleazy covers, and dumb jacket copy (see the foul, lurid, irresponsible third paragraph printed in bold type on the first page of Signet's *Cast the First Stone* under corny head, "James Monroe Was A Cool Cat") which afflicted Himes's career make the promotional abilities of his publishers seem a step below those of the man who hawks hot dogs at the football game. (At least he doesn't sabotage his product by packaging it in poison.)

Of course, some will say, "What do you expect?" and say that this is an "integrationist" consideration, as a young black female student said to me (she's enrolled in California's exclusive, mostly white European-oriented Mills College, incidentally—if this isn't having your cake and spitting it out too I don't know what is). I expect more. Why should so many people be hamstrung by words like "integration" invented by politicians? I call it *participation;* as long as we are in *this place* our painters, writers, and musicians should receive the awards commensurate with their talents. Vladimir Horowitz, who plays, as Cecil Taylor remarked, "other people's music," rarely performs, while our original composers are under so many contracts they become monotonous; and if our young black painters depended upon the patronage of black people who could afford it (anyone who makes over $10,000 a year ought to have at least three originals; they're 50 per cent tax deductible), they would surely starve.

The fact that *Lonely Crusade* isn't in paperback at this stage of the game leads me to believe that some of the people who thwarted the book in the first place still have undue cultural power. One wonders how the careers of our intellectually inquisitive young people, like Angela Davis and George Jackson, would have been had they been exposed to *Lonely Crusade* along with the numerous Chinese Ping-Pong Manuals, Algerian Clinic Gossip, and European Haze. How dare anyone come between our young people and their wiser ones; between our *griots* and their apprentices.

Despite the setbacks, the sheer hatred directed at him by everybody, it almost seems, Himes has carried on. One has the feeling that had he remained in the United States he would have been destroyed by whites, and by blacks, some of whom will proclaim their blackness to any available listener, yet seem so destructive about the best of their own culture.

The Quality of Hurt, Vol. I, reveals Himes to still be his cantankerous, irascible, feisty, brilliant self and predictably this first volume will draw him some more hurt.

For Third Worlders here's a doosey, ". . . I wanted to leave . . . all the United States of America and go somewhere I could escape the thought of my parents and my brother, somewhere black people weren't considered the shit of the earth. It took me forty years to discover that such a place doesn't exist."

On women: "Outside of her body, of course, the most appealing thing about a woman is a sense of humor."

On money: "I don't know what effect money has on other people, but it has always given me a confidence that nothing else has."

There are many observations concerning black and white women, Himes going so far as to enter a comparison of their coital abilities which students of the field might find instructive.

Small touches proliferate. We learn of Himes's fondness for dogs (indicated in the opening paragraph of *If He Hollers . . .*) and his skill at killing rattlesnakes in California.

I believe that it will be left to a young generation of black and white critics to assess the importance of Chester Himes as a major twentieth-century writer. "Serious" works, *Lonely Crusade, If He Hollers Let Him Go, Cast the First Stone, The Third Generation, The Primitive, Pinktoes,* etc., are of such high quality that their worth is only resisted by critics who have little interest in writing, a near pathological contempt for writers, and only care about evangelizing for some particular ideology. Europe freaks, black and white, have long denigrated the detective novel, probably because it is an American invention (Edgar Allen Poe), but things are changing. Nowadays people pride themselves on how much Chandler, Himes, Hammett, and Cain they know. Ross Macdonald's *The Underground Man* escaped the cloak-and-dagger sections of the book reviews and was praised up front. It won't be long before Himes's "Harlem domestic series," now dismissed by jerks as "potboilers," will receive the praise they deserve. (Many thought that when black critics began to assert exclusive control over critical chores for black writing the idiocy of diehard white critics, like the man Gore Vidal calls "Rabbi Howe," would be retired. Much to our dismay we found some of the black ones to be worse.)

Many major black writers have been influenced by Himes, whether by consciously using techniques Himes used earlier or by using similar story lines, characterizations, point of view, setting, and action. Episodes which occurred during Himes's visit to Paris have been dramatized in John A. Williams' great suspense novel *The Man Who Cried I Am*. The scenery and action which occurred at a southern college in *The Third Generation*, the Communist Party's suspicions concerning Lee Gordon, the black agitator in *Lonely Crusade*, are similar to scenes and actions in Ralph Ellison's *Invisible Man*. The way both authors approach these scenes and situations is a difference in style.

Younger novelists, Ronald Fair (see allegorical ghetto world of *World of Nothing*), Charles Wright, Al Young, Steve Cannon, Kristin Hunter, Clarence Major, and Cecil Brown (interracial love), are all taking for granted techniques and situations Himes and a former generation were chastized for using. He taught me the essential difference between a black detective and Sherlock Holmes.

The writing battles Himes fought may seem odd to a younger writer who, in a day of permissiveness, can say almost anything, write formerly taboo words, describe any sexual act, defame political leaders in the boldest language. A Doubleday and Doran editor prevented Himes from obtaining a writer's prize because she considered *If He Hollers Let Him Go* "nauseating." *Lonely Crusade* came under fire because a character described President Roosevelt as a "cripple bastard."

Included in *The Quality of Hurt*, Vol. I, are many instructive comments on the politics of American writing. We find that black American writers have always been objects of the most vicious, cruel, and lacerating scorn. After Richard and Ellen Wright sublet their New York apartment to some fickle college girls, the *Daily Worker* carried the headline: "Richard Wright's House Is A Pig Sty." (Bad headline writing, should be Richard Wright's House Pig Sty.) Himes points out that black writers receive more respect abroad than at home; while *Lonely Crusade* was critically abused at home it was chosen by Paris critics as one of the five best books from America published in France that year—along with books by Herman Wouk, William Faulkner, Ernest Hemingway, and Scott Fitzgerald.

When jealous liberals and radicals (he could have mentioned some of the "Nation time" bunch, and black "revolutionaries," too) see a black writer receiving adulation they will always get sore. When Wright received special attention from the patrons and staff of a Parisian restaurant, a visiting liberal publisher accused him of being a "big frog in a little pond," and suggested that Wright had deserted the struggle of American blacks.

On American media's ability to impose cultural "leaders" upon blacks, Himes refers to the Baldwin-Wright encounter.

On the American literary scene, the powers that be have never admitted but one black at a time into the arena of fame, and to gain this coveted admission, the young writer must unseat the reigning deity. It's a pity but a reality as well.

The Quality of Hurt, Vol. I, as you may gather by now, is a big book; big as the career and as the man. It's a good sign that black writers are beginning to write their autobiographies. The black autobiography received a bad name during the black gold rush days of the sixties. People seemed more interested in testifying than writing. (Substitute Christ for black in some poetry and prose and one can clearly see this old American Christian form peeking through in which the "sinner" related how he found Jesus; the day, the time, and his mood at this divine moment. Another Christian form given a veneer of blackness in the sixties was what Dr. Benjamin Mays, in his book *Born to Rebel,* terms "churching," in which backsliders in the congregation are reprimanded for their errant ways. This kind of poem usually went something like this: "Nigger, you ain't nothin/Never been nothin/Scared of this/Humbled by that/Why don't you take off them bell-bottoms?")

Now, with the trickle of journals, diaries, letters, glimpses one gets of their past in short essays, and books from writers like Himes and others, perhaps the black American autobiography will be restored to its former grandeur—the tradition of Walker, Wells, Booker T. Washington, and Douglass.

These writers are no pitiful mimicking caged parrots but swans, eagles, condors, hawks, owls, wrens (and a few ravens too).

Chester Himes is a great writer and a brave man. His life has shown that black writers are as heroic as the athletes, entertainers, scientists, cowboys, pimps, gangsters, and politicians they might write about. Many blacks have given Himes a bad time but his belief in the excellence and uniqueness of American blacks continued unmitigated. "Obviously and unavoidably, the American black man is the most neurotic, complicated, schizophrenic, unanalyzed, anthropologically advanced specimen of mankind in the history of the world. The American black is a new race of man; the only new race of man to come into being in modern time."

After the treatment of Chester Himes, the disaster

which befell Albert Ayler, and the way our painters, intellectuals who dare follow their own loa or assert the unpopular thing are treated, one might reply to Himes's praise: Are we?

The achievement of Volume I is even more staggering when you realize that another volume is on the way. Surely, that will be an additional monster destined to mind slam the reader.

Black World
March 1972

Music: Black, White and Blue

The trouble with much criticism of Afro-American art is that politicians control it and usually approach music, painting, writing, sculpture, and dance with their minds already made up.

When Frantz Fanon (popular, presumably, because he was born, not in Detroit, but in Africa and spoke French) wrote, *"Without oppression and without racism you have no blues,"* the anti-exploiter was himself exploiting a great music by using it to promote one of his pet theories. Ortiz Walton, author of *Music: Black, White & Blue,* would ascribe such a generalization to ". . . a failure to include and conceptualize purely instrumental forms of Blues in traditional analyses, and a much too literal interpretation of the poetry of lyrics of vocal Blues."

Walton, a musician, composer, and sociologist is just the kind of super-scientist, super-artist an investigation of Afro-American music requires and so his book is the best work on Afro-American music to date. Cecil Taylor, the pianist, recently commented: "Walton has raised points never before analyzed."

"Walton sees important differences between what he calls "Classical European Music," and "Classical American Music," by which he means "African music transmuted by the American experience." These differences are stringently documented by surprising information (can you imagine Johannes Brahms humming a ragtime tune and yearning to use its rhythms?), marvelous graphs which complement points made in the text, and personal experience (Walton has performed with a "Major" Ameri-

119

can symphony orchestra, the Boston Symphony, as well as with leading Afro-American musicians).

The book is full of cogent, cool comments and saturated with precision. Take this line interpreting the Blues, for example: ". . . being neither wholly melancholy nor wholly joyous but rather, in most instances, a combination of polar opposites which results in a tension of mood. Juxtaposition of major upon minor tonality resulting in the production of what has become known as "blue notes," is a musicological correlate of psychological and physiological tensions . . ."

Music: Black, White & Blue traces the European and African traditions and offers original theories on how they got that way and how they were influenced by differences based upon religion, culture, ecology, and geography. For Walton, European classical music is "rigid, unalterable, predictable and a fixed phenomenon," while African music means collective participation, improvisation, richer scales and rhythms. European music wasn't always that way but changed when the Christian Church triumphed in the West, inaugurating ecclesiastical music, and repressing the ancient pagan music of interesting scales and rhythms produced by European tribes. "The culminating achievement toward complete rationalization of music was the development of the symphony orchestra," Walton argues. "Here specialization reached its peak, for every man had a specific sheet of music to play the same way each time. No melodic, harmonic or rhythmic deviations were to be allowed, and an assembly-line type operation was set in motion by a foreman, the conductor."

Afro-American music (American classical music), Walton says, can be enjoyed by anybody while European classical music is designed for the elite. "Imagine a symphony audience snapping its fingers or saying 'yeah, baby, swing'?"

Lest the reader think that *Music: Black, White & Blue* is a ponderous, abstract, cold, theoretical work, be assured that the writing is excellent, witty, and jammed with interesting insights.

To me, one of the most fascinating discussions in the

book concerns unique contributions made to world music by Afro-Americans. Walton sees the need for people to realize their own cultural heritage and not hitchhike somebody else's.

The notion that no Afro-American culture exists and that history ends, for Afro-Americans, when they were, to put it in Mr. Walton's words, "captured, packed in ships, and thrown into America," was behind the bogus, light "identity" discussions of the early 1950s and early 1960s carried on by Afro-Americans who ignorantly denied the existence of Afro-American contributions to writing, music, and the other arts and craved identification with other cultures. At that time it was Europe, still is for some. Their successors, equally contemptuous of the Afro-American mind and equally moony when it comes to tough thinking have adopted Africa (which they often speak of as one country). There's no denying that Afro-Americans have benefited from a rich African heritage; a continent which contains cultures going back two million years is bound to be very wise; but often the African heritage is used to undercut the considerable achievements in the arts made by Americans of African heritage. Charlie Parker was born in Kansas City, the town we homeboys call K.C., not Lagos, and Chicago's contribution to world writing and music equals or surpasses those of any number of European and African cities.

Thus when Ortiz Walton writes, "Although the social conditions peculiar to America have obviously been an economic disadvantage to Blacks, they have coalesced with African retentions to produce a new and highly influential cultural world view," he is departing from the current Fashion Show, and when he writes that Afro-Americans took African music and *recast* it into "forms having an independent character of their own," our team greets this as the tie-breaking run at the bottom of the ninth. That *recasting* has occurred in writing, painting, dance, and the other arts too and those who don't see this either don't want to see it (people who call themselves scientists but banish any information that might upset their wobbly hypotheses) or aren't looking hard enough.

What Afro-Americans have done with what Walton calls those "essential qualities" derived from African art is one of the mightiest achievements in human history.

Music: Black, White & Blue contains interesting chapters on these homegrown forms like slave Music and blues, Ragtime, New Orleans Jazz, music of the twenties and thirties, and the strange career of that hermetic movement Be-bop, the music that was forced "underground."

Walton writes indignantly about the Public-Enemy-Number-One cast of characters who've wielded considerable control over Afro-American music in the past and present; the kind of rascals who drive around corners real fast and love machine guns.

Afro-Americans themselves do not escape the blame for the low esteem in which Afro-American music is often held. In a moving chapter, a tribute to Edward Kennedy Ellington ("The Duke"), Walton recounts how, after a symposium held at the University of California at Berkeley and devoted to Ellington (for which Walton wrote a handsome chapbook with graphics by Glenn Myles*) a black Californian wrote: "Ellington's music, on the other hand, is for the white community. It always has been . . ." The anonymous symposium member and author of the remark, cited James Brown's music as being for the average black man and woman. Another example, to my mind, of a black critic leaning over backward to tell the black masses "you got it," instead of risking charges of elitism by challenging them into developing their senses —developing the most powerful equipment they have on the planet and then some. James Brown, to my ears, has merely learned the same lesson as the creators of *The Great Train Robbery:* that is, you can play the same scene over and over merely changing the titles and still get a gullible public to go for it.

Music: Black, White & Blue also includes a section concerning the suit waged against the New York Philharmonic by bassist Arthur Davis.

Walton appeals for more Afro-American musical train-

* *The Coronation of the King, Edward Kennedy Ellington's Contribution to Black Culture.*

ing programs in a country in which Walton sees "too many symphonies." He criticizes funding policies of such institutions as the National Endowment for the Arts which he feels are geared to sustaining European culture instead of what he regards as the true American classical music.

Traditional "black" and "white" politics in America have been based upon catastrophe. Eagleton and McGovern were doomed from the outset because the public felt they weren't steady enough to commit what was an essentially insane act. Black politics have been based upon revolution, extermination, or exodus. (Objectives which are masses-oriented therefore sensationalistic [for the same reason the masses of people will continue to like loud and wrong films and music regardless of how often a handful of intellectuals sound off about "blaxploitation"].) Those who've tried to build a politics or culture based on the assumption that we're going to be here have been regarded as Uncle Toms. These "judgment day" assumptions have been enervating and wasteful but few intellectuals have dared to challenge them—Afro-American inintellectuals meekly follow "the people" instead of asserting the many directions open to them—directions "the people" may not always be aware of. Therefore it took considerable courage for Ortiz Walton to write what amounts to a call for the transvaluation of Afro-American values: "The Afro-American has become heir to the myths that it is better to be poor than rich, lower-class rather than middle or upper, easygoing rather than industrious, extravagant rather than thrifty, and athletic rather than academic. Accordingly Afro-Americans, unlike other ethnic groups, are viewed, and often view themselves, as being better off not owning property, business and land. This capitalism is good only for Jews, Italians, Poles, Lithuanians, Irish, Germans, Wasps and other ethnic groups residing in America who are in the process of striving to better their lives." Walton's book ends with a proposal that Afro-American music is a huge industry and that Afro-Americans should be in charge of—not telling the artist how he should do his work, the traditional Communistic approach—but packaging, selling, distributing, and billing for that industry. Walton has done his HooDoo Work in *Music: Black, White & Blue;* a major event in Afro-American cultural history. A book that can't be recommended highly enough.

Black World
December 1972

Bird Lives!

The most successful American composers between-wars were New York City boys like Aaron Copeland and George Gershwin and Roy E. Harris of Utah, who applied symphonic methods to jazz and *translated this folk art into music* [!] (reviewer's italics).

> *The Oxford History of the American People*
> by Samuel Eliot Morison, Vol. 3, p. 252;
> paperback edition

A recurrent theme in world myth has to do with man becoming God. When people actually accomplish this feat they are regarded as monsters by ordinary folk. You're supposed to aim high, not be high, and so when confronted with someone who makes us common we either deify these extraordinary people or destroy them. Charles Parker saved us the trouble of destroying him and he did such a good job that he died, it seems, from nearly everything.

His life reads like those of the fabled Giants; the humble origin, the legends, the ability to accomplish what was thought impossible. And as a Giant he was able to perform wonders equipped with little more than junk. "It had rubber bands and cellophane paper all over it and the valves were always sticking and the pads always leaking." A description of Charlie Parker's first alto, an 1898 saxophone, made in Paris. It was carried in a case, Mrs. Parker, Bird's mother, made from "pillow ticking, white and blue stripes, bought at a goods store and stitched firmly together on the family sewing machine."

Parker, nicknamed Bird because of his fondness for chicken, Ross Russell claims in *Bird Lives!* (New York: Charterhouse), was black and so we read the familiar story); the early marriage followed by separation; the degradation: "He had not eaten in several days and was phantom figure in much of black writing who, one hopes, will someday be accorded equal time to tell his side of the story); the early marriage followed by separation; the degradation: "He had not eaten in several days and was subsisting on a diet of California port wine . . . The wine was Charlie's food, drink—and medicine"; the frequent depravity: "A door stood ajar. Inside was a small cell, large enough for an iron cot, a white wooden night stand, the far wall had a single window, fitted with iron bars and, inside the bars, chain-link grating. Charlie Parker lay on the iron cot. He was wearing gray pajamas and a gray strait jacket."

He endured constant humiliations like "sulking majestically" with Lester Young, in the background, while Willie Smith and Charles Ventura were being awarded plaques, for best tenor and alto players, by *Downbeat* magazine. He was a black musician in a country whose official music establishment despises Afro-American music unless it is tucked away in barely recognizable form in the music of "A Major American Composer," whose music would collapse without copious infusions of ragtime, blues, spirituals, work songs, rock and roll and other elements associated with Afro-American music—a music that has paid for many a swell home and valet. The "serious music" of Europe has also benefited from dosages of Afro-American music: Hindemith, Milhaud (who at least admits it), Stravinsky, as early as 1918 with his "Ragtime for Eleven Instruments," and others, Charlie Parker praised when they should have been praising him.

The jazzman Charlie Parker was born in the right place, at the right time. Kansas City, August 29, 1920. A wheat and cattle town; headquarters for the distribution of cocaine, morphine, and heroin throughout the Southwest. He grew up hearing people like Lester Young (his idol), Oran "Hot Lips" Page, Jimmy Rushing, Big Joe

Turner, Pete Johnson, and bands like Count Basie and Jay McShann's Orchestra who performed in clubs, under the lenient political regime of HST's pal Tom Pendergast.

Billy Eckstine was on the scene as a member of Earl Hines's Orchestra. "A guy comes up that looks like he just got off a freight car, the raggediest guy you'd ever want to see . . . and he asks Goon, 'Say, man, can I come up and blow your horn?' . . . He blew so much he upset everybody in the joint" is the way Eckstine remembers the young Charlie Parker.

Charles Parker experienced the kind of special artless savagery of which Americans are often capable but his way of dealing with these outrages was to don the mask of cunning one associates with the trickster. Once while on a southern tour, he was able to jive the policemen about to give him a traffic citation into instead escorting him to an engagement. When introduced to Jean Paul Sartre he congratulated him on his music. He was always up to pranks and "put-ons," some of the farcical drugstore variety. Herb Gold once proposed that novelist Richard Wright played the fool to put his inferiors at ease; maybe the same was true for Bird, but his clowning didn't prevent him from working hard at his art. It seems that music was all he really cared about: "He was not as many were later to believe a maverick genius . . . He had learned at first hand from the masters of his art, had listened to every important soloist in Kansas City. He was determined, dedicated, tireless, ambitious. Charlie had put not less than fifteen thousand hours in on an instrument by a conservative estimate."

Parker became a legend very early in his life and by the end had been consumed by the dingy, febrile, frequently abominable world in which jazz is allowed to thrive by a society not only hostile to it but from time bent on outlawing it for reasons still considered funny and weird by some. ("The Cabaret Card" placed jazz under such distinguished trustees as the New York State Liquor Authority and the Narcotics Squad, enabling them to have power over who could and couldn't perform in New York.

Although Charlie Parker was never found in possession of narcotics, after undergoing the most degrading searches, his cabaret license was revoked at the "recommendation" of the New York Narcotics Squad. His unanswered letter to the New York State Liquor Authority, begging for the right to support his family, makes pathetic reading. You could write a book on specific laws which have been used throughout American history to repress Afro-American music.)

Then there were the avaricious and venal promoters, beside whom California used car salesmen appear eloquent and highminded. There were the drugs, alcohol, bad contracts ("Now's the Time," a Bop classic, was had for fifty dollars), and the harassment by the kind of police who dig getting up in drag in order to entice "suspects."

Some of the financial exploitation Bird experienced was due to his own business incompetence; unlike "The Major American Composer," he didn' have the accountants, the limousines, the plane tickets already taken care of and the plush university residency when he wanted to contemplate.

Although publications like *Life* magazine and *The New Yorker* viewed others as the most valuable players, Bird was the father of the new music condemned as Be-bop by its critics, a name that stuck. Be-bop brought technical innovations to music which were thought impossible in an earlier time and provoked amazement as well as scorn: "Be-bop has set music back twenty years," said Tommy Dorsey; but young pianist John Lewis, a student of the new music as well as an admirer, said of its chief proponent, "He was into a whole new system of sound and time." Be-bop also influenced the American style in fashion, manners and language. Be-boppers invented words long ago consigned to the slangheap by out-of-touch grammarians whose favorite writer is Robert Louis Stevenson; their demise has been kept from them because they are still with us, prospering in the highest places: "Cool it!" Dean Rusk once warned the North Vietnamese.

Russell's book is occasionally marred by extraneous details concerning Charlie Parker's sexual and eating habits. (He seems fascinated by the information that Bird balled three women in one night, for example.) Igor Stravinsky, a composer with whom Russell compares Parker, once advised his White House host President John F. Kennedy that he was "drunk," but Robert Craft's book *Stravinsky,* concerning the composer's life, was mostly about Stravinsky, the artist. When Russell makes a connection between Charles Parker, a flawed, though independent spirit, and Gus Hall's Angela Davisoid, he loses me completely. His characterization of an incident in which Parker urinates in the public telephone booth of a nightclub as a "revolutionary" act is way off the beam and merely an example of the kind of fashionable namby-pamby which regards any slop as a true main course.

I am annoyed when he judges Louis Armstrong's music as "archaic minstralsy." Such politically motivated statements deny an Afro-American musical tradition and have the effect of encouraging younger musicians to shun the past; as a result many sounds, rhythms and instructions have been discarded, much to the music's loss. When Russell blames Charlie Parker's hard drugs troubles on "oppression," that may very well be true to a degree, but it was heroin that eventually did him in; his choice and his responsibility—a habit which, due to puritanical inhumane laws, led him to squander much of his time in search of drugs and cut deeply into his ability to earn a living. (Of course, he didn't have a fancy licensed doctor to give him a legal "up" whenever he needed one.)

Where Russell appoints saxophonist Phil Woods as "The Keeper of (Charlie Parker's) Flame," others might nominate Ornette Coleman, Archie Shepp, Jackie Mclean, and the underrated Sonny Stitt as the chief burners. It is downright embarrassing when he tried his hand at novelistic "empathy" in attempting to replicate Parker's mood during certain situations—information he couldn't possibly know. But in terms of facts, dates, letters, documents, important material from insiders (Russell himself has headed Dial Records); in terms of a comprehensive discography and data concerning a major movement in American music and its chief prophet you can't beat Ross

Russell's *Bird Lives!,* a formidable biography about a fabulous, calamitous life.

You wonder what would have happened if so many people hadn't spoiled him. If some were as straight and firm with him as Charles Mingus and Babs Gonzales were. Would Bird have lived if the Baroness Pannonica de Koenigswarter had insisted he go to the hospital when he was lingering in her apartment, a human wreck in need of round-the-clock treatment?

Perhaps you can only relate to a monster in terms of awe, especially the Monster Bird, whose talents were so immense he could invent classics standing on his feet and whose appetites for life were as enormous—like a wounded monster full of gaping holes, he kept stumbling towards that life, getting up, grappling with life until he was down for good. At the moment of his death Russell claims there was a clap of thunder. The gods' tribute to a fellow god.

New York *Times Book Review*
March 25, 1973

A Westward Movement

Last year while walking down Euclid Avenue in Berkeley I ran into Cecil Brown, a novelist and playwright, whose *The Life and Loves of Mr. Jiveass Nigger* is an international big seller. While chatting with Cecil I noticed across the street James McPherson, a prize-winning short story writer and the author of *Hue and Cry,* a book which has earned him the praise of some of the sterling names in American writing.

Not only were over a million words in print represented at the intersection of Virginia and Euclid, but the scene was taking place in California, long considered the bane of the Afro-American writer.

"Salvage California," Zora Neale Hurston wrote bitterly in her 1942 autobiography, *Dust Tracks on the Road.* Chester Himes and John A. Williams also have some uncomplimentary things to say about the state. Williams writes about his bad experiences in California in his most recent book, *Flashbacks,* a collection of essays published by Doubleday.

But something's up. There seems to be a shift taking place as more and more Afro-American writers gravitate toward the Bay Area, many from New York.

Traditionally, New York has been considered the capital of United States culture and the center of Afro-American artistic expression as well. At the Schomburg Library, reputed to house the best collection of Afro-Americana in the world, you may rub elbows with some of the foremost Afro-American intellectuals. Larry Neal, Nathan Huggins, Addison Gayle, Jr., Harold Cruse, and Askia Muhammed Toure are frequent patrons of the library.

Walking down St. Mark's Place in New York's East Village I was often able to observe key members of several generations of the American "avant-garde," before breakfast, or chat with Archie Shepp, Ornette Coleman, Sun Ra, Bill Dixon, Albert Ayler, Cecil Taylor, and members of a splendid generation of young painters. When I lived in New York, Henry Van Dyke, author of *The Dead Piano*, lived across the street from me and W. H. Auden was my next-door neighbor. (The lions who stood guard before the durable bard's brownstone didn't have any jaws.)

The Black Arts, The *Umbra Poets*, N. H. Pritchard's "Transrealism" and several other important movements in Afro-American writing of recent years were begun in New York. *Essence, Encore, Freedomways* and *Black Creation* (currently contemplating a move to the West Coast), Afro-American magazines published in New York, regularly feature original fiction and poetry by Afro-Americans.

New York is also the home of "Soul," a public broadcasting program which, however mediocre, will be remembered as the place where many of the younger Afro-American poets were exposed to a nationwide audience.

And for some strange reason more money seems to be allotted to writing workshops, poetry-in-schools programs, and university residencies in New York than in the West and the South.

In the last few years, however, something has occurred which threatens to challenge New York's reputation as hub of Afro-American artistic and cultural affairs.

The presence in the Bay Area of such talents as Al Young, Buriel Clay II, Claude Brown, Cleo Overstreet, Ernest Gaines, James McPherson, Sarah Fabio, Ortiz Walton, David Henderson, Adam David Miller, Francisco Newman, Alison Mills, Jon Eckels, Maya Angelou, Pat Parker, Anthony Stowers and, although his supporters are quick to point out, "He's half Jewish," Bob Kaufman, has contributed to such a flourishing art scene that now whenever I return to New York I am asked, "What's happening on the Coast?"—a place formerly viewed, by New Yorkers, as the locale of rattlesnakes, Stetson-wearing hicks, and society pretenders who become involved in hairpulling fights, in the front row, on the first night of the Opera.

Some of these writers live in the Bay Area the year around, others reside here, seasonally, in between working stints at eastern colleges. They don't constitute a movement —they write in different styles and are of diverse generations and viewpoints—but their presence here is significant.

Cleo Overstreet is the dowager of the remarkable Overstreet clan which is to Berkeley what the Kennedy family is to Hyannis Port. Her book *The Boarhog Woman* (Doubleday) has been compared to the work of Damon Runyon. Ms. Overstreet is constantly writing and has three other books ready for publication including one about her recent trip to Africa, where she was shocked to learn that slaves are still being sold.

Sarah Fabio has taught at the University of California at Berkeley and Merrit College. Her recording, "Boss Soul," on which she reads her poetry to the instrumental accompaniment of three of her talented sons, Thomas, Cyril Leslie and Ronald, was recently released by Folkways. An authority on Afro-American culture, she lives in Palo Alto and is in demand on the college circuit.

While the Overstreets and the Fabios are long-time residents of the Bay Area, David Henderson is a newcomer. In 1970 he taught "Black Literature and the American Vernacular," a course which Dr. James Hart and I founded at the University of California, Berkeley, in 1968. The editor of *Umbra* magazine, his first book of poetry, *De Mayor of Harlem* (Dutton), showed promise. He is currently working on a biography of Jimi Hendrix for Doubleday and relaxes by bicycling through the streets of Berkeley.

Music: Black, White and Blue (Morrow) Ortiz Walton's first book, has been called "the best book on Afro-American music to date," by the prestigious *Black World* magazine. A doctoral candidate at the University of California, Berkeley, Walton was the first Afro-American to perform with the Boston Symphony and, regardless of his busy schedule, still finds the time to perform solo and with local orchestras and combos.

Maya Angelou, author of *I Know Why the Caged Bird Sings* (Random House), a widely-read autobiography, and *Just Give Me a Cool Drink of Water 'fore I diïe* (Random House), a collection of poetry, also lives in Berkeley.

Laney College teacher Adam David Miller was recently awarded the California Association of Teachers of English Award of Merit for his anthology *Dices or Black Bones* (Houghton). It was one of the first nationally distributed anthologies to include the work of Afro-American writers living in the Bay Area.

Anthony Stowers' profoundly Baldwinesque poetry has appeared in the pages of the *Paris Review* and the *Evergreen Review*. A colorful poet who reads his work in the velvety tones of a matinee idol, Stowers lives in Berkeley. He is the son of Ivy Anderson, who, though neglected, was one of the great female blues vocalists of all time.

In San Francisco dwells the semi-reclusive Ernest Gaines, whose recent book *The Autobiography of Miss Jane Pittman* won a Black Academy of Arts and Letters Award and a Common-wealth Club medal.

Claude Brown, author of *Manchild in the Promised Land,* lives in San Francisco about three times a year. He claims he is able to get a lot of work done out here.

Also in San Francisco is Buriel Clay II, who not only has distinguished himself as a playwright and prose writer but is also known for his work with the San Francisco Black Writers Workshop.

Carl Thompson, part-owner of the Toulouse, a Berkeley restaurant, is the president of Yardbird Publishing Co., Inc., a publishing firm organized in 1972 to serve as an outlet for Afro-American writers and the growing number of Asian and Chicano poets, among whose ranks are such talents as Jose Montoya, Victor Cruz, Roberto Vargas, Pedro Pietri, Frank Chin, George Leong, Curtis Choy, Shawn Wong, Cyn Zarco, Janice Mirikitani, and Jeff Chan.

Yardbird Reader, Volume I, which was assembled under the direction of graphic artist Glenn Myles and myself, has become a national favorite. *Yardbird Reader,* Volume II, will be published later this year. Organized by sculptor Doyle Foreman and writer Al Young, it contains work by Charles Wright, John A. Williams, Lawson Fusao Inada, Bob Fox, Jack Micheline, Cyn Zarco, Alison Mills, American Academy of Arts and Letters Fellow Michael S. Harper, Robert Gover, and an excerpt from a major novel by Al Young, *Who Is Angelina?* Sarah Fabio's dauntless *Phase II* magazine is also published in the Bay Area.

I'm not saying that these writers are "the bestest writers that ever was"—indulging in the kind of mutual back slapping that's become so popular among American writing cliques. That judgment I reserve for their readers and critics. But I feel it's important to document the shift that has taken place in Afro-American writing from its traditional home in the East to the West Coast, the Midwest, and the South.

This tendency, part of an overall trend to decentralize American cultural power, may in the end prove healthy. Or it may fizzle out. Some may succumb to the traditional fear held by both Afro-American writers and others of "perishing on the Coast," in the tradition of such distinguished casualties as F. Scott Fitzgerald and Nathanael West. (I recently called reporter Bill Cook of *Newsweek*'s San Francisco office to complain about the omission of Asians, Chicanos, and Puerto Ricans from *Newsweek*'s list of guest writers for a new feature called "Our Turn." "You didn't see any writers west of the Hudson included either, did you?" he asked. I had no comeback.)

Whatever happens, I will always prefer walking down University Avenue or its parallel streets and seeing that Bay and the mountains to staring from the window of a New York apartment at a warehouse that hasn't been painted in a hundred years.

So what if the Marriott Inn and Solomon Grundy's look so much alike that you don't recognize you've come to the wrong place until you've parked your car. So what if there thrives here a political element whose robotized members are illiterate, bellicose, and frequently insane and prone to consider everyone who disagrees with its views reactionary reactionary reactionary (the needle's stuck).

It's nice to be able to reach the sea gulls within fifteen minutes. It's a pleasure to look up and see the sky.

Sunday San Francisco
Examiner/Chronicle
May 26, 1973

Before the War, Poems as They Happened

When I read Victor Hernandez Cruz, Roberto Vargas, and Felipe Luciano I am impressed by the startling effect created by an admixture of symbols, textures, images, and rhythms arising from the poet's exposure to more than one culture.

The poetry: Afro Indian Latin and English seems to coexist in harmony as if they were meant to be.

Last year, when I picked up Lawson Fusao Inada's book *Before the War,* subtitled "poems as they happened," I was struck by the same thing, only this time it was a mingling of Asian Afro English allusions. Pheasants, pagodas and Japanese gardens "A desert tortoise—/something mute and hard—/something to decorate/a desert Japanese garden . . ." or "one whole whole tree/goes groping like a squid," go well alongside "Then bass was woman;/I, her master./She was black, Africa's/shape," from the poem *The Great Bassist,* which is dedicated to Charlie Mingus. The book contains a good parody of the baaad black poem which begins, "I am a mad mother—/fucker or in other words, a very irate citizen—"

In Inada's poetry a reference to *Ebony* magazine has no difficulty making out eight lines above *Madame Butterfly Rag;* and look where Miles Davis stands in the tradition of Basho, Buson, and Issa: "Miles was waiting in the dock/his trumpet in a paper bag." Malcolm X, Bud Powell ("Chases rainbows"), Gene Ammons ("Blow it,

137

Gene"), Clifford Brown, Lady Day, Prez, Count Basie, Ornette Coleman ("Una Muy Bonita") show up in *Before the War* as well as "three old-kimonoed men," and a dragon licking its lips.

The Afro-American influence on one of America's tiniest minorities (the entire Asian-American population is slightly under one million) isn't new; all one has to do is listen to Toshiko's Horace Silver-like attacks on the piano to apprehend this influence. Lawson uses it and uses it with care, but above all Lawson Inada is a Japanese-American poet who is concerned with what has happened to Japanese-Americans while here as well as what has happened to himself, his loves, his family.

The book jacket says, "Lawson Fusao Inada was born a Sansei (third-generation Japanese-American) in Fresno, California. He lived through the war with his family in "evacuation camps," resettling afterward in the black and Latin section of Fresno.

A frightening event, even by the standards of American history, perhaps explains why so many science fiction writers are located in California. One day in 1942, school-children found their Japanese-American classmates missing; their families' businesses boarded up. Japanese-Americans were routed from their homes and herded into "internment" camps in Lake Tule, California, because of some creature called The War Relocation Authority, ordered by President Roosevelt, and executed by then California Attorney General Earl Warren with the assistance of commanding officer John DeWitt, the FBI, and the military. This infamy was necessary, its supporters claimed, because of fear of Japanese "sabotage" since the Japanese dwelled near "ship yards and oil refineries"—read: in the poor areas of the cities. (They also irritated white farmers by their ability to undersell them.) Inada was a child then but he remembers this incarceration with the poignancy one hears in the voice of Ray Charles:

> Have you ever lost your woman?
> Have you ever lost your crops

and had to move?—
packing up without your woman
some evacuation going on . . .
Have you ever been wakened
by blue eyes shining into your face?

You wondered who you were.

You couldn't move.

Inada describes the degradation in these internment camps: "Mud in the barracks—/a muddy room, a chamber pot" and when he writes, ironically, sardonically of the brutish guards ("Because there was little else to do,/they led us to the artillery range/for shells, all that we gathered,/and let us dig among dunes/for slugs, when they were through"), we are reminded that the design for "The Flintstones" was executed by a Japanese artist living in New York named Isamu Kawai.

Inada lives in the West ("the pagoda of San Jose") and so he can strum out a little country western as in, "and bits of the cowman's tune,/alone and strumming/to a cactus, cows at grass/under a scavenger's moon."

It is said by people I trust that the "Japanese evacuation left such a scar in Japanese-American consciousness that since this ignominious fact Japanese-Americans have kept their peace for fear of exciting the vigilante mob, always in the back of the American mind, cutting up, looking for some whoopee." Lawson Inada has broken this peace and I should add broken it beautifully. Blow it, Lawson.

Lawson Inada and Frank Chin are Asian-Americans who employ allusions identifiable as Afro-American; poet Lorenzo Thomas, and novelist George Davis (*Coming Home*) are Afro-Americans who employ allusions identifiable with Asia (Vietnamese in those cases). Lawson and Chin got their black here, while Thomas and Davis got their Asia in Asia. What all this goes to show is that anyone who tries to keep his cultural experience to himself is like a miser, moribund in a rooming house, uneaten beef stew lying on a table, and lonely except for the monotonous tick tock of a drugstore clock—all that gold stashed in the closet doing no one any good.

June 2, 1972

The Song Turning Back
Into Itself

Novels, poetry, and political programs of an apocalyptic nature emanate from the Eastern Seaboard perhaps because it always looks like the final days there.

If a huge dark photochemical cloud was constantly hovering above your head (New Yorkers only see one third of the sun), wouldn't you just shrug your shoulders and say what's the use? However, on the east and west side of New York lie two rivers in which if you dropped a ham it would come out a bone like the victim of a piranha attack; and what about the air you breath: miasma from dog wastes; the people's faces: notice that tense, curlish, shrewish snarl about the lips of many New York women.

What am I saying is that ambiance influences writing. You can be sullen gloomy pessimistic or you can have a sunny disposition. Al Young's poetry has a sunny disposition.

A complete man, Al Young has spent his life refining and improving his sense, therefore, his work is about seeing, hearing, smelling, and good things to eat: pecans, crabs & shrimp, chicken with calico, strawberries . . . He loves nature and so the woods ("scruffy palm leaves") and insect life are restive in his words.

Knowing other languages introduces a poet to other ways of viewing the world. Right now, Young is studying Japanese but has had a well-developed Spanish voice for some time, which he implements effectively in his poetry:

"Carmel Valley/the Zoo at the end/of the Judah line/
Tomales Bay/McGee Street/Smith Grade Road/Avenida
Cinco de Mayo/Guadalajara Guadalajara/the beach at
Point Reyes of/saying goodbye. . . ."

Another of Al Young's consistent themes is: what is a
poet? Sometimes he is "The Prestidigitator": "I draw hats
on rabbits, sew women back/together, let fly from my
pockets flock of/vibratory hummingbirds. The things I've
got."

To say that Al Young is exhilarating, zestful, and
bright does not mean that he doesn't have his moments of
bitterness, and self-deprecation. He can be "a firstclass
fuckup/who but for divine mercy/would have gone/out
of commission/long ago/would have become/the original loveboat/cracked up against rocks/in fog or funk."

In this day when you can't pick up a magazine without reading a critic (usually black) soured on black writers; accusing them of failure or being imitative (the first
duty of a revolutionary critic is to read) or lacking tradition; it's a pleasure to read someone who is aware of the
integrity of Afro-American culture both present and past:
"Where you once walked or ran/or railroaded your way
thru/I now fly, caressing the sturdy/air with balls of my
feet/flapping my arms and zeroing." This is dedicated to
the Brothers who "invented jazz" but could just as well be
a tribute to those ancestors who wrote Afro-American
language before there was any discussion of an American
literature, and when most American writing was European derived.*

An interviewer called and asked me, "Are you angry?"
which had something to do with an essay on black writing
which ended up as a Jules Feiffer cartoon with these
dudes, in shades, beards, and arms folded, looking men-
acingly. He seemed vexed when I told him I experienced
the whole range of human emotions not just one.

Same way with the poetry of Al Young. People will
get sore because he is experiencing with his entire sen-

* . . . there was no consistent body of literature in America until
well into the nineteenth century" (Robert B. Spiller, *The American
Literary Revolution 1783–1837*).

sorial equipment attuned to what's around him like a radar dish. They would want him to be like the song say, "Deaf dumb cripple and blind." A limited dwarf, raging in his emotional chains, a psychological paraplegic spewing phlegm. Al Young's poems would answer, "Not on your life." "I violinize peace/in the Nazi era."

June 1, 1972

The Greatest, My Own Story

I was prepared to dislike this book. Hadn't Dr. Lawrence D. Reddick in his *Improvement of Race Relations in Motion Pictures, Radio, the Press and Libraries,* published in the 1930s, listed among the principal stereotypes of blacks, "the superior athlete," along with "the vicious criminal," and "the perfect entertainer"? Hadn't Henry Bibb, a fugitive slave writer of the 1800s, described a "sport" the slave master enjoyed, in which he would get slaves to ". . . wrestling, fighting, jumping, running foot races, and butting each other like sheep"? A "sport" urged on by ". . . giving them whisky; making bets on them."

Besides, a sport which attracted Christopher Lehmann-Haupt, who seems fascinated by blacks who are into boxing, encaged, or into rhetoric, and Norman Mailer, who, in a *Rolling Stone* interview, came as close to unequivocally endorsing Charles Manson's anti-black schemes as a liberal would be expected to, had to be pretty strange.

Esquire didn't give John A. Williams the assignment to cover the Manila fight because they, perhaps, felt Norman Mailer best represented the slave master's point of view.

The joke going around was that the rumble of both Mailer's and Ali's career would happen when somebody read to Ali what Mailer had written about him.

It was a bad joke because a Palooka, Muhammad Ali ain't. His book, *The Greatest, My Own Story,* is a splendid action-packed hurricane of a book which, like George Foreman, takes off and runs uphill goatlike. And it packs the same kind of wallop Floyd Patterson must have used to KO Ingemar Johansson. It is a good old two-fisted country thumping in words; a bone-crushing quality thriller which belongs to the same class as autobiographies written by Booker T. Washington, Frederick Douglass, and James Weldon Johnson.

It is a book that portrays Muhammad Ali as generous, heroic, and intelligent—possibly a genius—and quite capable of discerning that some people are drawn to him for perverse reasons: "Then there was this nightmarish image I always had of two slaves in the ring, like in the old days on the plantations, with two of us big black slaves fighting, almost on the verge of annihilating each other while the masters are smoking big cigars, screaming, and urging us on, looking for blood."

The slavery metaphor is used throughout the book.

One of the reasons slaves were brought to the New World in the first place was because they were considered heathens; it was a Christian priest, Bartolomé de las Casas, who convinced the Europeans that black "subhuman pagans" could harvest the sugar better than red heathens. Therefore, Muhammad Ali's point of view concerning Christianity is bound to differ from that of the arch-bishop who recently refused to share a platform with the Champion because of Ali's unchristian behavior in Manila. You see, in a Christian country, which the United States is, regardless of what it says about Freedom of Religion in the Constitution, you're supposed to *sneak* around.

Ali's problems began when he rejected Christianity and it was discovered that he was a Muslim. As long as he was an all-American boy, denouncing Africa, he was all right. He refused to enter the Army out of his religious as well as his political convictions, which were genuine and sincere since the book reveals that the Army, secretly, offered him an easy way out. He's had constant difficulty with whites who insist that he use his Christian name. Even a "doctor" threatened to hold up emergency surgery unless Muhammad Ali said Cassius Clay the same way you say "Uncle"; Muhammad Ali refused even though it meant painful suffering from a hernia. The very title *The Greatest* is likely to upset Christians because, for them, you can hustle as greedily and as unashamedly as you desire as long as you come on meek. Who me?

The book is honest, and so fair that he invites his first wife to give her version of why their marriage went awry. She blames it upon the austerity required of Muslim women.

In a day when people pretend to be so sophisticated, so jaded, so liberated, so free of ancient, vital passions, Muhammad Ali admits that he becomes jealous. He quarreled with his first wife, Songi, causing an ugly, violent scene before celebrities of the political, entertainment, and sports world, even threatening his idol, Sugar Ray Robinson. He objected to her wearing mini-skirts.

Ali has become not only the Black Hope, but the White Liberal Hope as well, mainly because of his stand on the war in Vietnam. A stand whose repercussions take up a good deal of the book. Here again, it's risky to confuse Ali's views with those of some of the people who admire him. If it had been white people the Viet Cong were massacring, the liberals would have probably criticized Lyndon Johnson for being soft on barbarians. Now that the Vietnamese are here, pathetically herded into various camps around the country, you don't see these same liberals inviting them to cocktail parties on Long Island, do you? The liberal pressure against the war only intensified when *their children,* in college, got drafted, not when poor blacks, whites, browns—fellows we went to high school with—were sent over there to be maimed and wasted—people who didn't have the same options, or resources, as a college kid or a Heavyweight Champion of the World.

But Muhammad Ali is their hero. Just as he is the hero of the poor, and the "oppressed," and the hero of the glamorous and affluent, Governor Reagan's son Michael, Elizabeth Taylor, Lady Bird's daughters. He is the "heavy" to a lot of people too. It seems that he enjoys his role as the "heavy" as much as that of the "people's champ."

He studied Gorgeous George's techniques of villainy: a role that has filled up the stadiums at his fights and has made him the biggest drawing card in the history of boxing.

Among some of the weirdos attracted to Ali is Miss Velvet Green, who attends every fight in a chauffeur-driven limousine and yearns for the day when he's carried out on a stretcher.

Muhammad Ali believes that the majority of "white America" desires such an event.

After refusing to take the step at the induction center, he received bitter criticism from patriots like Governor Otto Kerner, who recently served time for defrauding the citizens of Illinois; Congressman Mendel Rivers, who, according to Jack Anderson, used to get so pickled that he went about giving away Pentagon secrets to airline stewardesses; and true statesmen like Spiro Agnew, and Richard Nixon, who hated his "guts."

Jimmy Breslin described him as "a Muslim and a bedbug" for his stand, the kind of religious intolerance that recalls the "no-popery" hysteria of the 1840s which resulted in the Riots of 1844. Catholic churches were burned and many Irish-Catholics were murdered in the streets of Philadelphia.

It took Lester Maddox to say, "There has been a lot of controversy about this fellow Clay. When he rejected the draft, I'm sure it hurt him. He's paying for it. Well, we're all entitled to our mistakes. This is the way I see it. I see nothing wrong with him fighting here."

He is a complicated man who once called Bertrand Russell "dumb" before they became pen pals, yet he can be so Nebraska-green that when he had an opportunity with a prostitute he didn't know what was required of him.

His poetry is as competent as any of that produced by the New York School although literary critic Joe Frazier commented "Shhhiiiit!" Bud Collins says, "Robert Frost went to his grave with a smile on his face. Your poems don't threaten him at all."

The harassment Muhammad Ali has received from

what nineteenth-century writers called "mobocrats" is the best argument I've read for the establishment of bedlam clinics on the corner of every street in America in the same way the French have built toilets. He has been shot at and he has received evil packages containing dead animals. He is the subject of sexual fantasies that would shock Krafft-Ebing. He has been fleeced of his possessions by people posing as friends.

He is the dangerous "crazy nigger" and "bad nigger" rolled into one. The kind they used to lynch and castrate for stepping out of his place or for reckless eyeballing; for daring to ignore the limits imposed by the slave master's society.

Not to say that he is without flaws—flaws he readily admits. Not to say that he's Superman. This symbol of religious and political tolerance has advocated death for those black celebrities of whose life-styles he disapproves, which reminds one that blacks who are freedom fighters to whites are often slavers and bully boys to Afro-Americans.

I suspect that when he describes his black opponents as "bears" and "King Kongs" he might be invoking the skin privileges of his caste. When he refers to himself as "pretty" he might mean his Caucasian features.

Mr. Durham had done a very professional job in getting the Champ's style and tone down on paper, though one gets the impression that a considerable amount of the book is unghosted. The dialogue between Ali and Joe Frazier that Ali taped during a car trip to New York is simply terrific. Often, the prose becomes xenophobic, *Muhammad Speaks* editorialese. There's an episode in which Ali persuades Libyan President Qaddafi to lend the Muslims one million dollars, but there's no mention of the report that when the Muslim representatives returned for a second loan and were turned down they referred to the Arabs as "slave traders."

He seems to accept the Muslim doctrines, uncritically, and one misses the healthy skepticism and intellectual curiosity of his first wife.

There is a chilling remark from Joe Louis concerning

the possible murder of Sonny Liston that could have been developed. I expected more material about Ali's relationship to Malcolm X.

Muhammad Ali has kept boxing alive. And now he has brought writing-about-fighting above its usual depraved level in which black pugilists from Jack London's day to the present have been viewed as savages, as lustful machines, and as meatheads. It indicates that some boxers are capable of writing superior books about their sport. "My logic, my dear ex-student, is that the quiet cunning and deadly patience of the Spider Family, in this case the Tarantula Family, whose game is really big bananas, will settle this time for a mouthy, noisy bee," wrote Archie Moore, in an eloquent letter to Ali, warning of George Foreman's fistic talents.

When asked about the book at the time he signed the contract at Random House, Muhammad Ali said, "Writing is fighting." You can say that again.

Finally, there is a scene in which the Champion jokingly tells the present occupant of the White House that he, Ali, might take his job.

I don't think it's such a bad idea. He certainly exudes more intelligence and sincerity than the present field of dreary candidates. He could run on a ticket of religious freedom in the 1976 Bicentennial year. If he runs as well as he writes he might just throw the election into the House of Representatives.

New York *Times Book Review*
November 30, 1975

A Treasury of Afro-American Folklore

Some of the fiercest battles in history have been fought, not over economics, but culture. The subjugated resist the conqueror's language and riots ensue. His religion and culture are brought in with troops, not so much as tools of "civilization," or for "quality" or "excellence," or because they are "classics" but as fetishes—sacred objects requiring veneration; occasionally, irreverence has meant death.

The fact that, despite sometimes brutal suppression, syncretic cultural systems based upon African religions claim millions of adherents in this hemisphere, is not exactly shouted from the rooftops, therefore Harold Courlander's *A Treasury of Afro-American Folklore* (New York: Crown) is worthwhile if only for passages like the following, dateline, Rio: ". . . Tens of thousands of white-robed voodoo believers jammed into the famous Copacabana and Ipanema beaches tonight for the traditional New Year's Eve homage to Iemanja [Yemoja], the mystical goddess of the sea. . . . The cultists included men, women, and children of all races and income levels."

Yet *Afro-American Folklore* cannot receive my overwhelming approval because it contains avoidable flaws. Its main flaw is its one-sidedness.

After receiving the book I skimmed it, pausing here and there over an interesting song, or political satire included as examples of what Courlander refers to as Afro-American Folklore. An examination of the book reveals that none would exist without influences from Vodoun, or as it is called in the United States, HooDoo; systems based upon modifications African religions underwent in the New World.

At this point I was impressed with the book. I took it to Haiti with me and I think it was the trip that convinced me that Mr. Courlander's book, no matter how diligent the author appears to have been, is a tourist's book, and not, as Ralph Ellison writes on the jacket, ". . . the most important collection of Afro-American folklore compiled." That tribute still belongs to *Black Song,* by John Lovell, Jr., a book passed over in Mr. Courlander's bibliography. He includes instead "eyewitness" accounts by white tourists including some racist documents by Hern, Cable, and others which have been reprinted many times.

The other point of view doesn't come through. For example, Mr. Courlander uses material by Maya Dern, an author deemed curious by the Haitians, but ignores *Evolution of the Doctrine* by ethnologist François Duvalier, a Houngan who became President of Haiti. He refers to one book by Jean Price-Mars but omits Her-Ra-Ma-El's *The Daimons of the Voodoo Cult.* The Marcelin brothers and others equipped to provide material on Afro-American folklore from the Haitian point of view are also ignored. His material on HooDoo in New Orleans is inadequate and dependent upon tall tales spun by biased tourists, one of whom described Africans as "inferior and ignorant." Such opinion is more appropriate when presented in a book on the types of mental illnesses racism breeds, but not in a book concerning Afro-American folklore. Like someone attributing the building of Stonehenge to white savages.

The "ceremonies" described in the book are probably frauds anyway, rigged for gullible tourists; it's extremely doubtful whether an outsider has ever witnessed a Vodoun ceremony, in the Caribbean or in the United States, a claim made by Lynne Fauley Emery in her book *Black Dance,* the best book on the New Orleans the Africans made. This book is also neglected by Mr. Courlander.

There is an abundance of literature on HooDoo including documents and works left by participants which Mr. Courlander overlooks. So much that the legendary Harry

Middleton Hyatt has compiled three volumes which will be published in a book to be released by Oxford University Press and edited by Henry Louis Gates III of Yale.

To his credit, Mr. Courlander does include Zora Neale Hurston's *Mules and Men* but ignores her important *The VooDoo Gods of Haiti.*

In the United States section he does the same thing: anthologizes reports by Europeans on the nineteenth-century South and ignores narratives by the ex-slaves themselves. Miss Fannie Anne Kemble's reminiscences, for one, have been over anthologized.

There's some unoriginal poking about for "retentions," all of which is unsubtle since the United States is immersed in African retentions. All one has to do is visit the Miami International Airport and observe the fabrics and colors the Cuban and black women wear. African retentions are coming out of the car radios on the freeways of America.

The style of *Afro-American Folklore* reads like an edition of *Time* edited by "educators." This is because it's hard for an outsider to pin down Creole, which simply means the fascinating, exhilarating, and innovative "English" black speakers put on other languages. Not "Black English," but Creole, a survival language of fluidity and camouflage. Mr. Courlander believes that Creole elaborates on French vocabulary and syntax, although when one President of Haiti made up words as he delivered his speeches he was *perfectly understood!* Like gumbo, the flavor, rhythm, sound, and unpredictability of Creole gets lost in the translation.

A Treasury of Afro-American Folklore then is a worthwhile book that fails. Perhaps Mr. Courlander's method was wrong. He attempted to treat something as complex and sophisticated as Vodoun as folklore when its philosophy of Nature parallels that of modern physics. In other words, our stuff is science, their stuff is superstition. Cultural boasting has no place in an objective study of other people's cultures.

Washington *Post*
August 6, 1976

Ishmael Reed—Self Interview

Q. What was your most experimental writing?
A. *D Hexorcism of Noxon D Awful.* It was based, not upon other writing, but upon examples of dolls I had seen in books and museums. Gris-gris dolls. I wanted to make a crude, primitive fetish and that would put a "writing" on an individual considered an enemy to the tribe. In this "writing" I wanted to encapsulate his essential characteristics and through the inter-telepathic energy of the readers aim a psychic "fix" at this individual. A year or so later copycat Dan Greenburg came up with a "Noxon" and it was published in *Playboy* and another man named Seelye recently wrote a "Noxin" and it received major backing in advertising. Roth's *Our Gang* came out a long time after mine appeared and it was even set up like mine. His is being reissued. You begin to sympathize with the Georgia slave whose invention was ripped off by Eli Whitney—is also similar to Jack Johnson, who wasn't allowed to knock out a white man. Muhammad Ali had a point when he said: "Writing is fighting."

There is a taboo in this country against a black man besting a white man unless it's in sports, because, as they see it, "niggers" are brutes anyway. Blacks are also kept in line by social workers and socialists because whenever they have participated in business with a fair chance they've proven to be "lucky." In California they were so "lucky" in striking gold the state almost passed a "Negro exclusion act" to keep them out.

Notice the number of black plays which are anti-black middle class, read anti-achievement class, that are spon-

155

sored by liberals whose own group is 80 per cent middle class. You don't hear them putting their own people down. We see this in many fields. For example, if Sam Ervin had wanted to develop the Watergate case logically, as he said, he would have called Frank Wills, the black guard, who busted the case. Ervin wanted to spare powerful whites the humiliation of being busted by a nigger just as Grant intervened to spare Lee the humiliation of surrendering to black troops.

They put a "black" social realist critic on me who said he thought the piece was "cute" when the piece was solidly in the tradition of African and European witchcraft (he called it "sophomoric" because I had Noxon eating cat excrement for breakfast; I didn't put that in to shock, I put it in because that's what old fashioned "HooDoo" and European witchcraft formulas say you're supposed to feed a fiend). His calling it "cute" was one of the events that convinced me that you can't apply the Marxist reading to what is happening here in this country—"cute" was what the slave claimant called the especially devious fugitive slave. So this critic has more in common with a nigger catcher than with a, to put it archly, "student of Marx"!

The piece was published in *Amistad I* in 1969 and in *19 Necromancers from Now* (1970), an anthology of mine, that was censored for an entire year by two black teachers at Sacramento City College who claimed that it "wasn't for the people." Notice how some of these people who are so much for "the community" spend a lot of time at upper middle-class white colleges which resemble cities in paradise.

Anyway, a critic in Spain who is a *Noxon* . . . fan recently wrote and told me that a congressman priest from Massachusetts received a letter from a constituent saying: "If you can't impeach him, exorcise him."

Q. What went into the writing of *Mumbo Jumbo?*

A. Intuition, intellect, research, maybe even communicators from the psychic field. I was amazed the number of times I would play my hunches about a particular historical event and then be able to go out and prove it. I wanted to write about a time like the present or to use the past to prophesy about the future—a process our ancestors called necromancy. I chose the twenties because they are very similar to what's happening now. This is a valid method and has been used by writers from time immemorial. Nobody ever accused James Joyce of making up things. Using a past event of one's country or culture to comment on the present. Of course when an American writer does it it's called "nostalgia" by people who see the American past as unworthy as a subject. I bet if you were writing about England of a hundred years ago—the kind of programs they broadcast on so-called Public Television, where they're using taxpayers' money to promote the "grandeur" of the Western past, they wouldn't call it "nostalgia." Or if you were writing about nineteenth-century Russia, the literature a whole wing of eastern criticism champions because that's where their parents came from and it's their "ethnic literature," their "homefolks" literature (the same people put down others for promoting their ethnic studies and ethnic arts and turning away from the "classics").

Anyway, getting back to the parallels—there was a post-war economic crisis, you had government scandal (on page 69 of the paperback edition of *Mumbo Jumbo* there's a photo of the Watergate conspirators and the book was submitted on *January 31, 1971!* which is written after the last line in the book), there was an epidemic of "negromania" sweeping through America then, "The Jazz Age," there was a black writing renaissance, Egypt was on the ascendancy as it is now—important excavations were made in the twenties. And there are other parallels. The black cultural and political spectrum was similar.

I think I might have a touch of sync or synchronization ability (the ability to have insight into the similar form emanting from disparate entities or mediums is the way I see it). I get an average of three sync flashes per week. Last week I was trying to remember the name of a historian who was the best on the Monroe Doctrine. It occurred to me that he was heir to the Fannie Farmer candy fortune and I said Fannie Farmer and somebody on the radio said, "Fannie Farmer."

My mother is the clairvoyant of the family. She has the

gift of precognition and she communicates with apparitions of deceased relatives who bring her important news, prophecies, and, of course, fortune.

Thousands upon thousands of blacks have these abilites. The slave masters always marveled at their communications system. I am beginning to believe that a large number of blacks are able to communicate with each other telepathically. I wouldn't be surprised if it turns out that Afros have a larger percentage of people with these *psi* abilities than other groups, among whom we find about 10 per cent of the people with these abilities. It may be that a large percentage of Western people with such abilities were slaughtered (nine million people in two centuries). When the Catholic Church wiped out those who rivaled its authority as the supreme residue of "supernatural" powers—you know, witches. Natural selection set in and most of the people who remain were benumbed.

Hotbeds of paganism, like Germany and Russia, resisted. Notice how Solzhenitsyn recently referred to Marxism as a Western idea. As Ionesco recently pointed out, Marxism is rooted in the Christian tradition. Solzhenitsyn's remarks can be interpreted as those of a Russian pagan getting back at the Church of Rome.

My reading leads me to believe that HooDoo or as they say in Haiti and other places "VooDoo" or "Vodoun" was always open to the possibility of the real world and the psychic world intersecting. They have a principle for it: Legba (in the U.S., "LaBas"). Physicists have discovered an element called neutrinos that can pass through walls (ghosts?). When I said this at Queens College some of the students and their Marxist teachers sniggled. You see, Marxists know all of the laws of Nature. They have the knowledge of the theoretical god of Western philosophy; this is why they can call people and events "irrelevant"—they're omniscient.

Anyway, there were sections of *Mumbo Jumbo* which were written in what some people call "automatic" writing or the nearest thing to it. Writing is more than just the act of typing. I think you get a lot of help from heritage, you know, "voices," the existence of which may be proven through the use of tape recorders. Work in this strange field began with a scientist named Friedrich Jurgeson.

One of the strangest events that happened about *Mumbo Jumbo* was the refusal of a museum in Rome to give me permission to use the picture of a Negroid Osiris they chipped off the wall of an Egyptian pyramid like the vandals they are; yet they got the gumption to call people "uncivilized." When they first received permission forms to use it they were delighted but when they saw the author's photo they refused. My agent went to Rome and called the director about using it and the director wouldn't even reply. The photo appears in a book called *Black Eros* published by Lyle Stuart, I think. They let him use it but refused me permission.

Another mysterious episode occurred when Doubleday held up the book for a whole year. The book was submitted on January 31, 1971, and was supposed to be published in August of 1971 and it was held up until August of 1972. It would take an Archibald Cox to find out the reason why. I think I know. Of course, Bantam ruined the cover I did for *Mumbo Jumbo* just as they ruined Yvonne Williams' cover for *Yellow Back Radio Broke-Down*. The vice-president of Bantam called me and wanted to know what I was doing for the Soledad Brothers. He was calling me from his air-conditioned office in Manhattan. I told him that I sympathized with the Soledad Brothers but my main job I felt was to humble Judeo-Christian culture. He said, "Oh."

Well, Bantam ruined the cover and messed up the book I guess because when you come down to it they are loud and don't have too much class. I just did a book with little bitty "chump change" that makes their whole list look like a thirteen-cent hamburger you buy off the New Jersey freeway.

It always amazes me when some jeremiad hi-yellow "black" person would say, "Niggers can't do nothin right. The white man is the one." Did you know that Nixon wanted to retaliate against the Premier of North Korea when he shot down an American plane and killed over thirty men? Nixon couldn't because the Sixth or Seventh

159

Fleet was being used for the filming of *Tora Tora Tora*.

Anyway *Mumbo Jumbo* got through despite an attempt to bury it.

Q. Were you on "dope" or "drunk" when you wrote *Yellow Back Radio Broke-Down?*

A. The title *Yellow Back Radio Broke-Down* was based upon a poem by Lorenzo Thomas called *Modern Plumbing Illustrated,* which was published in a magazine called *East Side Review* (1966) which lasted one issue. I based the book on old radio scripts in which the listener constructed the sets from his imagination—that's why radio, also because it's an oral book, a talking book; people say they read it aloud, that is, it speaks through them, which makes it a loa. Also radio because there's more dialogue than scenery and descriptions. "Yellow Back" because that's what they used to call old West books about cowboy heroes—they were "yellow covered books and were usually lurid and sensational," and so the lurid scenes are in the book because that is what the form calls for. They're not in there to shock. "Broke-Down" is a takeoff on Lorenzo Thomas's *Illustrated.* When people say "Break it down" they mean to strip something down to its basic components. So *Yellow Back Radio Broke-Down* is the dismantling of a genre done in an oral way like radio. The "time sense" is akin to the "time" one finds in the psychic world, where past, present, and future exist simultaneously. A generation from now, when people read my work, they will say—ho-hum, so what else is new?

That is because they will have become accustomed to a way of thinking that's considered "way-out" or even "crazy" now, just as Be-bop was considered "way-out" in the forties, but is now used as background music on very conventional television detective shows.

The funniest thing that happened about *Yellow Back* was its rave review in a magazine called *Western Round-up,* a rodeo magazine. I've never rode a horse in my life. That's really rich because "Yellow Back" writers were usually dudes from the East like me. The cowboys would read their books and begin to ape the exaggerations of themselves they read. A case of life imitating art. And so you see I wasn't "crazy" or "on dope" but extremely conscious of form when I wrote that book as Roland E. Bush and others have realized and pointed out.

Q. Did you write a book on Adam Clayton Powell?

A. No. I didn't write a book on Adam Clayton Powell. I organized one in 1966—there were four of us who wrote a book on Adam Clayton Powell, each contributing essays, and I was considered the managing editor. We did it in a month. I contributed a muckraking essay; Myrna Bain contributed an essay on Adam Clayton Powell's background; Steve Cannon contributed an essay on historical parallels between what was happening to Powell and what happened in Reconstruction; and Clark Whelton contributed a reporter-essay on the rally that was held in defense of Powell at Abyssinian Baptist Church, and I'm very pleased with this book because it was the first to link Powell's problems to what we shall call, euphemistically, organized crime. It's very interesting that he got his most difficult time from judges with Italian surnames. The Jewish judges thought the suit that Ms. James brought against him was gratuitous and dismissed it, but the judges with Italian surnames were the ones who relentlessly persecuted Powell. And it's interesting that his problems began when he made a speech in Congress called "The Immorality of the New York Police Department," and that's when he started naming names, many of which were Italian surnames—all of the police who were on the take in Harlem—and this was a long time before the Knapp Commission or "Superfly," which, if anything, was an exposé of what New York big-city police are really like. So I think he had a lot of guts doing that. The publisher deleted my long introduction to the book because I had uncovered information that the congressmen who were pressing charges against Powell were potential felons because of the kind of corruption they themselves were indulging in.

Anyway, Steve Cannon and I are presently negotiating to get the rights to this book and to reprint it with new introductions.

One thing about Powell. He believed that a congress-

man's job was to get bills through Congress, not rapping
or taking glamorous "New Left" type positions.

Q. Why are you so hard on James Baldwin and Ralph
Ellison?

A. I think that within the framework of Judeo-Christian
culture James Baldwin is a great writer. What annoys me
is the fact that he's a hustler who tries to come on like
Job. He is undeniably a very ambitious man and the way
he hops over here from the South of France and comments on "radical chic" issues—these junkets seem to occur always when he has a book coming out. Right now
he's lending his prestige to an upper middle-class liberal
hobby of going into jails and bringing out some of the
worst elements of blacks and setting them up as cannon
fodder, you know, not humans but "armed projectiles."
We just lost Marcus Foster, whose only crime was that
he was trying to do the best job he could do. But this
anti-middle class, read anti-black achievers, which comes
from places like Howard University and the South of
Paris is negative and poisonous. I don't know any group
in the world that would want to ice its most skilled people. The Arabs recently attributed their success to turning from "rijal al thiqa," people of confidence, to people
of knowledge, "rijal al marifa": engineers, physicians,
scientists, skilled navigators, and aviators. Did you know
that the woman who runs the computer controlling five
or so missile carriers is black? People should read *Ebony's* feature "Speaking of People" as well as rhetorical
losing prophecies of doom and gloom. I was in jail but
it certainly wasn't for mugging, raping, or hitting some
old person on the head with a brick or gunning down the
operators of a Mom and Pop store. I was there for telling
a cop he was taking a bribe. They beat me at the Ninth
Precinct. I had my Selma all alone and *Life* wasn't there
to cover it. I was just another nigger taking his lumps.

While some of my critics were reading Albert Camus
and Hegel at Howard University I was living in the no-
torious Talbert Mall Projects on Spring Street in Buffalo,
New York, 1960. My parents recently had their car
stolen and they saw it parked in front of Talbert Projects

but the police were scared to go in there to arrest anybody. Hard-working black people are the ones who are bearing the brunt of all of this intellectual romanticism concerning the "Policial Prisoner," read "The Street Nigger" or "The Field Nigger." This abuse of the term by people like Baldwin and Professor Angela Davis harms the cause of those who are truly political prisoners not to mention the 27,000 aesthetic and "occult" prisoners they have locked up somewhere in the Midwest in institutions. People the society judges to be insane because they challenge it.

Dickens said that you can judge a society by the conditions of its prisons. That must mean that American society is pretty scummy. I know about the Skinner-inspired "behavior modification" programs and the experiments that are conducted on prisoner guinea pigs. I know about the brutality and the sadism; I know all about what the inside of American prisons resemble, but what are you going to do with somebody who comes into your house, rips off your stuff, and hits your mama on the head with a blackjack?

Baldwin does damage, I think, by not being informed that the majority of blacks in New York City, Detroit, and Chicago want Law and Order because they're the ones who have to pay with brain concussions for all of this radical chic stuff promoted from places that are so staked out with doormen and electronic gadgets that only God can enter the lobby. Everybody can't live on Central Park West or be chauffeur driven through Harlem. So it's easy for him to hop on the plane, come over here, and take up a cause. Before I call someone a "political prisoner" I would have to know what they're in for first.

Ralph Ellison has given interviews in which he puts down younger writers for lack of "craftsmanship." He'll write sly attacks against Afro-American writers but from what he has said his idea of craftsmanship is merely giving the synopsis of a Hemingway or Faulkner novel he's read. Telling what the story is about is not "craftsmanship," that's plot, one aspect of "craftsmanship." In fact, if he were only interested in plot he might reward everyone with a technical discussion of whether plot is "story line" or whether plot is based upon causality, the way one event logically follows another. I hate to say this, but his comments on younger writers do not concern "craftsmanship" but are more like rhetoric, the kind of thing his friends accuse younger Afro-American writers of indulging in. They recognize rhetoric because they are champs. What I am saying is that someone ought to do an interview with him in which he is pressed to say exactly what he means about lack of craftsmanship, giving specifics, examples, and suggestions—I mean citing authors and the specific ways in which they lack craftsmanship. That way he would be performing a wise service—to these young authors who according to him lack craftsmanship.

Q. Have you ever received an honorary degree or grant or an award for your writing?

A. I haven't received an honorary degree or grant but I was recently made an honorary pope by the Savarian Illuminati, for the writing of *Mumbo Jumbo,* which according to the sealed papers I received in the mail was founded in A.D. 1090 by Hassan i Sabbah. They read the book and don't think it was "muddled" as one of the "Sister" critics thought. I get my strongest criticism from some of the "Sisters." I guess this is because they want me to improve and do better, God bless them.

Q. What happened to the film version of *Yellow Back Radio Broke-Down?*

A. I am confident that it's going to be done now. Twenty-eight-year-old Francisco Newman, a film maker out here, has the option and we've just completed the screenplay. Some of the other options on it didn't come to fruition. I was against somebody adapting it and insisted on writing the screenplay, which we've just completed. I didn't want the film version of my book to come out looking like *Birth of a Nation.* I have to live here.

Q. What are you working on now?

A. I've just finished a new book, *The Last Days of Louisiana Red,* that's supposed to be published later this year.

I'm working as editorial director of Yardbird Publishing Co., Inc. We've put out two issues of *Yardbird*

Reader and now I'm working with Frank Chin, the playwright, and Shawn Wong, a writer, on *Yardbird Reader* III, which will be an Asian-American issue featuring an interview with James Wong Howe, who invented camera techniques that a younger generation takes for granted. Glenn Myles, our art director, is working with Bob Onodera on graphics. Ms. Roberta Palm of Howard University Press went to *Publishers' Weekly* (March 4, 1974) and told them, "We didn't realize until we looked into it that Asian-Americans hadn't been published before," when she knew better and got the idea for publishing *Aiiieee! An Introduction to Asian-American Writing* from *Yardbird Reader,* Vol. I and II. In Volume II we printed, in 1973, an introduction from the very anthology they say they found first. In fact, she called Shawn Wong and asked him the identity of the Asian-American writers in *Yardbird*. They don't give us an acknowledgement at all in their edition. Isn't that gauche?

I'm working on a new book, a "ragtime" novel, and am studying ragtime piano so that it'll come out right. I have also nearly completed a book of new poetry called *Flight to Canada*. I am also working on a book of interviews called *Afro-Americans You Don't Hear About Because They Ain't Rappin Singin MUGGIN Boxin or Dressed Up Like Big Bird on Sesame Street*.

This idea came when Charles Harris phoned me to tell me that he was with Howard University Press and invited me to submit a proposal for a book. I sent the proposal almost two years ago and haven't heard whether they accepted it. I know they're busy down there so they must have lost it.

I have also begun Reed, Cannon & Johnson Communications Co. with two fine writers, Joe Johnson and Steve Cannon, and we've recently published our first book, a novel by Alison Mills, a twenty-two-year-old actress. The novel's entitled *Francisco* and already received praise from distinguished writers like Ms. Toni Morrison and Mr. William Demby.

Incidentally, all of the funds that went into Yardbird and R.C.&J. were our own. I guess we're not nationalistic or revolutionary enough to receive federal or state funds and generous aid from private foundations.

I don't say this out of malice. It's just some gentle ribbing of some people who say one thing in *Publishers' Weekly* and another thing in *Black World*. Call for representative democracy in *Newsweek* but issue threats against those who disagree with them in black publications. It always tickles me to hear some of these people come on so "field" when they're receiving $1,500 honorariums. Some of us are lucky if we get $100 and a ride from the airport: John A. Williams, one of the most formidable writers in American history in terms of craft, doesn't receive grants, and Charles Wright, who has consistently produced quality work, has to wash dishes to make ends meet. One of these "for-the-people" poets recently received a thousand dollars for a reading while at the same college, a week later, I was paid so little I had to pay my airfare home out of my pocket.

I think the way certain "Black Studies" organizations at some schools used the funds they controlled in the 1960s and early 1970s might in the end be the best argument against students controlling their affairs. They were crazy about sensationalism and would bring in sensationalists to make them secure in their own ethnic security bags—telling them what they already knew. Some of them were middle-class kids revolting against their backgrounds, you know, where their parents worked and sacrificed to put them where they were and give them a better break than they had received.

Some of them would try to embarrass other people of opposite viewpoints or writers of poetry of a different style or subject. At Syracuse University, when they heard I was coming, they scheduled an Angela Davis rally the same night, and other writers can give you similar horror stories. There's a schizophrenic nest down at Santa Barbara that's as evil as they can be, take up your time and then act sloppy. Some of the grownups who put these people up to these stunts aren't going to look too good when this whole period is evaluated. Why would some of these people who are so much for the people, so much for "Freedom and Liberation," only want to expose their students to maybe one idea or one type of poem or novel? Of course they're not too careful about the words they use —view language as decoration or sound—so when they say "Freedom and Liberation" they must mean slavery. You see, the sleeper of the whole thing is that when given a choice many people will tell you they like slavery. A friend of mine, Jeanne Wakatsuki Houston, who with her husband James D. Houston wrote *Farewell to Manzanar* about the Japanese incarceration out here, says that some of the Japanese said that their best times were had in those detention camps. This is the basic flaw of all of this "Freedom and Liberation" talk. People who read Marx and Fanon should also read Wilhelm Reich's *The Mass Psychology of Fascism*.

And why all this antagonism towards individuality? Insects have individuality, even ants. You can't predict the behavior of one shark by observing that of another shark, and each wolf has a different tone, yet these people will go about saying we are all the same, then shout down Shockley and Jenson when they suggest that we are sub-human or want to fight when somebody says they can't tell them apart.

The Afro-American's great asset may be his "unpredictability," an asset which may ultimately be proven to have a psychic connection. There's always been a final solution suggested against Afro-Americans and they've always had the means to carry it out. We're still here.

Q. What is your opinion of recent black poetry?

A. Much of it is successful. One of the glaring problems, however, is that there isn't as much variety among the critical approaches as there is in the writing the critics are examining. Of course some of the critics only examine the writing of a particular school of black poetry and play like that's the whole thing, like other schools and individuals don't exist. I mean, how could somebody look at the black poetry of the last twenty years (I'm reluctant to call it black since some of the most inflated of the reputations—inflated by a magazine that has been pushing skin lighteners for twenty years—were people who are by my observation very "fair-skinned" and some of these people come on the "blackest"; I have to bring this up but we're supposed to be "scientists" aren't we?) and say that black poetry is directed to the end of "Freedom and Liberation" and based upon "black speech and music" when an examination would show that the majority of language material is American or English and that the poets and novelists have been influenced by not only music but graphics, painting, film, sculpture—all disciplines and all art forms—and write about all subjects.

They say music because they are socialist realists and music is the most popular art form of the masses. You can be influenced by music while you're asleep but reading is hard work. Of course listening to Cecil Taylor, Bill Dixon, and others is hard work, too, but when these critics talk about "music" they don't mean those musicians; they wouldn't be calling on "the people" to do hard work, they want to make it easy for them and a lot of nonsense that goes down stems from this desire. They are basically social workers and not critics.

Now, if these social realist critics were so interested in "Freedom and Liberation" why would they jive around with the recent cultural history of a people they're supposed to be championing—depriving them of the knowledge of how rich and varied their culture is and was? Why, if they were so hot about "black poetry" would they omit any reference to major figures who were responsible for its development: Calvin Hernton, Lorenzo Thomas, Joe Johnson, Albert Haynes, Charles and William Patterson? Why do they hardly mention the *Umbra* poets, who were writing black poetry in the early sixties? Why would they leave out some of the excellent poets who've been writing since then in favor of promoting one particular school that originates from the screaming wing of the New York School of poets, "personalism," and borrows so much from the examples of the Black Mountain poets that you can't pick up an anthology without someone like Richard Ellman saying black poets would be nowhere if it were not for Olson, Williams, Ginsberg, et al., which is just about as mischievous as someone saying black female poets are superior to black male poets, as Kenneth Rexroth wrote in *American Poetry in the Twentieth Century,* published by Herder and Herder, p. 158.

Anyway, truth will out and already people are beginning to see that the 1960s was a richer period in Afro-American writing than most thought and that the tricksters' school of Afro Lit did a cover-up, put a cultural Watergate on the people.

One more thing. Typography is merely one aspect of poetry and one suspects that some individuals in this school, which the social realist critics use to support some weak thesis, employ noisy sensationalistic typography to conceal the rather banal intellectual content of their poetry—it's interesting that this school came into prominence in the middle sixties and coincides with the arrival of what is called "rock" music, which also used up-front bedazzling ear-excruciating music to conceal bad musicianship and poor performance. Art Tatum, Earl Hines, and Fats Waller with one beat-up piano have a wider range and a fuller emotional, intellectual, and aesthetic content than all of the "rock" bands put together. But of course you hardly hear about them because eastern musicians are futuristic and neglect anything before the 1950s. I'm beginning to think that the music before the fifties was better.

The sixties was a strident decade. I call it "The Decade that Screamed." It's going to take hard working critics to sift through all of this and separate the substance from the noise.

Getting back to typography, since critics view that as one of this school's big trumps—Norman Pritchard on those terms may turn out to be the best "black" poet of this school. His work makes people like E. E. Cummings seem very primitive, but of course Pritchard has the edge on Cummings since Pritchard has devoted his life to painting, roomed with painters, and befriended famous painters and took a degree in Fine Arts, and so he was able to bring the techniques of the visual arts to the page, which is the highest order of typography. His typographical inventions make those of this school appear crude and period. But the people who puff this particular school, one among many in black poetry, don't devote a line to Pritchard. They do not realize that he is the best of the typographical or concrete school because he realized long ago that words had become decoration and had lost their meaning (rhetoric) and that the poet's job was to render them on a page in an aesthetically eye-appealing way. He said: "Words are ancillary to meaning." Of course, I disagree and set my poetry up in a conventional way. His sound is that of jazz music and is not just incidental to the words, as you get in rapping poetry. His *Aswelay* and *Gyre's Galax* are probably the purest jazz poetry to come out of the sixties.

I don't agree with his approach and think that ultimately this kind of thing gets into an area in which the painter and musician are superior because it's their thing —but I understand Pritchard and can't understand why he doesn't get the play in the anthologies commensurate with his achievement. Anyway I think we are entering a hard period where sensationalism will be seen as just that. Peter Bradley, a painter, discusses something called hard art, hard to do, and hard to get to. The seventies are going to be a hard decade in art and culture. Hard criticism and hard knocks.

The writing establishment is now Afro-American and critics who can't see that are social realists and Christians who love to lose anyway. Notice how much they talk about losing: "Nigger, you incapable of doing anything, the white boys is the one that's smart." I cut out clippings of achievements of Afro-Americans for the last two years and I find them to be impressive, some staggering: Dr. Cooke, Afro-American scientist, part of a three-man team that isolated a human cancer virus at Cornell—I call him Dr. Cooke because UPI failed to give his first name. I'll bet if he was some unskilled liberator seduced into a wild scheme by upper-class carpetbaggers you would have gotten his first name and front-page picture.

Anyway, the field nigger got all the play in the sixties. This field nigger romanticism came out of places like Howard University, which is apparently a hotbed of lumpen, field nigger, proletariat, professional street nigger chic. Maybe it's about time people started paying attention to other types of slaves and free blacks from the past. Maybe this generation should listen to shoemakers, masons, bakers, brick and tile makers, inventors, butchers, scientists, cabinetmakers and upholsterers, carpenters and joiners, fishermen and oystermen, harness and saddlemakers, tailors, printers, dentists, barbers, physicians, teachers, musicians, architects, and others. They were there, too, and maybe they have a lesson to teach the present.

No matter what his critics say about him, Booker T. Washington's Tuskegee is still there.

Q. Why you so mean and hard?

A. Because I am an Afro-American male, the most exploited and feared class in this country. All of the gentlemen, all of the ones who tried to be nice, are in the cemetery or sitting on a stoop humiliated and degraded waiting for someone to hand them a bowl of soup or waiting for the law some woman has called on them. (I'd be willing to bet that half the men at Attica who were wiped out were there on domestic charges.)

With few exceptions, men of most races, not just whites, fear or are curious about his powers. Opportunistic Africans and West Indians like the one *Esquire* put up to call Afro-American intellectuals "empty-headed" (March 1974) are imported by mischievous whites to preside over his political and cultural life, and to stifle his rage and show him up. Even Derek Walcott permits somebody like Selden Rodman to quote him as saying, "There's nothing whiter than an American black, once he has money. . . ."

When will Afro-Americans learn that they are alone and no one cares about them unless they can use them? Russia sold them out; China sold them out; Cuba is preparing to embrace Nixon; the African countries they point to as "socialistic" buy ads in Western newspapers begging for Western capital. It's amazing how uninformed some Afro-American "charismatic" leaders are—they get away with it because Afro journalists don't ask them tough

171

questions and seem to bend over backwards to embrace their point of view.

Anyway, the tragedy of the Afro-American male is that he can't articulate the full extent of his oppression. If I say I am oppressed by "honkies" or "the system" the crowd roars and the popcorn is passed all around and gulped down. But if I say that "whites" are not the only ones who believe in the cultural and intellectual inferiority of the Afro-American male, if you get what I mean, and cite evidence, I'm censored by both white and black publications. Maybe in these hard times ahead we can get into some hard questions about this other oppression—this silent oppression.

March 10, 1974
Berkeley, California

Betye Saar, Artist

Betye Saar is a working mother who skitters about California in a Saab usually accompanied by the three daughters she raised: Alison, seventeen, Tracye, twelve, and Lesley, twenty, a student at San Francisco City College. She is the recipient of awards from The Downey Musuem of Art, Downey, California, the Fifth Annual California Small Image Exhibition, the Pasadena Artists' Society, the Watts Summer Festival, the Los Angeles County Museum of Art, the Whitney Museum of American Art, New York City, and her work is included in major American collections—private and museum. She has designed costumes for theater, motion pictures, and has made two films: *A Colored Spade,* and *Eyeball.* Her work draws its sources from Africa, Oceania, as well as Afro-American folklore. The following interview was conducted in March 1973, after the completion of her successful show at Berkeley's Live Oak Park.

IR: Betye, why do you call your show, your recent successful show, Black Girl's Window?

BS: Well, actually the gallery director thought of that title, after that window that I have—it's kind of a takeoff from a line by Matisse which is "Art is a window . . . a way of sharing. . . ." And that was kind of like my whole feeling about the show—the way I see things. Like looking out from my head, from my eyes, and the way the viewer sees. And since the majority of the works were windows, that's why we decided on that theme.

IR: Is this the reason you have a play on many kinds of eyes? I notice a persistent element in your work was the eye—the Egyptian eye—different kinds of eyes. Done on leather and using all kinds of materials to construct an eye. You've talked about the seeing, the idea of the visual and seeing through a window.

BS: It relates in part to that. I have selected certain symbols that I repeat in my work, and the eye is one. And the eye also serves as looking at one, or one sees the same thing as one eye sees another eye. It's true I use the Egyptian eye, which is the "all-seeing eye," the protective eye to ward off the "evil eye." I like the form, the shape, the design of the eye. And I use many materials—paint, rocks, eye shapes—openings—this means a looking out, an attitude as well as the graphic image.

IR: In my mind I mentally divided your work into three or four series—this particular show we're discussing. One section of it dealt with the way blacks have been depicted, especially in entertainment and in popular culture. And to achieve this effect you used elements like, for example, a real banjo, and you used old advertisements for toothpaste, and things like that—soap—things that give an ironic commentary on history. Then at the same time you're able to take essential forms that one sees in a survey—you know—of a history of blacks in America and connect them with what's going on now. For example, I saw one piece you had in which two people were holding banjos and the final—it was like a triptych—and the final panel showed a man with a rifle. Were you saying that things haven't changed very much in history?

BS: The title of that piece is "Let Me Entertain You." And my reason for that window was that the black in his traditional role has been the entertainer—the dancing darky, the banjo player, or whatever—that was the first panel of that window. The second panel was a lynch scene, which is another form of white entertainment. So the reverse is that there's a new form of entertainment—the black's entertainment. (I guess it could be interpreted as that.) And instead of the musical instrument, the instrument is now a rifle. The reason for the black imagery is—well, it started three or four years ago, and I started collecting those images in postcards and sheet music, and other forms of advertisements—I guess it was around the turn of the century when a lot of that was prevalent. So many of those images were hurtful. I mean really painful, like a watermelon that explodes and there's like a nigger's head in it—that kind of thing. Just horrible jokes and things. This is a really negative thing, and how can I, as an artist, change that to make it into a positive thing, to make it a thing of beauty, a thing of interest? So I started using those images in my work.

And then a kind of revolution or social statement evolved from that—it's because I worked in a kind of stream of consciousness way, things just fall into place. And it just seems to come out that way—that it [turns into] revolution, and it also has—but this idea didn't come to me until after I had finished several works, and I could look back at them and say, "Hey, I'm kind of in a trance and this is my creative revolution because I can't participate any other way," I just can't because of my makeup and my personality. So I do it this way. And this also serves as an explanation to whites or others as to why blacks react the way they are because they have all that [hate] behind them.

IR: You know, you said something very interesting. You said you worked on a stream of consciousness level, but there is an order in your work—a consistency and a kind of rationalism, but maybe a different kind of rationalism —a kind of reasoning that we may not be able to explain —as beyond reason. You understand what I mean?

BS: Sure.

IR: I mean there may be another order, and you may be one of these unique individuals who are gifted to tap another dimension or another universe or a world most of us aren't able to see yet! You do use a lot of ideas, and in your work you use objects that we associate with—for want of a better term—African religion. Do you see yourself in that tradition?

BS: Well, my art is very personal. It's like what is in my head at the time I'm doing it, although several pieces are worked on at the same time. About this stream of consciousness thing, I do tap a source because in the last two years I have developed a technique from a technique that was taught to me of using the alpha and the theta brain waves for creativity. And it's like a kind of self-hypnosis where you get rid of all the input of other shit that's going around and just let it flow. And it's so automatic that you're not even conscious that it's happening. I don't have any trial-and-error kind of business. Sometimes two things really catch my eye, but in the end I always really know the right one. About the African thing, it's not so much African as what we call Primitive, because I use Egyptian and Oceanic and American Indian and African, any kind of culture that is related more to the earth or to nature and I use those kinds of materials. That's where that theory comes from, that evolves with putting materials and symbols and colors together so that in one piece you may find materials or symbols or signs or designs from several cultures, but it all works together as a tribal thing. But then, it's a secret tribe.

IR: So then it's like Betye Saar's window and not a Black Girl's window.

BS: Right.

IR: I want to get back to this series that really interested me. I thought the other work was craftsman's work—one of the series was leather—and designs painted on leather. That was so intricate to me that I thought that it would take someone who went through the process of doing that to really appreciate it, because I could see there were different kinds of knitting involved. You must have gotten into like the encyclopedia of world knitting to put that together like that. It is an Afro-American tradition because you took bird feathers and you took organic material and you took found material and you linked it up together. It's a very sophisticated version of the old quilt making in the Afro-American South, where the women would use disparate materials and make a quilt, which was like one unity. But that series, I guess I like it because it was very literary. For example, you had a panel, you had four panels—cartoon panels on the washboard.

SB: "National Washboard."

IR: Yeah, and so you do use this in some instances to create a debunking effect on American history as we see it. I notice, for example, you use authentic photographs from the same period that the caricatures were derived from. So you saw how things were actually at that time and how they'd been caricatured. So do I see like some muckraking going on?

BS: Right, right. The series that I have—they're like the tribal things, like the past. So far I've been dealing mostly in the past and in the future and some of the things in the past touch the present, like in the "Black Series." Like they have the panel with the revolution and things like that. In one you're speaking of "National Washboard"— the washboard itself was a symbol of the black woman— her Aunt Jemima role and the washerwoman, whatever. And it was a cartoon series from a newspaper which I painted and added collage—I took words out and added the watermelon and the Aunt Jemima head and things like that. And on the other side of that—because that piece is exhibited suspended—there's a black hand and a red fist, a clenched fist, which give the other side of the washboard scene, or the other side of the coin.

IR: There was another one you're speaking of, the Aunt Jemima figure, the archetype which you find in other work of yours. I saw a few of those images. In one you had the two measuring cups and in the one measuring cup there appeared to be flour and in the other measuring cup it appeared to be dynamite.

BS: Right. That's "Measure for Measure." And also behind that was "Aunt Jemima's Finest Flour" and on the other side was "Revolution" or "Africa" or "Right On"— or what ever.

IR: It was a very versatile show. Many people get into a rut, but I could see where you experiment with different ideas and different cultures and different media. You had some phrenology art, like using different offbeat occult systems to make a point. And you had a person's brain and instead of the signs that were usually associated with phrenology you had Prince Albert Tobacco can coverings and apples, things like that. This was done in 1967?

BS: Yes.

IR: So you've been consistently interested in offbeat sciences. Like what we call astrology.

BS: Yes, like the occult arts.

IR: Yes, occult arts. When did you get interested in that? Have you always been interested in this?

BS: I've always been interested in it, but it never entered into my work graphically, I guess, until 1965, when I was into drawing zodiac signs and star charts and that led to palmistry and phrenology and then the phrenology went from the head of a phrenology chart to a man's head to a black man's head and that evolved into the black thing. But even in the pieces that are the black pieces they still have some reflection back to the occult sciences, even to the star and the moon, which to me represents how the stars rule our lives, or destiny or fate or whatever. But I like a flashback from the tribal hangings to the black images to the occult sciences or to have them all in one.

IR: I went to the show twice. The first time I got a very superficial reading of the show. I was reading the show being—coming from another field, coming from another attitude—someone who has not developed his eye as well as an artist has. The more you look at it the more you see. There are hidden elements in it. It will trick you. I'm sure if you went back every day, you'd have a thing where you go to see it thirty days or something and just take notes. What was so hip about this was most of the time people exhibit. The old idea of an exhibit is where you go to a museum and you look at the stuff and all the art is there. You did have some hidden pieces. Would you like to explain some of the stuff that the audience didn't see? The patrons didn't see? For example, what was in those vials?

BS: Oh! Well, the whole "Mojo" series or the tribal hangings, each one of those pieces has a secret, a secret root that only the person who buys it or the person I know knows about. And the piece you're speaking of now is called "Gris-Gris Box." You open a panel and inside there are some little wooden boxes—little columns of wood—and you open them and inside each one is something that could be used for a gris-gris or to make a kind of magic thing. They are organic materials.

IR: Like what?

BS: Shells, bark from a tree, bones from a small bird, and pods. I don't know what that pod is—it rattles, it has a sound. Another thing I tried to do with the mojos, with the whole series, was to get into a sensitivity thing. Certain materials would have odor, like sandalwood, or carob pods have a distinct odor. They are also very tactile, like fur and leather, things to touch and pods with seeds that make sounds like pieces of wood or pods with seeds that would rattle or bones that would rattle. So it would be more than just the sensitivity of sight. One woud get into smell and sound.

IR: Incidentally, have you ever gotten into trouble with the ecology movement over those dead birds? (Joke.)

BS: No.

IR: You also like a lot of precious little things. *Stuff.*

BS: Stuff you're supposed to throw away.

IR: Well, but they look very big—they glisten—they look very good. What is some of the stuff that you have in there? I saw throughout the work like little bits and pieces of things—like marble, with all kind of jewelry effects and things. It looks so busy. What was that?

BS: Well, it's just like—I guess some of it could be junk, but I try not to collect junk. I like old things. Old things have secrets of where they've been before, people that they've related to. So I go to thrift shops and flea markets and things like that—some things people give to me, some things I just find. In a parking lot you can find little bits of tin or something that somebody's lost—and it's just the way that they're put together that gives that jewel-like quality, because isolated it's just nothing. It's the way that they relate to each other. Certain things have a certain look about them that's enhanced by what they're placed next to.

IR: I was interested in one that seemed to stand out. Let me go into this other thing first. In Vodoun they have a thing called grosben-age which allows each individual to bequeath his essential qualities to the world. I guess it's kind of like your soul, the ka of a person. I was reminded of this when I saw that piece you did on your grandmother. "Grandma's Garden." And it was like everybody's grandmother. I was thinking of the petals and the old rusted photo and the idealized picture—I'm talking about "Grandma's Garden," 1972—close to "Grandma's House" and in "Grandma's House" you had her glasses, all the lace, everything that you associate with that. And it gave it a spiritual quality because the stuff you used in it was kind of like ghostly—the soul of Grandmotherhood.

BS: Like faded memory.

IR: Yeah, too much.

BS: The thing about "Grandma's Garden"—I was flashing back. Sometimes an artist has to see their work all out there to realize what they were really doing. And when I made that box I had these dried petals and dried flowers and this old photo of two ladies in this garden and this piece of sheet music that said "My Garden of Memory" and then the butterflies. But when I put the petals down I found little beads and little pieces of glass and I glued those in. Because when I was a child my grandmother had this house at 117th Sreet, in Watts, and I would spend my summers there. And I would be in the yard digging with a stick all the time. And I would find little pieces of glass and beads, and it would be like pulling up weeds, and there would be some little thing that would be like a treasure to me. To a five-year-old kid it's a treasure. And I think that's where I became a junky, that's where I started collecting that stuff, because I would always go home with a bunch of that stuff.

IR: So as not to be misunderstood, you weren't collecting heroin, you were collecting these little pieces . . .

BS: Yeah, junk—like junk.

IR: Junky.

BS: Right, right. Well, that's my own inside joke. But that's what my studio's like. It's like, it's filled with stuff, junk—junk, but when I put it all together—when I made that Grandmother's Garden, to make that I had to hide those things because those were the things that I found. But not everybody sees that. I have to point out—that's another secret.

IR: There's one piece that really stands out. From this show, like a sore thumb. What piece am I going to talk about?

BS: From what series?

IR: It's called the "Vision of Cremo, 1967," in which you have a figure from Greek mythology—Pegasus. And it's not a red horse—it's a green horse this time, and there's a fisherman thing there. A green horse.

BS: Oh, that Pegasus thing. That actually is something that I found and I didn't think of Pegasus when I put it in. Remember, there used to be a gas station called Flying-A?

IR: Yeah.

BS: That was the symbol there. See at that particular time I was working [in] a stream of consciousness where there was no direction. That just like took over—I'm not going to say that I was possessed or anything like that. But things just fit in.

IR: It's like looking for the well with the witch's stick where you go all over the place until you find the well.

BS: Right, right, right—it's that kind of thing. So that piece kind of evolved that way. I'm still trying to figure out why I use things like that—those pieces in that one. Sometimes I know exactly what I'm doing, but a lot of times . . .

IR: I'll bet'ya I know . . .

BS: You do?

IR: I'll think about it more though—I think I can read the artist from reading the show. Not in a Freudian sense, but trying to use all the knowledge available. You do draw from many cultures, like there was a Chicano piece called "Fiesta of the Dead." Where did that come from?

BS: The idea comes from the basic piece. And that was like a wooden tray of early California. I based the thing on that. It has a horseman in it . . . that horseman could mean time passing or whatever—and then sometimes I

just have a feeling, like there's a dancing couple in it—
I guess that's to indicate music or whatever to make the
fiesta, Los Murdos or something like that, with the skulls
and skeletons . . .

IR: That's another recurrent element in your work—skeletons.

BS: Right, right. Which is death, because death is part of
life.

IR: I'm glad you told me . . .

BS: No—or it could be Halloween, or it could be anything. That's why I use that.

IR: I want to get back to why you use what
people popularly call "Third World" materials and subject. But "Lama, 1972," in which you used these ivory
pieces, these dicelike objects with ancient characters on
them—were they done at any particular time in connection with your new ideas, or—how did they come in there?
Do you work on a series of work and all of a sudden an
alien idea comes in and you go to that and then come
back? How does that work?

BS: Well, if it's all in your head, how can it be an alien
idea?

IR: I mean alien to the project you're working on.

BS: But the head is always working on projects. But I
know what you mean. That particular work is the work
that I really enjoy doing. That one, "Lama," "The essence of Egypt," and "Wizard" are three of a series where
I deal with the mystical philosophies or secret societies of
other groups.

IR: I saw one of the men with the white paint—white
body paint on them!

BS: Oh, that's in the mojo, "Ten Mojo Secrets"—that's
another secret. I'm talking about those little boxes—that
was a special series, secret societies, like the "Tibetan
Book of the Dead," like what that involves with lama
and those ivory squares are from a mojo—everything is
like common things, but when they're put together, they
get into a special thing. So that's a lama meditating with
his particular secret society.

IR: A critic saw your show, and he described it as explaining why black people are angry and bitter. What would you think of that assessment?

BS: Well, it's something that I have said that comes from those derogatory images, even though they aren't particularly used during our time, like today, because most of those things have been destroyed or put back. But it's like if it happened in your father's time or your grandfather's time, those hurts are still passed down to you, and it's just kind of one way of explaining why the anger is still within the black man—it's because of all that other stuff that happened before and those images are part of that. They're just comical graphic things—it's not the real thing except for the lynchings. Those are the photographs of the real thing.

IR: Your show has been very well received, critically. How did you think the criticism ran? Did you think the criticism was very bright or was it intelligent or . . . ?

BS: No, because it was just based on things I said. There was one review in *Art Week* where the woman really looked at the work. . . .

IR: What was the woman's name?

BS: Lynn Hershman. She reviewed the work and compared it with other artists who worked in the same technique.

IR: Like who?

BS: Joseph Cornell and . . .

IR: Arthur Dove.

BS: Yeah, and to me her review was more meaningful because she departed from my own statement about my work. You read four other reviews and there are certain things that are said in each one of them, which meant that either the man wasn't thinking or he was lazy when he was writing it.

IR: I was at a conference, and a gentleman said—I was proposing that some of these cultural organizations use their foundation money to open up gallery exchanges that would deal [in] Afro-American artists, that would promote them and guarantee gallery space all over the country—and the gentleman said that some of the Afro-American artists were doing things that the "community" couldn't relate to, and he thought that what they should really be doing are like charcoals. What do you think about that kind of statement?

BS: Well, he had limited vision because he evidently hasn't seen what's going on. True, there are some artists who do things that "the public" or "the community" couldn't accept, but there are just as many artists doing other things. "The community" hasn't seen—particularly "this community" hasn't seen—the kind of thing that I've done until I had it up there. So I didn't know whether they would accept it or reject it. You have to take a chance.

IR: We've gone through ten years or so—these have been years of people finding their racial identity in an era of black pride and many symbols like the clenched fist have arisen. I was reading where the national income of blacks in this country is up to forty billion dollars, so with all this enthusiasm for racial pride and all this I'm sure blacks are flocking to buy works of Afro-American painters. In your discussions with other painters do you find that this is what's happening?

BS: No. Now, with my particular pieces I try to keep the prices so that people who really like them will buy them. Of course, they're not always shown where people with money [can] come. But I know of several collectors who think it's more of an investment to buy white art. I understand a certain famous black athlete has a big million-dollar house and it's filled with non-black art. . . .

IR: What does he have in his house?

BS: I've never been there. All I know is some artists who say he hasn't bought black art. And they're black artists.

IR: I hope he's careful about what he buys. There's a re-attribution thing going on in the Metropolitan—they're finding fakes all over the place. Well, not really fakes, but [work] attributed to people like Goya, and they were done by Goya's brother or the dog—Goya's dog or the gardener.

BS: Right, right. Well, a lot of those people had apprentices who painted in their style.

IR: So this really, like Vietnam, collapsed, and now the

Watergate. When they talk about standards they don't really know what standards are. This scandal is kind of the equivalent to a tuberculosis outbreak—a political, economic, and cultural epidemic, you know. Sophy Burnham wrote a book called *Art Crowd,* showing the Watergates in the art world run by people who think they are superior to Nixon.

BS: Well, it's time for a new art scandal.

IR: But I mean, they say that Afro-Americans don't have standards. I'm talking about this reattribution thing— what does it say about Western standards?

BS: But all Western art is based on African art.

IR: Would you go into that—like all of it?

BS: It's based on, let's say, non-European art because it's either Asian or African or Egyptian. Like there was a book sold during the time of the Olympic Games. A great amount of study had been gone into where they compared contemporary European artists and where they got their technique. For instance, everyone knows Picasso was doing landscapes and portaits until he saw some African art. Of course, you see you really need an art historian to go into that. Because I'm not going to lie and make a comparison because I'm into doing it, not comparing it.

IR: When did you become interested in being an artist?

BS: I picked up a sketchbook that I made in 1942—funny little sketches. So I know I was doing it then. And then I have also drawings from when I was in kindergarten. So I was always into art and drawing and my mother was interested in art, and she always encouraged me to take special art classes and things like that. However, it wasn't until maybe '60, '62 when I decided that I was an artist. Before then I was like a designer or a craftsman or something else like that.

IR: So you've had a very successful show here in Berkeley Live Oak Park Gallery. So what's up ahead? Next?

BS: This exhibit goes in part to Humboldt State College and part to the Los Angeles County Museum of Art. And to other small shows and galleries and places where I've been invited to participate.

IR: You've also been lecturing. You went to Oberlin College? How was it there? How did you like it?

BS: Oh, that was nice. I like that because I'd do a slide presentation which allowed the students to see what I am doing. And I just talk about my work and what I think about when I do it. And how I do it. And I usually just relate to whatever questions they ask me—you know—whatever feedback I get. What materials I use or whatever they come from—that's what I extend from. The direction that my art is taking (as well as the graphic things that are in the gallery) is film making, because I'm interested in films about my art, an extension—like you see a piece, you look at a window and there's a picture of a sun or a face or a skeleton. So from that I would go to all things that relate to that kind of image. Other astrology signs or whatever. It would be like a kind of animated thing, but it's just like film is art.

Max Bond and Carl Anthony
on Afro-American Architecture

Max Bond is the principal of his own firm, Bond, Ryder Associates, and a member of the Architect's Rehabilitation Center for Harlem.

He has taught architecture in Ghana, and is currently professor of architecture at Columbia University.

His commissions include the new Martin Luther King, Jr., Center in Atlanta, Georgia, and a new building to replace the "outmoded" Schomburg Collection site.

On the evening of January 28, 1974, before a packed audience at the University of California at Berkeley, Mr. Bond delivered a lecture entitled "Architectural Mumbo-Jumbo" in which he discussed, among other things, a connection between my novel Mumbo Jumbo *and trends in contemporary Afro-American architecture.*

I invited Mr. Bond to my home, a cottage on Edith Street, to discuss further parallels between the art of writing and the art of architecture.

We were joined by Carl Anthony, assistant professor of architecture at the University of California, Berkeley, who teaches energy conservation and community design.

Mr. Anthony has traveled widely and is writing a book on the roots of Afro-American architecture. He is art commissioner of Berkeley.

Mr. Bond's Berkeley schedule was very heavy and so he soon had to leave. The discussion was continued by Mr. Anthony and me.

REED: Why don't we go into that point about buildings

having to express the culture of the people who use the buildings?

BOND: Okay. Well, I think that to do that the people have to have some say about the buildings—about the creation of the buildings—and so inevitably they will express it either through the shape and the form of the building or through the content of the building. For example, in housing, it's really unlikely that if black people were building housing for themselves they would have the same kinds of divisions of homes that we find in—say, housing provided for them; say, public housing, or any kind of subsidized housing. You know, I am not sure where this will go, but I think the evolution would take place if we could respond directly to the needs and habits of the people rather than responding to the rules that are set by banks or by the federal government.

REED: Do you mean carrying that as far as the people helping to design the buildings?

BOND: Yeah, in a sense; I think that if people could really express their needs and be made aware of all the implications of their needs I think they would. It's not so much their designing for or with the architect but that the thing becomes a mutual process whereby the architect is so in tune with the people that he can reflect those needs, accurately.

REED: Last night you were contrasting that approach over against—you mentioned two schools: the New York School of Beautiful Objects and "The Frozen Thing" —and you were saying this kind of approach was not related to the lives of the people and that—I almost got the idea of an American fortress idea, that buildings are arranged so that people can defend themselves. Fortress suburbia.

BOND: That's right. These are the two kinds of things that architects are doing. In New York for the very rich —for their vaction houses—they create these beautiful objects which have very little to do with the people, the way they use them, but have to do with a bunch of preconceptions; they're all living a lie. The architects are supporting them in living a lie; they take people who, in typical fashion, made some money by hustling, all kinds of things, while creating for themselves a serene environment, telling them they are gentlemen, they are great lovers of the arts, and all of this bit, in purely European fashion; yet these people's lives, whether they made their money through whiskey, or drugs, or the garment industry, or whatever, have nothing to do with that. That is absolute discordance. It's all about pretense! It's all about a young American cat who made some money portraying himself as a European gentleman. On the other hand, the defensible space thing—you know, they're saying that for housing in cities and so forth we have to worry about defensible space—spaces that you can control, that you can be secure in.

REED: And probably fire at people from?

BOND: Well, dig it, if it's necessary. But where you know the people around you so if any stranger comes in he is immediately spotted. The implications of that are just fantastic. One: it says that all strangers are hostile and obviously, the easiest way to recognize a stranger is if his color's different. So if you get into a little enclave and a man of another color comes in, he is immediately a stranger and an enemy and the whole thing is based on the idea that, in fact, we deal with each other, unless we know each other, as enemies. Instead of another kind of concept of city and of urban life which is the opportunity to welcome meeting strangers. It has to do not only with people, but ultimately, with ideas, because what it says is that you become closed to these ideas just as you are closed to strangers, so it, symbolically, represents this sort of division of the society into these various camps where you know the people whose ideas are the same as yours, your life-styles are the same, your habits are the same.

REED: Condominiums—?

BOND: Yes, in effect, all of this kind of thing and you emphasize your place as opposed to somebody else's place. And I think that's very political because, on the one hand, it represents in a kind of measure the anti-intellectualism of America, in the closed things, but also it is very political because it says we have a society that's full of problems . . . it sets people apart. Let's just deal with that instead of trying to change the society and make it an open society, a society which welcomes differences and variety.

REED: That relates to some points you made in your book, *Architecture and Slavery in the South*, Carl. From reading that I get the opinion that you feel it was meant that way in the beginning. I mean, separation of class. The plantation is a paradigm of that.

ANTHONY: Right, in fact, as Max was talking about the image of the successful gentleman, the European gentleman—that tradition goes all the way back to the first coming of slaves in 1619 and the plantations were built on the backs of slaves. The Europeans were really trying to imitate the fashions which were contemporary in Britain at that time. They were not that much interested in what the American continent was and, in fact, one of the reasons they had slaves to begin with was they needed somebody really to conquer the place and domesticate it. They didn't want to be bothered with it, so in the sense you look at an early plantation you can see this very schizophrenia about the American continent. They were really trying to extend Europe and part of that, instead of accepting the fact that this was a new world and therefore required a new kind of architecture and a new kind of coming to terms with the realities here.

REED: Some architects have imitated Native American forms, their cliff dwellings and—

ANTHONY: Yes, there are a few.

REED: There *are* a few.

ANTHONY: Max, I think your point about Frank Lloyd Wright that you made last night was quite interesting. He is one of the people who, in fact, was more aware of the new world. More aware of the Japanese traditions, more aware of the Mayan traditions; in fact, in a curious way, he became an outcast because he was never the establishment.

REED: They must have said, what kind of white man is he?

BOND: That's right. At the same time Wright was doing his stuff and trying to develop American architecture, the real power, the architects who represented power, were trying to do either the Italianate buildings or neo-Renaissance buildings or classical kinds of buildings—McKim, Mead, and White in New York, and their sort of descendants as opposed to Wright, who was in fact an outcast at the time.

REED: You mentioned related arts, like jazz, and you may have even mentioned dance and I was thinking—of course an architect works with space, and rhythm, and all the arts work with form. I was wondering what would be the architectural aesthetic equivalent to, say, be-bop or ragtime? Could there be like a ragtime building or—?

BOND: Well, I think there could be. I mean, it could be but the problem is that we haven't gotten enough into our architecture truly to know, but there are certainly architectural equivalents in America of classical music, because that's the establishment music. So that there have been architectural equivalents in America representing the same types of cultural orientation a particular kind of music represents, a particular kind of writing.

REED: They say John Milton was trying to build a cathedral when he wrote *Paradise Lost*.

BOND: There are these certain mind-sets when you approach things in a certain way and you find expressions of that in all the arts. I think that if you could build one it seems inevitable that you would get parallel expressions to bop and to ragtime and to all kinds of things. I have a sense that is hard to put into words directly, but I think that if you listen to some of Miles's things when he had the group with Red Garland on piano—their stuff is so urban it really conveys the sense of the urban environment, and *without the pretense,* and that's the fundamental difference between what the black art forms are doing and the establishment culture—they really deal with what the people are. For example, while the plantation master was listening to some sort of version of classical music the slaves were singing their work songs, about what they were doing. In the urban areas, the music reflected directly what the people were concerned with, what they were about. There is just this fantastic kind of difference!

ANTHONY: There is one point which I want to make about that. Since I haven't done much research and I doubt whether anybody else has. My guess is that if we went back and really looked at the environments of the people who played ragtime we would find the answer to your question and I think that probably there's a very strong kind of correlation between the world that they lived in and the music and a sense that's lost to us because we've been looking in slick magazines for images rather than understanding what our transition has been. So, in that sense, I have a kind of vague image in my mind, you know, of just listening to this guy with his upright piano and the kind of environment in which he can be playing. It begins to suggest that a whole range of images has been absolutely excluded from the architectural tradition—the Afro-American tradition.

REED: So this reconstituting of values is something that is happening in all the fields.

ANTHONY: Sure. It's the same as in your work. In the sense that just being out here on the West Coast and seeing what you do with the regional difference between the West Coast and the East Coast—we find the same thing happening in architecture except that now we have a new generation of black architects who will bring a new dimension to that exploration, so that, hopefully, we will begin really to appreciate the qualities that make a place real to people who inhabit it in the same way that I can pick up *Chattanooga* and I can, in a sense, see the places evoked just by reading poems.

REED: I want to go into this—problem—the government built these projects, the people call them "socialistic programs" for underprivileged people, and then they say, well, we built you these buildings and you piss in the hallways and throw the garbage out the windows—like in Harlem. What do you say to somebody like that? Now, here is Harlem, beautiful, you look at the early pictures of it in the twenties, a desirable place like that—what do you say to people like that—blacks are peasant people and Puerto Ricans just can't keep their stuff up?

ANTHONY: Yeah, there is a real interesting kind of confusion in the last fifteen to twenty years that entered into architecture because as the profession became aware of blacks there were a lot of people running around pretending to be experts on blacks. I remember one class I attended where there was a guy who said he was documenting black life-style and he had gone into the project buildings and he had seen black people pissing in the elevators, because that was black life-style.

BOND: I think there are two things in that. There is one sort of economic stability and there's also a pride in one's self and one's environment so that you have contrast to the way people treat public housing, which is made to regiment. It's very much like barracks with very little design in terms of the people, with very little chance for them to influence their environment and modify it to suit them. People react one way, but on the other hand if you go to black communities where the people have control over that, you find tremendous care.

REED: Like in parts of Brooklyn.

BOND: Yes. Or even here, or in Atlanta, wherever the black people have the sense that this is where they belong and it will not be taken away from them, where they are not subject to all sorts of rules. There is a great difference in the ways in which they approach it. In America, if you took the people's jobs away, the community would immediately start to deteriorate. There is a famous example of some town out on Long Island that was making jet planes, fighters, and they were going to phase that plane out, and the town got up in arms, and the government finally had to give them a new airplane to make. Because all the people in the town said this would destroy the town. And that was really the truth, but—so when you're talking about white people everybody's aware of that but when you're talking about us, they say: Well, shit, they should be able to keep up the neighborhood even when they don't have any jobs. No . . . no one else has been able to do that. No one has been able to maintain an environment and improve it without money. Without means, without some sense of worth that comes from having a job, having money, being a productive element of the society.

ANTHONY: There is another interesting contrast to be made in the sense that buildings are really an outward expression of people and they're the thing that mediates between us and the natural environment. And so is clothing. And one of the things you find is the black people's really rich sense of personal adornment, which will obviously carry over into a larger realm if people really had an opportunity to express that. What I certainly look forward to in the next twenty years in this country and also around the world is a kind of renaissance of the kind of expressiveness that Max showed in his slides last night that we find in traditional African architecture. That stuff is really incredible. I think that Max's point is well taken. The issue was not to imitate the traditional African form but the issue is to understand the truth in it, which is that people who have control of their environment will make a counterform that really expresses what they're trying to do.

REED: On looking at different buildings and photos it seems to me that American architects are eclectic anyway, they have a tradition of eclecticism. You would even use European techniques if they proved useful?

ANTHONY: Sure. Yes. Absolutely. In fact—there's a passage I'm sorry that you didn't mention in *Mumbo Jumbo* which really ties that whole thing together; I don't really have the citation but there's a part in which you talk about taking some of this and some of this—[Abdul's speech, pp. 37–38, hardcover *Mumbo Jumbo*—I.R.].

REED: Yes, yes, the collage really flowered in this country. I see a theme running through your remarks, Mr. Bond, that if you change the economic system, there will be a flowering of architecture.

BOND: Yes.

REED: A more socialistic—?

BOND: Yes. An economic system more adapted to the means of the people. I think the other thing is to deal with the fact that there is a cultural war going on in this country and that the availability of more power, more control, more means for us, the oppressed people in this country, is another key to the flowering of a whole new thing. In fact, America's culture is our culture.

REED: [At this point, Bond prepared to leave, saying that a socialist society would lead to the flowering of architecture.] In spite of what Bond just said, some of the pictures I've seen of architecture in socialist countries seem pretty standardized, bland, and gray. I want to ask you, do you think a person like Frank Lloyd Wright, who is probably considered an eccentric as you described him, would be tolerated in a socialist regime?

ANTHONY: I think that he probably wouldn't find any clients. I don't think that he would necessarily be subject to any kind of personal problems but I think that it would be rather hard for him to find clients. I just want to make one comment about that. I found that—in fact, I've had some correspondence with a man named Roberto Segre, head of the history department of the Architecture School in Cuba and he indicated to me in the correspondence that they are taking a second look at Frank Lloyd Wright because they think there is a place for his kind of thinking in Cuban architecture.

REED: So there's a possibility of variety . . .

ANTHONY: Well, I think that essentially the history of socialist countries up until now has really been competitive with capitalists, so therefore the standard has really been established by capitalist countries and we don't know what that'll be.

REED: Yes, I see. The leaders in the socialist countries always seem to be able to find a nice villa or a beautiful vacation spot.

ANTHONY: Sure. That's right. True. Indicates the spirit is not dead.

REED: Right, and I understand that some people who talk socialist talk in this country, when they go to Cuba they stay at the rich resorts the Rockefellers left behind.

ANTHONY: I do want to say, however, there is a very deep kind of spiritual problem involved in most ideologies of socialist architecture. It really does, in fact, kind of follow a compulsive model which is based on the idea of trying to make everybody the same and that really does come through in the architecture; I would think that if a new spirit emerges, that perhaps in China you would begin to find the beginnings of it, because the people are really involved in a kind of self-reliance and the regional architecture building out of that is much stronger than in most socialist countries.

REED: I see. I want to ask you a question about the new homesteading. Where people are going back into the cities and are refurbishing abandoned tenements and houses. Would you encourage an Afro-American with capital to participate in this?

ANTHONY: I think that would be a good idea. Not only in the cities—to acquire a stake in the land is an important step in shaping the environment in a way that really meets your own needs as opposed to having to be subject to whatever the landlord wants. So I would encourage that.

REED: Do you think that Afro-Americans take advantage of all the housing aid, loans, and openings that are available to them?

ANTHONY: No, they don't.

REED: Why is that—lack of information?

ANTHONY: Lack of information, also there are some programs that are tailored for Afro-Americans and for poor people in general. These programs are essentially designed to fail, so that in a sense one would be better off in the open market than with those programs that are designed to destroy people's morale and keep them hung up for years trying to get a small amount of money to do minor kinds of work in the houses.

REED: Before I turn to your paper, I want to ask you this. We were talking about the possibility of having a style comparable to ragtime. Ragtime apparently was a collection of folk forms that were stylized by the composers, and I was looking at—well, this is really a two-part question. Also the idea of Western architecture. Can we say there is such a thing as Western architecture when, for example, a style like Art Deco, epitomized by the Chrysler Building on Lexington Avenue in New York, borrows from jazz, Asian, Aztec, Egyptian art? In fact, it was referred to as "Jazz-Modern."

ANTHONY: Well, I think that you've really touched on a

problem. I mean, there's a mythology of Western architecture and the pretenders to that authority would like people to believe that only one thing has been going on for thousands of years. But, in fact, there have been hundreds of regional architectures that have been ignored by the tradition which reports on a sort of one line of development. If you begin to analyze it—I think Max made the point in his lecture. When you begin to analyze in detail the different parts of that so-called Western tradition, you find not only Art-Deco borrowing from the Aztecs and the Egyptians but you find Le Corbusier borrowing from the Africans, you find Frank Lloyd Wright borrowing from the Mayans and the Japanese, so that, in fact, the so-called Western architecture is simply a response of a certain group of people to other groups of people and it's very effective.

REED: And then you can see Islamic forms in European architecture.

ANTHONY: Oh, obviously.

REED: I want to turn to your paper. You talked about the differences between the two styles of architecture with which colonial America started off—the plantation architecture and the frontier architecture. This is a very interesting comment here—you said, "The planting class discovered that it was cheaper to move on to new territory than it was to practice conservation of the land." So bad ecology goes back to an early date in this country.

ANTHONY: It's one of the interesting things about studying the history of this country. You find that in many ways it was the South which was responsible for the irrational and wasteful land practices. The reason it was possible for those southern planters to be so wasteful was they had an army of slave laborers so that they could actually exploit the land in a way for which they were blameless. In fact, the first energy crisis came with the abolition of the slave trade. Because then people really had to figure out what to do in order to maintain their standard of living when they didn't have the source of energy that up to that particular time was free. And then, of course, some of these other new developments came with the Industrial Revolution which meant that they no longer had to rely on human labor in that particular way. So now we are facing the same spiritual syndrome, but it's based on another kind of irresponsible exploitation of resources.

REED: There is an interesting historical point connected with what you are saying—in your book called *Architecture and Slavery in the South*—that is, by practicing bad conservation, they always had to keep expanding.

ANTHONY: That's right.

REED: Okay—where Negroes, mulattoes, and Native Americans were judged as real estate themselves.

ANTHONY: That's right.

REED: Also this kind of planting in the South led to a social distance between the master and the slave so that a Virginia estate was almost like a little nation.

ANTHONY: Right. Actually, what happened in the South is that when they first came the planters had an image of how they were going to develop settlements based on European experience that went back for a long period of time. However, they soon found in the South that because of the presence of enslaved Africans they really needed to invent a new form of settlement pattern. In fact, the plantation grew out of this and the plantation was a unit of government as well as a town in its own right, and so that you find that all the things that were required to support the economy of the plantation were really supplied by the slaves. Kind of a self-sufficient economy

REED: Uh huh. There was also another point you made—where slobs come in all classes and all races. I was reminded, when you said that some slaves had high-post bedsteads, mosquito netting, chinaware, mirrors, trunks, and chests. And there were some slave-carpenters, who made some marvelous furniture—I was reminded that when I worked on a poll in Manhattan and I had a chance to go, it seemed to me, to every home in Harlem, I found this variety where you go into a slum and you go into somebody's home—especially the older people— where everything was very neat and they had fine cloth and chinaware and you go to somebody else's house and it reminded you of the women's dorm in some middle-class college where people don't clean up after themselves. I guess you just find all these types.

ANTHONY: Depends on the individual.

REED: And the individual can really find that under some of the most adverse circumstances he can make a pleasant environment, like some people have certain negative opinions of hippies, but some of the hippies have moved to the slums and have built some swell apartments. [Black artists are doing this in Oakland. I.R.]

ANTHONY: That's true. In fact, one of the interesting things about New Orleans I noted when I was there, I had the occasion to be visiting the older section of the city and there are many hippies and bohemian types who consider it very arty to live in what used to be slave quarters. They are fixed up quite nicely and, of course, one of the things that makes a difference is that in the slavery period you had maybe fifteen or twenty times the number of people living in the slave quarters.

REED: The congestion was there even then. You say that you have traced some African survivals in architecture—and this has probably been the scoop of your paper—that they have been overlooked by European-American scholars when investigating the origins of American architecture, because they're not architects, they're sociologists.

ANTHONY: Well, it's partly because they're not architects. It's also because most architectural critics have operated under the assumption there is no architecture in Africa.

REED: I see.

ANTHONY: They were not capable of recognizing its appearance in the New World because they did not appreciate the fact that it existed in Africa.

REED: And you make a point that a recent study has shown that the wrought-iron work in New Orleans was done largely by blacks, who dominated the building trades in that city.

ANTHONY: Incidentally, that study was done by a black, I guess he's considered the poet laureate of New Orleans —a man named Marcus Christian.

REED: Marcus Christian. You give some examples—for instance, you talk about a house built by Metoyer, who was a freeman of color in the early nineteenth century, and it was known as Africa House. You say the roof structure with the deep pitch and steep overhang recalls houses of Bamileke in the Cameroons.

ANTHONY: One of the interesting things about my visit to the South was that I actually had been prepared to do a study of the repressive institution of slavery and I didn't expect to find anything that reminded me of the research I had done in Africa. I had spent a year traveling around West Africa making drawings and documenting traditional villages. When I came here to do research in the South, I really had accepted that most of the material survivals had been destroyed with the exception of a few portable items, and when I began visiting plantations I noticed that behind the big houses there would be small buildings that seemed to be reminiscent of the size and scale proportion of the buildings that I remembered from my research in Africa. Finally, when I got to Williamsburg, I was almost crying because I looked here and there and saw really large numbers of outbuildings that unmistakably were of African derivation and the thing that was the most frustrating about it was there was nobody to tell, so I went to talk to the curator of Williamsburg. Williamsburg, Virginia, as you know, is a historical development, it's been made into a museum with seventy-five million dollars of Rockefeller money, and I asked him if he had any idea what was going on, because half the population of eighteenth-century Williamsburg was black. They were all either artisans or domestics, and his official literature said they didn't leave any kinds of material survivals, and I asked him if he knew anything about the outbuildings, who designed them, and he said there were no records of who designed or built them. I asked him if his research in England had seen anything like that, and he said, no, he hadn't seen anything like that. Then he proceeded to tell me the black people couldn't possibly have done it because they had been so "broken" by that time. So I think that a thorough study of the South from this point of view has still not been taken and I think it would yield a lot more. On my own trip I was only able to make visits of less than one month so that I was unable to go to very many places.

REED: How do you tell influence in architecture—I can understand how you can tell influences in writing or music or painting—do you look at the roof or the—?

ANTHONY: Well, if you understand something about the typical layout of the African compound you begin to recognize certain recurrent patterns. One thing, the life of the people, essentially the social life, takes place outdoors as opposed to indoors, so the structures themselves do not have to be as large as the houses of more northern climates. Then you begin to notice the roof pattern, the way the openings are oriented, and so forth. A lot of details reveal that kind of carry-over. Of course, you have to study it—I think there's a parallel that occurred in some of the earlier anthropological studies of African forms in music and language where there were lots of people running around saying there are no survivals of African grammatic structure.

REED: The only people who're able to maintain a culture are Europeans. Is that the assumption?

ANTHONY: Right.

REED: That's because they're smarter than anybody else.

ANTHONY: But then they found out that the people who were making these pronouncements didn't know anything about it. So they weren't qualified, and it's the same thing in architecture.

REED: Same thing in literature. They say there was no real Afro-American literature until the nineteen-forties. Well, that's interesting. May I ask you, I was reading a book here called *Shelter*** and it seems to be giving the message that we should bring back handmade houses using minimal technology, and "Shelter" architects have been influenced by structures from all over the world. Like houses built of driftwood; house-trucks; house-boats; houses made of thatch; treehouses, towers, domes, barns, teepees, and igloos. The teepee looked like it could serve every need of a shelter.

* Published by Shelter Publications, P.O. Box 279, Bolinas, California 94924.

ANTHONY: It's an amazing device.

REED: And it was built for sixty-five dollars. Some of these houses can be built in a day for one thousand dollars. This has profound implications for people who don't have much money in this country—have we come to the point now where you can get an acre of land and build some kind of a cheap house?

ANTHONY: Well—

REED: Or is that just sort of a pie-in-the-sky—

ANTHONY: I think it hasn't really come to that point yet. I think that most of the people building these various constructions are essentially middle-class white kids, and there is no place for them, so they are willing to take a risk which, say, your average welfare mother is not in a position to take. The movement is really very healthy because these people realize that this reliance on the establishment and on government to provide decent shelter is in many ways really a mistake because people who sometimes go out and do it themselves many times do far better than the government can do. It is also very valuable in that it shows the number of hidden traditions that exist in this country, so the thousands of solutions of particular environmental problems that have been worked out over the centuries have been ignored largely by the experts who are essentially hooked in with banks and real estate agents whose interest is not in the solution of environmental problems but in just making money. In coming back to the question, one of the reasons that their houses are so inexpensive is that they don't go through this whole financing number. Most of the cost of the house, two thirds of the cost of the house, is the cost of obtaining the money, so I don't think it has come to the point where everybody can just go out and get an acre of land. But I do think it's come to the point where most of the sort of conventional wisdom has completely fallen apart. We all will have to take a fresh look at what our resources are and what can be done with those resources we have. I'm very enthusiastic about that stuff. I mean most of it, those domes and teepees are indigenous solutions and are architecturally far more satisfactory and exciting than most of the stuff produced by the architectural establishment.

REED: I was reading an article where people were having a political conference—blacks—and the same week I saw an ad in the New York *Times* where they could have had maybe eight hundred acres in North Carolina for the amount of money that went into their conference. [One hundred dollars per acre—I.R.]

ANTHONY: Right. In fact, when I was working in Harlem we had a contract—it was for a high school in Harlem—and the contract was for one hundred fifty thousand dollars to do a feasibility study for this high school, which the community was given because the city had no intention of building a high school, and if that money had gone to purchasing the land we could have had a plot of ground in Connecticut the size of Harlem, with a seminary on it. We did the research and we found the place, but people weren't thinking in those terms then, so essentially a great opportunity was lost.

REED: In my reading I found that it may be that blacks are kept in one political viewpoint, or politics, lopsided, you know, because mainstream America is really afraid of their competition. And that they really don't want a free enterprise system because—and this may sound crazy, but I've been able to trace this to 1849 California, where blacks are considered to be just too damn lucky. Put them on a bar and they strike all the gold. So they encourage the blacks they can "rehabilitate" or do missionary experiments on, and obstruct the independent ones. Thomas Dixon, who wrote *The Klansman*, feared Booker T. Washington because Washington was talking about economic independence.

ANTHONY: Sure. One of the things that is really ironic about the whole slavery period (and this really came as a surprise and shock to me) is that many of the economic political forms which were built into slavery were very much like socialism. That is to say, if a worker had his arm cut off, that is, a white worker, people would say to hell with you, you lost your arm, that's your problem. But the master of a slave wanted to insure his investment—if a slave lost his arm the master would be out a certain amount of money, so as a consequence he'd put into the plantation hospitals and all these various other things to maintain the health of the slaves; and of course the brutality and all that was another feature, but what is really interesting to see is that kind of paternalism.

REED: Of course, you have to realize that some people enjoy slavery. People today, many of our contemporaries, enjoy slavery. I want to ask you one more question—because this is the kind of question we all get when we go out to the campus and I'll ask you as an architect: Do you think your ideas about the future of architecture in this country are relevant to the Afro-American struggle?

ANTHONY: Yes, I do, because first of all, I am an Afro-American architect. It's my struggle. I think that there are a number of dimensions of the struggle which have not been explored, and are very little understood. And one is the physical environment, really very little is known among Afro-Americans about the built environment. We generally take it for granted the same way we take the trees, mountains, and sky for granted. It's something that's here that was built by somebody else for some other set of reasons. We have not really moved to the point in the twentieth century where we have begun to manipulate the environment in any significant way to reflect our own aspirations, so that I take it upon myself to become a part of that struggle to really come to terms with the physical environment and begin to shape it so that it gives us back positive images of ourselves and our aspirations.

Yardbird II
1973

Doyle Foreman, Sculptor

Introduction

*I met Doyle Foreman when I came to Berkeley in 1967
from Los Angeles. He lived with his family: Selma, a court
reporter, and his son, Doyle, Jr. They dwelt in a solid
house, on Fairview Street near the Oakland-Berkeley border, endowed with beautiful woodwork, vaulted ceilings, a
fireplace, and a backyard. Doyle was working on his
bronze pieces then, and I found his work strange and
charming. For pets he had a raven and a iguana, and in
his Toyota truck, hanging above the dashboard, were gris-
gris made of bird feathers, bones, and leather. He was the
real first Western documentary I'd seen and when he described the land he sounded poetic.*

*I still hadn't shaken off New York City when I arrived
in Berkeley from Los Angeles. Bob Gover, the author of*
One Hundred Dollar Misunderstanding, *invited us to his
Malibu home on weekends. I was so uptight that the first
day on Malibu I walked out onto the beach without dis-
carding my black boots, which had seen a couple of New
York winters, and my gray double-breasted sports jacket.*

*His neighbors would startle me by walking through his
living room to the kitchen, removing things they needed
from his ice box, and then returning to their apartments.
Wha'? I thought. In New York if you didn't have nine
police locks you were out of business. Things in the West
were slower than New York, where everybody seemed engaged in a high-wire act to keep from falling into the
Bowery. A Californian told me that everyone he met*

from New York acted like a cop; New Yorkers say, If you can survive in New York you can survive anywhere.

So Berkeley was strange to me, a New Yorker. I couldn't get used to everyone smiling at me; every day was like the most wonderful spring day and you could see mountains and water. With the influx of Easterners it's beginning to change, but you used to be able to step off the curb and be assured that all of the cars would stop. You do that now and you're taking your life into your hands. New Yorkers can only see a third of the sun, which is why all of the headache commercials come from there, the aspirin and drug commercials, too.

Doyle had come to Berkeley from Oklahoma and seldom talked about his background, but when he did would point to a life that I, a strident, nervous, talky, fast Easterner, couldn't fathom; but when I did I could see that there were other examples we've yet to explore and by denying such a model we are robbing ourselves of our diversity and amputating our total experience.

Teacher, sculptor, horticulturist, Survivor Doyle Foreman's thoughts are in From Woodcarving to Bronze.

They say out here, "You have to get up pretty early in the morning to get ahead of Doyle Foreman," and you'll see why.

ISHMAEL: I want you to really go through this thing about walking through the sand dunes that were mountains.

DOYLE: Well, we were just driving through, and then later on I was describing the desert as an environment and I was saying that the desert is not as desolate a place as it seems to be.

ISHMAEL: You were describing the sensation of walking on the sand dunes.

DOYLE: Oh, you mean the canyon? Well, I was saying the sand dunes are like hills.

ISHMAEL: And then the sand disappears?

DOYLE: Yeah, and then there's actually agriculture.

ISHMAEL: I was saying that the desert is always seen as being barren and arid.

DOYLE: Yeah, and I was saying that the equivalent of life

is very high in comparison with places that appear to be more lush because the life there supports the kind of animal that lives off a sparse diet. That's why most cactus have thorns. It's survival of the plant, you know, or the survival of life, like it's the kangaroo rat that manufactures its own fluid and doesn't drink water.

ISHMAEL: You were also talking about visions that people have in the desert.

DOYLE: Yeah, well that's a question that needs deep research.

ISHMAEL: Once you told me about a cavalry you saw.

DOYLE: That happened one morning in New Mexico. It was near Deming, between Las Cruces and Deming, New Mexico. I was traveling through there one winter and I had a generator go out on my car and I thought I was completely isolated, but then I saw this service station. But when I got to the station, it didn't have any gas. It was just all these pumps and all these rooms. I went inside and met this woman and she told me she didn't have any gas and that it would probably be the morning before I could get my car repaired. They offered to take me back into Deming.

ISHMAEL: That's when you saw the vision?

DOYLE: Well, as I sat there I realized that I was going to have to spend the night on the road. This woman had given me some coffee and she was talking about the history of her family, that they had come from Tennessee to the desert and the first place they had moved to was White Sands, and the Atomic Energy Commission had taken all that area so they were uprooted and moved to this particular site. At that particular time the state freeway was going to run right through the place they had, so somehow their fate was always in the way of this thing, which in this case was the state highway.

In the process of having this conversation, she said you could see a mirage every morning from this particular site and that somehow had something to do with why they had stopped there and chosen this place. Well, in the process, I spent the night in my car and the next morning she showed me this mirage of cavalry. I don't know what it was.

ISHMAEL: You both witnessed it? Describe it.

DOYLE: It just appeared as a group of mounted people riding down this kind of draw, off this kind of mesa down into the lower part of the valley. It was a long distance away, you know—not like a hundred yards away.

ISHMAEL: How did you know it wasn't a real cavalry?

DOYLE: Because there's no real cavalry there—real cavalry don't even exist any more.

ISHMAEL: Did they have period uniforms on?

DOYLE: It appeared to be a uniformed group. Now, this was at a distance, you know.

ISHMAEL: Have you ever heard of a cavalry being wiped out around there?

DOYLE: I don't know New Mexico history.

ISHMAEL: What town was it near?

DOYLE: Between Deming and Las Cruces.

ISHMAEL: And people have seen this cavalry riding out?

DOYLE: Well, this woman has seen it.

ISHMAEL And you saw it with her?

DOYLE: Yes. She said it happens only at a certain time of the morning, so I would hypothesize that the light would have to be just right every morning at a certain time.

ISHMAEL: I was thinking, we were talking about the barren places which have been mistakenly thought of as not having life. Would you say that the ghetto was like a metaphor for an extension of that? A barren place that's not supposed to have life but has life anyway?

DOYLE: A ghetto? No. I would say a ghetto is a true desert. You see, a ghetto is a place that can't support itself—it's fed from outside. It's like an island that doesn't support life—like an island, once under water, that doesn't support any life—like, dig, you see what I mean?

ISHMAEL: You grew up around the desert? You're attracted to it?

DOYLE: Yes, Arizona.

ISHMAEL: Why were you attracted to nature?

DOYLE: Well, my grandmother taught me about the woods. I lived with my grandmother one winter.

ISHMAEL: How old was your grandmother?

DOYLE: I'm not certain—she was in her sixties.

ISHMAEL: Was she one of the first people coming to the West?

DOYLE: She was part of the Choctaw Removal of 1821 or whatever it was called. You know, the Wounded Knee Treaty, when they told the Choctaw that they had to move west of the Mississippi River and into Western territory. I don't recall what all that history is about, but I think it was a General Cook that started the first mission about 1830. I'm not certain.

ISHMAEL: Was your grandmother the first of your ancestors to come out here?

DOYLE: My grandmother came to Oklahoma from Mississippi because she was part of the Removal. The Government told them they had to move.

ISHMAEL: Your grandmother was Choctaw Indian?

DOYLE: She was part Indian.

ISHMAEL: And your grandfather? What did he do?

DOYLE: Grandfather Black came from Texas. He and his brothers were farmers. They set up this community. I haven't inquired all about it. It was homestead land in southeast Oklahoma, which was Indian Territory at the time.

ISHMAEL: You known there's a joke in American black folklore that black people try to claim being kin to Indian because they're ashamed of being Negro, African, you know. I know that I have Indian background (Cherokee) and you have Indian background. Many blacks have Indian background. There was a great deal of intermarriage among Indians and black people. There are instances of blacks leading Indian tribes into war against cavalry and also blacks on the other side, too, fighting against the Indians.

DOYLE: Sure, that's what the whole 9th Cavalry was about, right?

ISHMAEL: This is a day of black consciousness, right?

DOYLE: Yeah, sure.

ISHMAEL: Do you think that consciousness is hereditary? Like genetic, maybe?

DOYLE: Genetic? Consciousness? I don't know. I've never explored it that way. I think the awareness of ancestors means a lot. It changes how far you push out and how far you set your future. Somehow you look to ancestors to be a model for something.

ISHMAEL: Well, that's a traditional black thing—African thing. What I mean is like there are certain tribes or cultures which practice reverence for ancestors. You look at a generation like this which has such contempt for the past and you can see where there's a lot of trouble, that must be the consequences of erasing your past memories. What do you think are the consequences of that?

DOYLE: What are the consequences of erasing memories?

ISHMAEL: You know, like knocking down a totem.

DOYLE: Well, I think everyone should have a sense of history. If you don't have a sense of history, you don't have much of a future. That's what I was implying, because somehow it doesn't give you any kind of motivation. I think the upsurge of black pride was to try to give some basis for even being proud. Okay, if you are separate and demoralized, what do you do? That's basically what created the potential of slavery. They knew once they had cut you off . . .

ISHMAEL: Slavery is not having an awareness of the past?

DOYLE: Yeah, sure, right. As a kind of model for future generations. Okay, so what happened was slaves immediately cut off from their background, cut off from language, and cut off from traditions, right . . . ?

ISHMAEL: But they created new things.

DOYLE: Yeah, but they were cut off from traditions, okay? They no longer had the same kind of framework for what they could do, primarily because that was one of the ways of making a person a slave. You definitely have to do that. You know what happened in Surinam: immediately they went into the bush. The same thing happened in Mexico, in the rebellion of Vera Cruz. It was pretty much like home. That's why you have places like Mandingo. You'd have to visit there to see it. There is part of that thing there. But where in Surinam the junta rebel at an early stage, meaning having organized groups, they immediately went into the bush, the bush being very similar to the Cameroons. They adapted very well. They also have their art forms—they maintained their visual arts. And that's another thing—the significance of visual arts—keeping the heritage of visual arts.

ISHMAEL: Visual arts were always destroyed by the colonialists. Why?

DOYLE: Because it represented the past, history, communication—like talking drums of the Congo can be heard for fifteen miles. Okay, now that's a form of communication, like Morse code, right? The Indians had smoke signals, right? Okay, that's communication in a picture form, or musical form.

ISHMAEL: So how does all of this come up to your art, like your sculpture? Now, first of all, I want to ask you, why do you use bronze? Why don't you use wood? Why do you call yourself a neo-African sculptor? What does that mean? Some kind of gimmick?

DOYLE: No, that would be like reaching back to early forms in Africa, using them as a basis, like a Caucasian would reach to the Greeks, right? You idealize your history. Like, if you have Grecian or Roman inheritance, you look to that, right?

ISHMAEL: Why not have a black African thing, a Greek thing, a Chinese thing, ragas—why not mix them all up?

DOYLE: I do that.

ISHMAEL: Why neo-African? Is that after Jahnheinz Jahn?

DOYLE: It's not the same thing.

ISHMAEL: That's what he means when he says neo-African.

DOYLE: Sure, okay, number one—I have a kind of feeling, right? Even when I was carving wood, I had a kind of natural feeling about it.

ISHMAEL: Woods or bronze.

DOYLE: Right. I started out as a wood-carver.

ISHMAEL: What was the significance of using wood? Because it was available?

DOYLE: It was available and it didn't cost anything, right?

ISHMAEL: If you had the money, what would you use?

DOYLE: At that stage, I wasn't aware of art supplies.

ISHMAEL: Suppose the New York State Council of the Arts or the California State Council of the Arts gave you some money. Would you be doing this engineering stuff, this electronic stuff, the white artists are doing?

DOYLE: I was getting to the premises on which I base my stuff and you asked me a question about why it would be referred to as neo-African. I would say that just by the feel of the approach, it's like how you first start visually accepting form that you're going to deal with. Now, my whole thing is like an animate kind of approach to things, right? And that leads back to like my grandmother teaching me about the woods, my experience in the Sonora desert, and also in Baja, which came later on. But all these things brought together along with the wood experience make it a very straight kind of communication with early African art, meaning like from the Ife bronze to the tribal bronzes that are done today in metal or brass, like the Fon people of Dahomey, or the gold weights of the Ashanti from Ghana. The Benin art also depicts aspects of West African life—the imagery is brilliant. They talk about it like a landscape artist would talk about, you know, his thing. Like Turner and all those English landscape painters. Okay, what they did was what they knew best. Like New England—this is the kind of thing that people push to a point of interest. You say it's history, okay?

ISHMAEL: Western culture, right?

DOYLE: Well, in American art, you're getting kind of a superficial art form. You're getting a transplant—European art, Anglo-Saxon art coming together. But in early American art, you're getting sort of primitive—people who never went to academies. So then they began to paint like Europeans. It was very difficult for America to be anything other than European.

ISHMAEL: There have always been alternative cultures. The Indian culture was here.

DOYLE: Yeah, but they totally ignored the Indian culture. Heathen art, man, has always been one of colonial powers' first scenes. Like, you know, no one respected heathen art—they collected it as curious stuff. They brought it back and buried it in their cellars.

ISHMAEL: But the mainstream of American culture has always been Western European.

DOYLE: Yeah, so when they began to accept it, they say it's primitive or something else; they have categories they want to put it in.

ISHMAEL: They call your stuff primitive even though it came from a great civilization?

DOYLE: They would say, "Oh African art, primitive art." Now, that was carefully laid down—that's no coincidence. It's because they never expected that they would have to bring African art (which was the name they gave it) and African expression out of the curiosity collection and take it seriously.

ISHMAEL: I look back at black painters in the last century and they're very European. They seemed to be doing the same things the whites were doing—landscape scenes and paintings of, like, scenes from Greek mythology.

DOYLE: Yes, sure, well, that was the big thing, but people like Jacob Lawrence . . .

ISHMAEL: I mean earlier.

DOYLE: Early Jacob Lawrence? Well, there was an upsurge in the thirties of kind of a self-pride thing.

ISHMAEL: I don't mean Lawrence and that generation. I mean the nineteenth Afro-American century.

DOYLE: If they were painting, they were painting like the Europeans. There was supposedly some early painter, a black painter in California. Someone at the Oakland Museum was telling me about that.

ISHMAEL: You're talking about earlier than when?

DOYLE: Well, 1900. Now, you know, California, up until about 1830, was very heavily populated with blacks.

ISHMAEL: There are people doing bronze casting in this country? How many people are doing bronze casting within an African context?

DOYLE: I don't know of any others.

ISHMAEL: Why bronze? Because of the Benins?

DOYLE: No, I was into bronze before I was totally aware of what the Benins really were.

ISHMAEL: Describe that process.

DOYLE: Well, it's the lost wax process.

ISHMAEL: And what is that?

DOYLE: That means that the wax is lost in the process of completing a piece, meaning the wax is burnt out.

ISHMAEL: You mean we got a sophisticated process like that from a bunch of savages jumping up and down?

DOYLE: You can see the Benin art form and you know it's not primitive in any sense. It's a highly sophisticated art form.

ISHMAEL: What do you say to a critic like John Canaday, whom they call the hanging judge critic of the New York *Times,* who makes some of what I would call the meanest racist statements about black painters, and he and this critic Grace Glueck, who is kind of like protecting the white man's civilization—I have to get to that. She attacks woman painters as well as blacks. Is that sexual and political? Is that fanatical? I mean, can't they see, I mean, surely these people know better, being art critics on a newspaper?

DOYLE: Well, if you would say he doesn't know what he's doing, I think you would be making a mistake. He's not there because he was accidentally thrown up there—he's there because he wants to be there. And he stays there with his wit.

ISHMAEL: So it really doesn't have anything to do with art at all? It's just like they're doing a job for the establishment—it's the same role as a general, or a priest.

DOYLE: Well, this is the thing. I haven't been able to really understand the whole concept of a critic in the first place. It seems to me like a retailer or someone you have to pay something to because he's in the middle. A critic seems to be only in the West, right? Do you think other people have art critics?

ISHMAEL: I notice there are some black artists who really believe that they're inferior.

DOYLE: Well, this would show is their personal work. I mean the work is going to reflect you. I don't care how zero you lay it down and how you try to deceive your viewers about yourself. What you need to do is be as scientific as possible. I would say you would be more into science than into art and therefore you would only show some kind of shape out there that would have no emotion whatsoever.

ISHMAEL: Why, when the critics go to a black painting show, do they always feature the social realists? I don't mean that in a pejorative sense. There are good examples of social realism. I consider myself a social realist in an aspect, but I mean social realism as . . .

DOYLE: You mean a style that was developed at a certain period and then passed off on people.

ISHMAEL: Social realism has been defined as any art which arouses indignation or concern for someone's plight, that provokes controversy or discussion about social evil.

DOYLE: But it also says something about how you can get that expression out. What do you call Russian art, man?

ISHMAEL: Social realism.

DOYLE: Okay, now what does that art do? That art . . .

ISHMAEL: It's pamphleteering art.

DOYLE: Right, it's propaganda art. Okay, then I would say that if you make it graphic in that sense where it's got to depict something or tell something in an everyday visual kind of way of human figures over the years getting shot, of human suffering, of people in the streets, okay, that's one way of saying it. It's sad. It doesn't hold the same kind of impact as if you really got into your art and came up with an inventive way of expressing yourself. You know what I mean? I mean, you can hit people on many different levels, right? Okay, now my things wouldn't be abstract in the sense that they would be geometric figures, right? No. Like what they do in an organic sense tells you what they are. I mean, like this is an animal and this animal happens to be a fish, pig, or something. It's going to say whatever that animal is and you can see it. If you can have any kind of . . .

ISHMAEL: You're working within a system like African mythology . . .

DOYLE: Sure, it's within a concept of that kind of animism. It's my adaptation, my bringing together my ideas in that sense. Meaning like early experiences made me familiar with these things I'm talking about, but it also gives me a premise in order to depict it.

ISHMAEL: But you said that before you even came into contact with African art, you were using these techniques unconsciously.

DOYLE: Well, in the first place, like I said, I started out carving, right?

ISHMAEL: The cheapest material?

DOYLE: Right, free. I started carving palmwood in grammar school. Palmwood that came from trees that were in the park. And it was soft material. Actually, I carved soap earlier. That was an urge to make something three-dimensional out of a fixed material. A method of taking away in order to get what the images are going to be. A carving is a whole visual experience in itself, because what you do is to form an impression of the image in your mind and then you work for that. It's not like modeling, building up or pushing something into shape as wax would be, or clay would be. So it's a whole process that you develop into a way of thinking. I mean a wood-carver is definitely going to be different from a painter. He's going to think in three dimensions. Where a painter is thinking about a three-dimensional thing, but it's always illusion. Like the sculptor has got to do the real thing—he's got to do a physical three-dimensional thing, right?

ISHMAEL: What do you say to a critic when he says you're mystifying your past? I was reading this critic the other day and she said that blacks have really no history or anything, that it's just mystification and all this stuff. I think a San Francisco radical woman said this in the *Evergreen Review*.

DOYLE: Well, I would say that that woman is a fool.

ISHMAEL: Because she lives in San Francisco or what? She was talking about how she was dedicated to the cause of the students at San Francisco State, and she talked about black students, and she was complimenting a black student because he was able to write a paper on Dylan Thomas, and she indicated that he wasn't like the rest of these niggers who mystify the past.

DOYLE: Yeah, well what she's saying is blacks don't have a past.

ISHMAEL: Why is it important for us not to have a past?

DOYLE: Well, it gets back to that slave thing again, you see. I mean, if there was no past, well, you know . . .

ISHMAEL: What do you think about the younger generation that would rather look at the European writers and theoreticians than rely upon the wisdom of their ancestors? I found in my travels that some of the "black studies" programs are shams, because some of the best scholars of black history are intimidated by politicos. I had a very difficult time with the black students because they're in a big contempt of the past, you know, it seems. Do you find that to be true or not? Maybe I'm wrong.

DOYLE: Oh, sure, I find it to be true, and I find black students being less artistic as a group than, say, they were when I was in school.

ISHMAEL: Was this a conscious thing? Maybe they should have built their own universities.

DOYLE: They already had their own universities. What was the black university modeled after? What is Howard modeled from?

ISHMAEL: Well, Christianity. Christian missionaries.

DOYLE: Right, missionary schools.

ISHMAEL: The university sells trained priests, in a way, from among the ranks. The universities of South America took the brightest of the natives and made them priests. It's just secular, really. It's not religious. Ostensibly, anyway.

DOYLE: Sure.

ISHMAEL: There is a black establishment in painting, isn't there?

DOYLE: A black establishment? Well, there's the people who were on the scene in the thirties.

ISHMAEL: What about now? Is there a younger black establishment?

DOYLE: Establishment? I'm not really sure what you're talking about.

ISHMAEL: When I say establishment, I mean are there black people in posts and museums and in other roles connected with painting and sculpture culture who make decisions on which black painters and sculptors get through and which don't get through?

DOYLE: Well, sure, this is the kind of favoritism that passes around. It's a clique.

ISHMAEL: There could be, like, creative cliques. Does this clique allow the wide diversity of painting and sculpture that's going on among blacks to get through their decision-making powers?

DOYLE: Sure, any time anyone sets up a show and eliminates the rest, they're going to have to make some kind of choice there, meaning like . . .

ISHMAEL: Do you know any examples of this?

DOYLE: Well, I know examples, but I'm not really interested in, like, discussing any of them.

ISHMAEL: I'm just a born muckraker, that's all.

DOYLE: I'm saying there's something someone had in mind when they set up a show and that gets back to the critic and like middle people—curators of museums—you know, it's like they say, "This year we're going to push this school of thing, so all the . . ."

ISHMAEL: Let me ask you something. All the people who are members of that school get through, right? Let me ask you something. This fellow, Henri Ghent, who's a black curator from the Brooklyn Museum, put on a show of eleven painters in Geneva and there were protests by the European students, who said that the show wasn't black enough, and there should have been more "Black Power" material in the show, and the mayor of Geneva, Switzerland, a woman mayor, said that the paintings were European-derived, were derivations of European art, and that it wasn't like black music, where black music influenced Europe, jazz influenced Europe, this art was like really derivative.

DOYLE: Well, it's like the transplant I was telling you about, like, of early American painting. This same type thing has happened with a number of blacks whose models were European painters.

ISHMAEL: Would you call your work black art?

DOYLE: I wouldn't call it black art. I mean, personally I wouldn't. I would say it comes from black expression which is based on history and research and identification.

ISHMAEL: In Africa, blacks did use art in religion or in a religous context, didn't they?

DOYLE: Well, all art wasn't used that way. The whole Benin thing was court art.

ISHMAEL: But I've seen an inordinate number of examples of masks and dolls from both East and West Africa.

DOYLE: Yeah, but that's where you get religion and art together and it's actually the European who is separating it and calling it art. Art is like extracted from something else and set aside and called art. I think it's not a legitimate category. Somehow it doesn't seem to be natural, but it was done that way. But Europe has less art than Africa, or than the Americas had.

ISHMAEL: Expand on that.

DOYLE: Say from Mexico down to regions in Central America, there was a highly prolific art culture, not to say that Oceania and some of the others weren't as rich, but when you compare what happened in other countries with what happened in Europe, Europe was zero, practically, on what they produced as art. Now you see the same people over and over and over. I mean you've got Michelangelo and you've got Rubens.

ISHMAEL: There's a black painter I know who told me he's crazy about Rubens. He said he would fight anybody who tried to put down Rubens. What do you think about that?

DOYLE: Well, somehow he's identifying with European art. I'd say at that particular time a person didn't have a soul; he didn't know who he was.

ISHMAEL: Let me ask you this: do you think you would be doing different work if you had grown up in a city?

DOYLE: If I had grown up in the city, I would probably be doing like all these hard shapes, because that's what a city is. A city is a place where everybody is pulled together to be used, right? They call it work force. You can call it anything you want to, but you're there to spend some hours making somebody else rich, man. That's what a city is, and, like, if culture comes up from that city by that city being there, I think it's very rare. I think people come there to try and get a buck, you know what I mean? And you naturally have to play all these social games in order to achieve that, you know. Okay, you think any New York artist lives there after he makes some bread? After you make some bread, where do you go?

ISHMAEL: To the country.

DOYLE: Right, where it's sanity, right, so you can have some house and some security and all that. Man, he's not down there on that street getting kicked in the ass all the time. No! I mean, you know, name some artists who are making some bread. There's a thing in here by Segal. Where does he [George Segal] live? I bet he doesn't live in Manhattan. I bet he lives out some place. But you know what that means. That means that you can say what you want to, but the main thing is being some place where you can have that thing or that quiet or whatever it takes to really hear your own self. The city is only a marketplace, man. It's not any place to live.

ISHMAEL: You're going into film now?

DOYLE: No, I'm not going into film now. I'm just experimenting with film.

ISHMAEL: But you're making pictures of what?

DOYLE: Makonde sculpture.

ISHMAEL: You just got a grant to do that?

DOYLE: No, I got a grant to do some films in some techniques of African sculpture. It's more than one film involved. But one reason I chose film for this is that it can give the idea to the people faster.

ISHMAEL: Rather than having them go to a museum.

DOYLE: Well, museum, curator shop, any place you can find it, you know. And also, by making careful selection, you can find very fine art in it. You have to be selective, because all of it is not good art. They're doing it for commercial reasons, primarily because it's one way of making some money.

ISHMAEL: Let me ask you something. Thomas Hoving just spent five million dollars for a Velásquez. Like some of the taxpayers' money, actually. We call it Hoving's SST.

DOYLE: Well, it was kind of like a stickup.

ISHMAEL: Yeah, and he had like blacks viewing the painting. Even *Time* magazine threw up over that.

DOYLE: It was kind of like a rip-off of the taxpayers' money.

ISHMAEL: He doesn't have many black painters in his museum.

DOYLE: Well, in that case, he's a racist. That's not new in the art world.

ISHMAEL: Now, you're making a film now. Do you have access to private collections? Are there big collections in the United States of African sculpture?

DOYLE: Yeah, there are fairly large collections.

ISHMAEL: What kind of people own them?

DOYLE: Well, Rockefeller owns some African art. Helena Rubinstein. She had one of the largest collections that was auctioned off about '68 or so.

ISHMAEL: She was influenced by African cosmetics?

DOYLE: Probably so, because, after all, what is talc and lots of that other stuff like lipstick . . . what was lipstick originally made from? Animal fat, right? Whale blubber or something like that. You begin to think of the origins of some of those things. What is talc? Talc is like what you dust yourself with, like birds taking a bath in the dust, you know, or lots of animals bathe in the sand dust. It's a way of cleaning yourself, or making yourself feel comfortable on your skin. The other thing is like the earth colors, you know, like burnt siennas and ochers and things like that that come from the earth, right? You can mix them with a little oil and rub them on your face and it really makes a difference. Everybody is into that body painting thing. Hippies sort of got the idea kind of wacky, because they don't really do anything with it. Body painting, body decoration is really an art form in itself. Like right down to scarification.

ISHMAEL: I get from this conversation, from what I've seen about your art, your work, which pervades your life, life being an art . . . say something about your garden.

DOYLE: Well, I grow a garden for probably the same reason I do art. It's been a kind of way.

ISHMAEL: And what do you have in there?

DOYLE: You mean, like food? What are the things I have? Well, you know, like tomatoes and all the regular things like carrots, lettuce. I really have a variety of stuff.

ISHMAEL: Many black people live in miserable conditions, but they always seem to have yards.

DOYLE: Horticulture is really an American and an African thing. It's not European. The Europeans lived on potatoes and rye and barley and oats and meat. But you take all of the domestic vegetables—most of them came from the Americas or from Africa. That means that high civilizations like the Mayans were on corn, on maize. Most of the large American cultures were on maize. That was like their staple. European was wheat, barley, or rye, you see. Well, maize along with yams and lots of other things the Europeans thought were poison, really not too long ago. Europeans were still thinking corn was for animals only. Germans were saying that in the fifties.

ISHMAEL: Let me ask you something. I've read a contemporary account, a William P. Kenn book called *Swallow Barn,* which Calvin Hernton turned me onto. It's a description of slavery, and it said that wherever they could be utilized, the blacks had gardens all around. You mean that's a lost art that blacks had until they got to the city or what?

DOYLE: Well, agriculture in America and Africa was really a woman's kind of thing? Small plots, meaning like the house was not very big, right? It was mainly for sleeping and eating, right? So the rest of the time she spent outside. What was she doing? In the garden. Doing the wash in the stream. So she spent lots of time outside. She wasn't inside as much as the European woman was because her house wasn't as big. Okay, now you go to Mexico and the Indian woman spent most of her time outside. She cooked outside. Some guy was going to do the Indians a really big favor in this little village. So he made them a stove that ran off the sun. Well, those Zapotec women thought that was really crazy, because they weren't going to be out in that sun cooking. They didn't cook in the sun. It was like, you crazy, you think I'm going to be cooking out in that sun? These things come together in natural kinds of ways.

Okay, what were the men into? They were into animal husbandry. They were herding the cattle.

ISHMAEL: Let me ask you something. In the last five years there have come out the *Whole Earth Catalog, Mother Earth,* a whole bunch of, like food conspiracy, where the kids go down and rip off the wholesalers' refuse stuff, man, and sell it cheap. Why haven't these kinds of ideas reached the black community?

DOYLE: They did. That's why black people used to get all the scraps. When I was a kid, I used to know a guy who worked at a slaughterhouse, and he would come by the house every day and he would have a bucket of blood. Now, that's kind of strange. Well, he worked at the slaughterhouse, but I didn't know that until later, and what he was doing was taking that blood and making sausage out of it, blood sausage, right? But, like, when I was a kid, we made our soap, we made lots of things ourselves. Like lye soap. That was the thing. You made that soap and that soap would clean all those clothes, right? That's part of those kinds of things that were carried over. Now, in many cases in Africa—if there's a potter in Africa, it's usually a woman, right? The women make the pots. The men weaved. It was the woman who took care of the garden, though, and certain other things, too. And I don't really see anything wrong with having secret societies, because in that you could really show people what life is and how it could be led in a groovy kind of way.

ISHMAEL: Okay, so now we've talked about the sun, we've talked about the desert, about growing up in the city as opposed to growing up in the country, about how you started out carving wood and about how carving wood expresses a particular kind of consciousness.

DOYLE: I think it brings forth a three-dimensional concept early. Meaning you can get into it with some very simple tools and really express a lot, in a piece of wood, because it's organic and it will respond.

ISHMAEL: So if anyone writes your biography, which I'm sure they will, it will be something like from wood carving to bronze.

DOYLE: Yeah.

ISHMAEL: And then we talked about the processes of your thorough knowledge of African resources. When you talk about black art, you know what you're talking about.

DOYLE: It stems from African art. Yeah, I'm not talking about what someone else told me, I'm talking about what I've been able to . . .

ISHMAEL: You can trace it, you know what you're doing.

DOYLE: I know African techniques.

ISHMAEL: Does your stuff have a message?

DOYLE: Well, it depicts certain things, and once they're all together they say subconscious kinds of things, you know, about what I feel about the subject I happen to be projecting in art form. Okay, just take that cat, for instance. What does a cat mean to you? What does a leopard mean to you? What does a jaguar mean to you?

ISHMAEL: Reminds me of African myths.

DOYLE: Well, it reminds you of African myths, but it can remind you of American myths, too. Have you ever heard any panther stories?

ISHMAEL: Yeah.

DOYLE: Like old people used to tell stories about panthers, right?

ISHMAEL: A fugitive slave was always supposed to cry like a panther.

DOYLE: Yeah, now where did this term come from? Do you know what a panther is? It's just a mythical animal. It doesn't exist.

ISHMAEL: What do you mean, a panther doesn't exist?

DOYLE: There's no animal named panther, man. A panther is a jaguar or leopard or mountain lion, especially black. It's not a breed of animal. It's not a species. It's a mythical animal.

ISHMAEL: A fantasy?

DOYLE: No, a mythical animal. Not a fantasy. A real animal in the sense that it is a real animal, but it is like a black sheep, do you see what I mean? It's like an albino.

ISHMAEL: That's what scared them so much about the panthers. It calls up imagery of horror. I mean, like being attacked by a panther.

DOYLE: Right, by a cat, and on top of that, that cat is black.

ISHMAEL: Like night. A demon cat.

DOYLE: Of course it is. It's the same thing in Clark's *Track of the Cat*. He was kind of gettting into it when he said that the Indian in the novel, Joshua, kept asking how large was the cat. He said, the cat is as big as the whole world.

ISHMAEL: So if a fugitive slave yells like a panther, it shows uniqueness.

DOYLE: Well, I'm not really sure about that. I haven't pondered that. The panther is a mythical cat, a mysterious cat. It's like unknowable—in the dark you can hear him, but you can't see him. You don't know where he is. He's deadly. You don't know where he's going to come from. Now, you know in all mythology there are some strange kinds of things—like women copulating with panthers. Well, you can see what it is. Someone knew a woman had a panther and he hated males. Like right away males became a threat to his territory. Okay, people are territorial animals. People get some of those kinds of things confused now. Okay, you draw your little square off. What are you going to do? Are you going to pee around it? How are you going to identify yourself to the other animals that that's yours? Okay, most of them urinate around it and that's their territory, and like when that other animal smells that urine he knows, he knows his urine from the other's. So this is people today, man. They call it my turf, and my this, and my that, but it's basically the same thing. My house. My casa. That means his territory, right? He's inside of it; it's his whole trip.

ISHMAEL: What are you going to do in the future? What are you going to do next?

DOYLE: Next? I don't really see it that way. Well, as long as there are resources of expression available, I'll keep doing it, you know. But I'm not going to be a fad kind of artist. I don't see myself getting into plastics, because plastics are inanimate. They don't have anything to do with me.

Encore
Spring 1972

George S. Schuyler, Writer

Ishmael Reed and Steve Cannon

George Schuyler, whose career has often inspired bitter controversy, was born in Providence, Rhode Island, in 1895. He is a distinguished journalist whose work has appeared in *The Messenger*, The Pittsburgh *Courier*, *The Crisis*, *The American Mercury*, *The World Tomorrow*, *New Masses*, *Modern Quarterly*, *Opportunity* and *The Nation*. He is the author of *Black No More* (1931), the first science fiction novel written by an Afro-American, and whose plot has been widely imitated. He is also the author of *Slaves, Today: A Story of Liberia* (1931), and *Black and Conservative* (1966), his autobiography. Mr. Schuyler is presently the book reviewer for the *New Hampshire Union-Leader*.

Mr. Schuyler discussed his stormy career and other matters with Steve Cannon and me in October of 1972 at his handsomely furnished apartment on Convent Avenue in Manhattan, full of sculpture, paintings, photos of his friends: authors, artists, and Presidents, and memorabilia concerning his hauntingly beautiful daughter, the late Philippa D. Schuyler. During the course of the interview Mr. Schuyler exhibited some of the spunk and bluntness that once required him to keep a gun next to his typewriter when threatened by some political opponents. When I asked Mr. Shuyler about the 1930s incident in which he was picketed for his comments on Angelo Herndon, a black Communist, he looked puzzled, trying to recall the case, saying "I don't know. It's hard to remember. I've been picketed by so many people."

227

REED: Mr. Schuyler, in an essay you wrote called "Dr. Jekyll and Mr. Hyde and the Negro," you talked about a Negrophobe who exempted his maid from being a Negro. You talked about that as a metaphor for the Jekyll and Hyde nature of race relations in the United States. You said it explains to a large extent how our largest minority "has been able to survive regardless of Nazi-like laws and customs." You talked about the discrepancy between private and public attitudes regarding race relations. Would you like to elaborate on that?

SCHUYLER: When did I write this?

REED: In the early forties, I believe.

SCHUYLER: I don't recall just what it was.

REED: How would you feel about that generally? Some people are always talking about a "final solution" for black people in this country. You said that blacks have been able to survive because of a kind of schizophrenic attitude with which white America—the way white Americans regard them. This was an essay that was published in Mr. Sylvestre C. Watkins' *Anthology of American Negro Literature* [1944].

SCHUYLER: I'm trying to recall it. I don't recall it now. However, you can summarize the conclusion I drew and I'll elaborate on that.

REED: You said that there seemed to be a love-hate relationship between blacks and whites. You talked about the certain paradoxes illustrating this relationship in the South. You mentioned one incident in which black people were standing on a train. A white conductor wanted to give them more space and he broke the custom by allowing them to go into the section of the train usually reserved for whites.

SCHUYLER: There are a lot of peculiar things going on on all sides. That is, the people are not all the same. You have immense differences between individuals, regardless of color. They both love and hate, sometimes at the same time. These things were apparent to me very early. There's really no validity to the generalization that white people or black people per se think a certain way. They don't at all. They think as individuals, unless they are childish, and then they rush to concede the generally accepted thing. But I find so many exceptions to the rule.

REED: You started off the essay—I'll have to send you a copy of it—by an amusing anecdote about this man suffering from what you called Negrophobia. He hated Paul Robeson and he hated black people. They asked him about his maid, and he said, "Oh, Ann, she's not black . . ."

SCHUYLER: "She's not a Negro." Yes, well, they don't regard people very close to them as Negroes, nor do Negroes regard white people who are very close to and intimate with them as white. That's the last thing they think about. I remember being asked down in Georgia, how did it feel being married to a white woman? I said, "I'm not married to a white woman; I'm married to Josephine. That's my wife. It doesn't occur to me; I know that she's white, but it doesn't occur to me except when somebody like you mentions it." I said, "I didn't marry a white woman. I married a certain individual." I think that happens in many parts of life and in human relations, that people don't think about certain individuals being Jewish, for example. Easily, I say, "So what? I don't care about him being a Jew. I'm interested in his character and his manner and whether we get along or not."

CANNON: That's what you were saying in the essay, that in interpersonal relationships judgments are made in relation to the person and not to ethnic background or anything like that. Can I put it that way?

SCHUYLER: Yes, I think you can put it that way. Of course, in recent years we have adopted certain words and have worn them out. "Ethnic background" really doesn't mean a damn thing.

REED: Can you give some more examples of words you think have been worn out, or have lost their meaning?

SCHUYLER: Well, "black" is one.

CANNON: Back at the turn of the century, that was a negative word for Negroes to use, wasn't it? Or I would say in the twenties.

SCHUYLER: Some Negores used it, although my recollection is of the struggle to get the word Negro capitalized, and I said at the time that it didn't make a damn bit of difference if it was capitalized or not. I'd just as soon have it an adjective or a noun, because it didn't change his position, it didn't change his character. Then with the "black" business going on, it was even less sensible than Negro.

REED: You use the term Afro-American in this particular essay.

SCHUYLER: Yes, I used it. I think James Weldon Johnson was the first one I knew to use it and I thought it was an accurate term, although even that is not completely accurate. Some colored people are of three or four different derivations. That is, they have Indian . . .

REED: You claim in *Black No More* that the real distinction, the real so-called pure African disappeared very early in this country and that most *people* are descended from Caucasians and Indians.

SCHUYLER: Yes, and a lot of whites are descended from Africans and Indians. As a matter of fact, these two anthropologists from Johns Hopkins University made a long study in Virginia about miscegenation of the white and Indian, and they found that there were no unmixed Indians in the Eastern United States. The only place you find unmixed Indians is in the West, and in some remote places in the South where they had a reservation.

REED: You satirize people like James Weldon Johnson and W. E. B. DuBois and give them satirical names in *Black No More*—also Garvey. There's always a touch of whimsy about it; it's not really vicious satire.

CANNON: It bordered on how absurd that situation really was.

REED: The thesis of *Black No More* was that if blacks became whites all of a sudden, the civil rights movement would go broke. You were suggesting that a lot of these civil rights groups really thrive on the misery.

SCHUYLER: They profit on the grief, although since they make a profession of it, they cannot acknowledge that there are others who do not, who do not give a damn. Some of the very masses that they're trying to win over don't care. They're not as frightened as many of the so-called leaders and spokesmen.

REED: Another thing about *Black No More*. I notice that on page thirty-two of the paperback edition (Collier African American Library), when you talk about how this individual Mac Fisher becomes a white man, all of this elaborate machinery Dr. Crook has around, reminds me very much of the Paint Factory section in *Invisible Man*.

CANNON: "Pure and White."

REED: Where the young man, the protagonist, underwent an operation. He was in this hospital and had all this science fiction type apparatus around him. You were the first one to do that in *Black No More*. I would call it a science fiction novel.

SCHUYLER: Yes, it was in the direction of most of the science fiction.

CANNON: But it went inward instead of outward; can I say that?

SCHUYLER: Well, *I* wouldn't say that.

CANNON: I mean metaphorically, in terms of him going down to Georgia to meet this family as opposed to going to the moon. That's what I meant.

SCHUYLER: That's where a Negro usually goes when he gets a little money.

CANNON: Down South, right?

SCHUYLER: . . . Struts around in his shoes?

REED: You had a scene where Fisher starts out being black and goes to this cabaret and sees this girl and falls in love with her. A Dr. Crook has the formula for changing black to white. John Howard Griffin did a book like that, *Black Like Me*. They never gave your novel credit for preceding that. I'll bring that up again. What Max Fisher does after becoming white is that he works for the most rabid, racist organization. Will you make comment on parallels to Sartre's *The Inauthentic Jew,* where the people who really probably hate Jews are their own group. I have just read that the head of Hitler's Luftwaffe was Jewish and so dedicated that the German High Command looked the other way. Were you trying to make that comment in *Black No More*?

SCHUYLER: No telling.

REED: Why did you have him become an anti-Negro organizer in this book?

SCHUYLER: Because it was a pretty good plot.

CANNON: I thought so, too. I enjoyed the book.

SCHUYLER: You can get drawn easily into the race nonsense by that device.

REED: I want to return to that first question. I live on the West Coast and we have a different intellectual environment than in New York. In New York you hear a lot of the black intellectuals talking about the holocaust . . .

SCHUYLER: What holocaust?

REED: The one that's always around the corner, like *The Fire Next Time*, or there's going to be a final solution, like Nixon's going to take everybody to concentration camps. You mentioned in your essay that blacks really stimulate this country.

SCHUYLER: You mean do they make a cultural contribution?

REED: Yes.

SCHUYLER: Of course they do; they always have. They not only made it in this country; they made it in ancient Rome, and in Greece. This man at Howard University . . .

REED: *Blacks in Antiquity?* Snowden's book?

SCHUYLER: Yes, he goes into that. The first man to do that, of course, was J. A. Rogers. He preceded all these people and was a better researcher and scholar.

CANNON: Plus he published his own work.

SCHUYLER: Yes, and now Macmillan has put out two volumes of his. What is the name of it . . . *Great Men of African Descent* or something like that. It's well done and they follow the text almost completely. They leave out some things, those which were convenient to leave out. I was responsible for starting that.

REED: Is that right?

SCHUYLER: Yes, I was the one who got Rogers to start writing about the Great Men. He'd been talking about them over at the YWCA cafeteria and so we sat down and talked about these things. I was the managing editor of *The Messenger,* so I got him to start writing it. Then, when *The Messenger* fell and I went to Chicago to edit Ziff's publication—it was a supplement that went into all of the larger Negro weeklies—this supplement, in order to get better advertising notes, was edited in Chicago and published there. The printers just put the names and titles of the papers on as many thousands of copies as they used. So I got Rogers to write for that. I left New York for Chicago because there was a much wider circulation; it took in almost all the country. I think it had about 300,000 circulation combined.

REED: You mentioned dining with J. A. Rogers. Were you part of a circle in the twenties? A circle of intellectuals, poets, and writers?

SCHUYLER: Yes, although the word wasn't in use then.

REED: "The New Negro," Alain Locke said . . .

SCHUYLER: I had very little association with Alain Locke because Alain Locke was teaching at Howard University and he just came up here on occasion. But I moved around in that circle, because we met at some of the places. At one time, Theophilus Lewis was in that circle, and Wally Thurman and Langston Hughes—we used to have dinner in Langston's home.

REED: Did you know Zora Neale Hurston?

SCHUYLER: Sure, I knew her very well. In fact, I published one of the first of her short stories.

REED: You have very rigorous standards for writing. You wrote an essay called "The Negro Art Hokum" which made everybody mad. Do you still maintain those views?

SCHUYLER: I don't know of any that have changed. I think that such art as Negroes produce will be American art, and all of the rest of this is hokum. Usually it's hokum because they don't know anything about Africa. They're not African. Knowing some African history doesn't make a person an African. Just as knowing Italian history doesn't make someone Italian. That was brought forcefully to mind when I was in Africa. Just being black didn't mean a damn thing.

REED: So even though an Afro-American may use African themes or African techniques like the young painters and sculptors are doing . . .

SCHUYLER: Painters and sculptors are a different thing. They could sculpt or paint Eskimo, and if they were good artists, they could sculpt or paint good representations of Eskimo.

REED: So you meant writers?

SCHUYLER: If you're talking about writers, now you're dealing with the culture of the people, and these people here don't know a damn thing about African culture. In fact, there are so many cultures in Africa that one would have to be historian, traveler, philosopher. I visited about twelve different tribes, or nations, as they call themselves —they're more honest than we are—in the back country of Liberia. They all had different hairdos, they had different language, they had an interpreter to talk through, and they stayed in their own areas. In other words, they were just small nations or tribes.

REED: There's a great deal of fanfare about a long awaited book by Alex Haley, the man who tape-recorded the autobiography of Malcolm X. He's doing a new book in which he traces his ancestry back to the Mandingo. But you did that already. You traced your ancestry back to the Mandingo tribe.

SCHUYLER: I traced them back on the maternal side to Madagascar. That's not so far back—a couple of hundred years. Then there were some Indians back there. Of course, there are some Indians in practically every Negro's background.

REED: I see a thread running through your comments on this which leads me to believe that by not acknowledging Caucasian or Indian ancestry, blacks are not being true to themselves and that maybe much of the politics and culture are based on false premises. Would you say that? Like, a lot of stuff that we hear today about the emphasis on "black pride" and this kind of thing.

SCHUYLER: I think the "black pride" ploy is horsefeathers. Now, people have pride, I mean individual pride. Usually it's based on something, not on nothing, like they make it now. A man has pride because of his family, because of his prowess or his accomplishments—that's what he's proud about. He can even be proud because he's got a small foot or something like that. He boasts that he thinks a lot of himself because of that. But what is there to think about being black or pink or red. So you're that. There's nothing to be proud about; you didn't cause it. If a man caused it, then he could be proud.

REED: It seems that a lot of our politics that we hear about—and I'll get to that in a minute, because you did a great study on certain liberal newspapers in *Black and Conservative* in which you talked about the lopsided ideological viewpoint in reference to blacks. It always seems to be the left-wing type of viewpoint that's promoted. There seems to be a lot, like today, on the campuses, you have teachers and professors who are pushing this idea of a collective, and "the people," and looking out for the group as opposed to the individual. They talk about the "luxury of individualism." Of course, my point of view is that individuals and secret societies have done as much to change history as mass movements. What do you see as the future of the black individual who does want to achieve things on his own terms and wants to express his gifts?

SCHUYLER: Well, I think he can do it. As a matter of fact, most of those who have accomplished something and have some kind of reputation have done it. You can't go into a man's factory or mill and say, "Here, I'm black"— he doesn't want that. He wants to know what you can do. For many years there was a Negro who worked over here at the Newark *News*. He was city editor, I believe. The Newark *News* is a very prestigious paper in this area. But, you see, he wasn't a race man and therefore only a few people knew about it.

REED: So he couldn't really go in there and say he's a race man; he has to be qualified as a journalist. And you made the comment: "Those who haven't accomplished something laud those who have."

SCHUYLER: Yes, and they also take credit for it.

REED: Take credit for it?

SCHUYLER: "Look what *we've* done."

REED: When they point to someone like Garvey, or Du Bois, or yourself, or Wallace Thurman? That's an interesting point. Have you read Professor Nathan Huggin's book, *The Harlem Renaissance?* Did he talk to you? What is your assessment of that book? He said that the movement failed because it depended on white patronage. I never heard of anybody describing a movement of white writers as having failed when there could be individual successes in art—say individual poems. It seems that his idea is that they weren't radical enough for his taste.

SCHUYLER: This "Harlem Renaissance" is pretty much of a fraud. A lot of people connected with it were phonies, and there weren't many connected with it.

REED: That's Thurman's viewpoint—"the Niggerati."

SCHUYLER: There was a man [Thurman] with a sense of humor and not chained to any racist chariot. He had ability, shown by the fact that even in that early day he was able to get a job out in Hollywood as a writer.

REED: We've noticed, Mr. Cannon and I, that those writers who were independent, Rudolph Fisher, yourself, Wallace Thurman, even to an extent Zora Neale Hurston, who although she had patronage did do a lot of work on her own in the South—she recorded folklore and went to New Orleans.

SCHUYLER: And to Haiti.

REED: And to Haiti. And she wrote *The Voodoo Gods of Haiti,* which you can't find, as you can't find *Infants of the Spring* or others. Why do you think the people who are more into the collectivist type of poetry and "for the people" have a bigger reputation than those who are independents?

SCHUYLER: Because they've been played up and built up.

REED: Who builds them up?

SCHUYLER: Well, people who are interested in building them up. It's a clique. Who would ever think of Malcolm X as a leader?

CANNON: Really.

SCHUYLER: Lead what?

CANNON: Every time we talk about that, we get shouted down.

REED: You can't say that. He's a holiday now.

SCHUYLER: This was a man who was so ignorant that, until I informed him, he didn't know that there were more white Moslems than there were black. I had to tell him on the radio. I used to be on this program—"The Editors Speak." He was on there frequently, and I had to tell him about this criticism, this denunciation of the white man—and you say you're a Moslem—that most of the Moslems were white. And moreover, I criticized him because of these people using *X* and *Y* after their names. You take the name Muhammad itself—that's taken from a white man. And these names that the Negroes have in Africa, that is, those that are Moslems, all come down from the white people who conquered them. I just told him, publicly, "You just don't know what you're talking about." And then when he went to Mecca, and saw it himself, it changed his whole outlook on things. Then, Mr. Muhammad fired him and that made him go off independently to be a leader.

REED: You talked about this clique. Would you describe this clique and how it works?

SCHUYLER: They use the same tactics, or similar tactics, to those they accuse white people of using. Now, you know, at my age and with my experience, I'm not eager to become a member of anything.

REED: What is your age?

SCHUYLER: I'll be seventy-eight in February. They have various organizations around here, this clique does, which they haven't invited me to join anyhow.

REED: Why is that?

SCHUYLER: Well, they know I won't. I don't regard them as top flight. I belong to the Authors Guild and things like that that are of some value to me. I belong to AS-CAP by virtue of my daughter having belonged to it, and I inherit her interest in it.

CANNON: I was sorry to hear what happened to her. I met her when I was a little kid: I must have been about sixteen years old, and she came down to Southern University to play—a very long time ago.

SCHUYLER: [*Pointing to poster on the wall*] That was her rehearsal at fourteen to play with the New York Philharmonic Orchestra at Lewisohn Stadium, which had never been done before by anyone except Marian Anderson. That was her standard, too.

REED: You were trying to instill a standard of excellence in your children?

SCHUYLER: Yes. Now, let's see. From whence did we wander?

CANNON: We were talking about the clique organizations, about the "Harlem Renaissance" being a fiasco.

REED: Langston Hughes was an excellent poet, don't you think? There were indivuals within the Harlem Renaissance who were accomplished. Countee Cullen was a fine poet. And Wallace Thurman was excellent; he's considered part of the Harlem Renaissance, for some reason. There were fine musicians, too, isn't that correct, like James Weldon Johnson, who wrote lyrics for Noble Sissle and Eubie Blake. You're criticizing the public relations aspect; the title.

SCHUYLER: You can put it on one way and say that there were many people in the nineties and the hundreds, and after that, who were exceptional. If you gather them all together, you could probably call it a renaissance. But some of these people they put in the Harlem Renaissance didn't even live in Harlem.

REED: Like who?

SCHUYLER: Well, James Weldon Johnson was associated with the NAACP; so was Walter White. They were here by virtue of the NAACP being here. There were others, like Clarence Cameron White, who was a great violinist and composer and had his work played by symphony orchestras.

REED: What about Claude McKay?

SCHUYLER: Well, Claude McKay was just a transient. In his late years, he lived in Harlem when he came back from Marseilles. His accomplishments were not particularly in Harlem. I think he wrote "If We Must Die" down in the Village somewhere. He was with the Max Eastman crowd. But of course, I know that there are a lot of people who want to claim every Negro in the world.

CANNON: Well, tell me this. During that period when you

were up here, in the twenties and thirties, was there much interracial intellectual gathering? Fusion of ideas? I'm trying to see if it was integrated on an intellectual level.

REED: They hung out at the cabarets.

CANNON: Yeah, well, I got that out of *Black No More.*

SCHUYLER: Well, they had cabarets all over New York. There were even some Negro cabarets downtown, but there were also other associations. There were labor union associations, there were forums of all kinds. In fact, there were more forums in the twenties and the thirties than there are now, although there are three or four times as many Negroes as there were then. But I would say that the intellectual standards have fallen, if anything, because I think the people who were trying to be intellectual were aiming at higher standards than they are now.

REED: You're talking about Harlem?

SCHUYLER: Yes, in Harlem, and, as a matter of fact, you can go outside Harlem!

REED: You know, we have some pretty good contemporary writers here now. William Melvin Kelley has been compared to you. His book *Dem* has a science fiction plot. And also your idea in *Black No More* of what would happen if all the blacks disappeared, is taken up in *A Different Drummer.* There are a number of good writers. We may say that the standards are better than in the twenties, you know!

SCHUYLER: It just happens that I've gone through this whole period of literature from the mid-twenties on to the present.

REED: And you think that the standards are lower now than they were in the twenties?

SCHUYLER: I should say that they are, not only for Negroes, but for whites as well.

CANNON: For the whole publishing world, huh?

SCHUYLER: Great art and literature has traditionally come out of and been supported by people of means and education, what is called the upper class. As a matter of fact, Upton Sinclair did a book once on that very theme and showed how all the Greek art and sculpture had been subsidized by people of means. Where a fraternity or a church has the means to subsidize an artist, they very seldom do it, because they don't understand it. Presumably, you've got to understand what you pay for, and know what it's all about. You can imagine, as in Rome, for example, Ovid and Horace were subsidized by the people who appreciated what they were doing.

REED: Would you consider Duke Ellington's music great art?

SCHUYLER: No, it's not great art.

CANNON: What's missing from it?

SCHUYLER: Variety, for one thing. Duke, whom I know and respect very much, has cleaned up on this trend. I think that some of the things Duke wrote thirty years ago are more pleasant to me than these growls that he puts out now.

REED: Do you think that what is called Afro-American music—or what's generically called jazz, ragtime, blues—that this . . .

SCHUYLER: That's a horse of another color. It's original.

REED: But original doesn't necessarily have to be great.

SCHUYLER: No. You make it great by the addition of artistry.

REED: *Time* magazine did a review of my book and then compared it to your work and they called you "the black Mencken." Did you know Mencken?

SCHUYLER: Yes, I knew Mencken well. I was his houseguest several times. Whenever I passed through Baltimore I would call him up, and if he was not busy, I would go by there for an evening, and try out his cellar. He had a wonderful cellar. There were other people, too, during that period who were prominent in the literary world, even in the South, that I visited and shared their hospitality. And they solicited me. This was especially true after I wrote for *The American Mercury* in 1927. At the same time, in 1927, my first piece came out, and it was the lead piece, too. I came to be known by a lot of people who were writing. I think that other colored people with skill can get the same respect and co-operation. It's being done all the time. It's probably being done more now than it was then, because there are more Negroes now and there are more Negroes of education and training now than there were then. Because, after all, a so-called intellectual, even if he was connected with church or with one of the race-saving organizations, was not much in the labor movement because there weren't many Negroes in the labor movement on a higher scale. Once in a while you'd run across some colored man who was secretary-treasurer of a union, but, you see, Negroes couldn't join most of the unions at those times.

REED: There are still some unions they can't join, like the construction union in New York they're having difficulty with.

SCHUYLER: Oh, yes. Well, the labor movement started out in this country on Jim Crow. Not on Jim Crow, but on exclusion. The first labor union in the United States was in Boston and that was before the Revolution. They specifically put in their constitution that they weren't going to have any men of color, whether they were free or not. At the time of the Civil War, there were only about three unions in the United States that permitted Negroes membership. And so in that field you had very little representation. But the fields in which you did have representation didn't produce so much either. That is in the field of education.

REED: There's a controversy now about "Black English."

SCHUYLER: Hogwash.

REED: You said there are no racial or colored dialects, only sectional dialects in *Black No More,* there are really no racial differences, only class differences, you said in *Slaves Today,* 1931. On the other hand, you do seem to hint that there is a unique style of African choreography or music.

SCHUYLER: I wouldn't say African choreography. I would say there's choreography in the dance, because I've seen that, and it was African, too; it wasn't any bogus thing.

I might say, to digress, that in 1960 I was in Nigeria celebrating the first black Governor General of Nigeria, and we were there for a week when they gave the dance festival, which included tribes of people from all parts of

Nigeria. When you say that, it makes it international because each one of those big tribes is a nation, you know. They got nothing in common. That's some idea they built up here in Harlem about that. As a matter of fact, half the Negroes in Nigeria enslave the other half. But now there you had marvelous dances and with no influence from anywhere else. It was indigenous. It came out of their lives. Now, as for the music, there's very little to African music. There are some tribes that make beautiful music. Other tribes are just percussion. In fact, I don't know why, as well trained as so many Negro musicians are, in the United States, that they haven't composed more on African themes.

REED: Still there are a lot of jazz musicians who at least use African titles.

SCHUYLER: Yes, but speaking of orchestral composition . . . they have to embody root music that comes out of the people that they are writing about. And they [have to] refine it and make something very artistic out of it. Now, they haven't done that. Somebody may have done it. I don't claim to know the history of music, but I know my daughter was the only one who did it. Because she wrote "The Nile," which was premiered in Cairo by the Cairo Symphony Orchestra on—this was 1965, December 10.

CANNON: Was that ever recorded? Or do you know?

SCHUYLER: Well, it was played here. At her memorial service. They played it here at her memorial service, which was held in Town Hall. And that embodied the music, the basic music of Ethiopia, Uganda . . . well, all the four countries that bordered on the Nile, so that was the name of it, "The Nile." It was applauded very highly there by the critics in Cairo. But those are my views about art and literature and all. And . . .

CANNON: Did you and Mencken ever get in heated discussions about American language or was he working on that at the time?

SCHUYLER: I gave him many items for his *American Language*. We discussed. We didn't argue about it, of course. There wasn't any argument.

CANNON: No, you know what I mean. Just differences of opinion.

SCHUYLER: Just contributions to Americana.

REED: Are you an optimist about the—this is the kind of question *they* ask—an optimist about the future of race relations in this country?

SCHUYLER: Well, in a sense I am. But they're not going to continue so good if it's left up to the Negro intellectuals to stir things up and frighten people. It's a very bad thing, you know—to frighten people—especially if you don't have anything. Like I remember a vaudeville skit, you know, and the blackface comedian makes a pass at his back pocket, you know, as if he had something in there, and then later when he got the other man scared, when the other man began to retaliate, he would say, "I was just joking."

CANNON: That means that you knew Bert Williams and George Walker, doesn't it?

SCHUYLER: I didn't know them.

CANNON: I mean, as far as having seen their performances.

SCHUYLER: *The Messenger* office was just two doors north of where Bert Williams lived on Seventh Avenue.

CANNON: How was their material? I've never seen them. How are they as comedians? Were they very good as compared to what was happening in the world at the time?

REED: You're talking about Williams and Walker.

CANNON: Because I think what's-his-name was just coming on the scene when he was a little boy . . . what's his name? Leon Earl and people like Eddie Cantor—they were very young at that time. Earl was older. He was close to Williams, I think. .

SCHUYLER: Well, Earl was better than most of them. You know, one time in one of the Ziegfeld Follies, Williams and Earl had a skit together and it was really immense.

REED: Bert Williams worked with Eddie Cantor.

SCHUYLER: I don't doubt it.

REED: Yeah, they had a routine. Williams was called Rufus the Red Cap. Of course Williams always upstaged him and you know that W. C. Fields said he was the funniest and saddest man he ever saw perform. But a lot of the younger black comedians, with the notable exception of Richard Pryor, who I think is a genius, consider the black comedians of the past to be Uncle Toms.

SCHUYLER: These people were comedians and they were good ones, too. And they took the life around them and made a joke out of it. As a matter of fact, lots can be said for Uncle Toms. I remember he said, "You can have my body but you can't have my soul."

REED: That's interesting that you would say that. Because it seems that Black-Negro-Afro-American behavior is always—always has to be restricted. You have to be angry. There's only one mask that you can wear. I was reading in the *I Ching* the other night that there is a kind of parallel in Confucius to what we call Uncle Tomism—what they call taking abuse from the outside by preserving your inner light all along.

SCHUYLER Well, now, how do you think these free Negroes—whose position was very difficult—in this country—how do you think they survived and, in some instances, prospered? And not only in the North.

CANNON: In the South?

SCHUYLER: In the South. Because, as I say, it was the individual. And if the individual has it within him then he can go to Harvard, Yale, Chicago, and all the other universities. And he'll just be a mediocrity. You run across them every day. Humpback with degrees.

REED: I notice in the universities, and Steve has too, a lot of the children are really undergoing an emotional, intellectual, psychological crisis because they've been badgered into thinking they have to be—you know—

CANNON: Well, use Mr. Schulyer's words, "race people." They think they have to be race people before they can be individuals.

REED: And some universities, instead of designing courses, they're like conflicts between those people who . . . really have like a Communist orientation when you come on out with it . . . and, say, those who want to make it within the system or treat Afro-American culture as a serious entity instead of using it as a political rally hall. How do you see us resolving that?

SCHUYLER: What other system is there for them to make it in?

CANNON: No, he means in terms of—let's look at it this way—in terms of Frederick Douglass and those people came up here. I'm going back now to the nineteenth century. Now, you had an awful lot of free Negroes living up around here. You mentioned one earlier in the conversation. You were talking about Thomas Fortune. Now, how did they react to the rabble-rousing Douglass and what those people were doing? I mean, did it affect their livelihood at all . . . or their "consciousness"?—that's the kind of word they use now.

SCHUYLER: Well, all of them were opposed to slavery of course. But they disagreed with the means which were being advocated. Douglass himself did not follow John Brown. John Brown, he gave him hell for not going along with him, but of course Fred Douglass was saying, in a way, in accordance with the old song Bert Williams popularized: "I may be crazy but I ain't no fool." And then you had a long debate among free Negroes in this country from the 1820s on about emigration to Africa.

CANNON: Yeah, right, that so-called Colonization Society. And if I remember correctly Douglass came out totally against it.

SCHUYLER: Yes, he was against it, but there were a lot of Negroes who were not against it. There were about ten thousand Negroes who went to Liberia and Captain Paul Cuffee had plans for an organization to carry a lot of them to Sierra Leone.

CANNON: The guy's name—you know who I'm thinking about—Delaney. Martin Delaney was another one of them who supported the movement.

REED : He always came back here though.

SCHUYLER: Well, he only went there once.

CANNON: Well, in other words what that whole Garvey thing was was nothing else than echoes and . . the rounding out of that whole thing that started in the 1820s.

SCHUYLER: Yes. What had been said and done before. Only he could get a strong voice . . .

REED: Only he could talk louder. Lots of style. Lots of style.

SCHUYLER: Louder . . .

REED: How do you think Garvey will be evaluated when all the fuss dies down? Historically.

SCHUYLER: Well, I think he'll be evaluated like others who have had this dream of migrating to Africa. There are many of them who have had it, you know.

CANNON: Well, Chester Himes did a pretty good job of doing parody on that. I don't know if you read that *Cotton Comes to Harlem,* which was a parody on that whole Garvey thing. The movie version wasn't but the book itself was.

REED: But of course, there are people in the country— leaders—who use African or quasi-African-based philosophies and have success like Elijah Muhammad and Amiri Baraka.

SCHUYLER: Well, now, Elijah Muhammad—he's another hustler. However, he's not bereft of ideas and has much more fruitful ideas than most.

REED: Like the farms and the businesses?

CANNON: In other words and from what you know about this country, being your age, would you see him as an American phenomenon somewhat similar to the Mormons? Would you be able to draw a parallel to them?

SCHUYLER: No.

CANNON: Because the Mormons are supposed to be an American religion—right?

SCHUYLER: No. Not unless he did as the Mormons did.

CANNON: Going out and getting some state . . .

SCHUYLER Yes. Some territory. But you see the thing is about Elijah Muhammad's followers, they don't want to go anywhere and they don't even want a segregated state. They just want to be aloof as a sect.

CANNON: That goes back to what we were talking about in that interview you had Ish, I think in *Changes* you were talking about this other guy who was around in the twenties, you know what I'm thinking about. Where everyone had cards saying they were Asians . . .

REED: Abdul Sufi Hamid?

CANNON: Yeah. He was up in Harlem at that time, wasn't he?

SCHUYLER: He was strictly . . .

REED: No . . . excuse me, I meant Noble Drew.

CANNON: Yes.

REED: The Moor.

SCHUYLER: The Moor. Well, they were authentic Moslems, weren't they?

REED: Well, they called themselves Moors.

CANNON: They had little cards they ran around with.

SCHUYLER: Of course the Moors had only been Moslems since about the seventh or eighth century, before that they had another faith.

REED: I want to ask you this question. In *Black and Conservative,* you talked about the hassle you had with the Angelo Herndon people . . . where you had to get a pistol because they were in the South organizing and you pointed out that he was a Communist too! . . . and that they weren't particularly ready for criticism, I guess, so they picketed your house.

SCHUYLER: I don't reall the name . . . I've been picketed by so many people. I knew Angelo Herndon. I also know that he turned against the Communists.

REED: He did, huh?

CANNON: Recently?

SCHUYLER: No, no, he's dead now. You see, they exploited Angelo Herndon as they do everybody else, only he detected it.

REED: You feel he parallels today. I'm thinking of Angela Davis, for example. Do you think she's being exploited?

SCHUYLER: Well, undoubtedly . . . she's been exploited and she has swallowed this mob-hokum hook, line, and sinker, and it's unfortunate, I think, because she seems to be a bright person. But she's gone too far and the thing she's advocating now, most of the intellectual rich gave that up years ago.

CANNON: Back in the thirties.

SCHUYLER: Well, back in the thirties and forties. I know very few real intellectuals today—I'm not speaking about color now—who swallow Marxism and Stalinism and that sort of thing. That's been discredited, even the Bolsheviks can't make it.

REED: They're building Pepsi-Cola factories now in the Soviet Union, I understand. China wants Coca-Cola.

SCHUYLER: Well, hell, everybody wants Coca-Cola well cooled. But I suppose you saw that comedy that James Cagney starred in—*One, Two, Three*—that was based on the rivalry between Coca-Cola and Pepsi-Cola to get a contract from the Russians? Oh, it was a classic! And it was laid in Berlin and so they were all trying to get these Russians' contracts and the Russians were trying to get the Coca-Cola, and so on. Well, I mean, that bubble has burst and I hate to see people at this late date, you know . . .

CANNON: Come out with archaic ideas.

SCHUYLER: I don't bother now. I don't have anything to say about it at all.

CANNON: Well, let me get back to that question that Ish tried to ask you about the school situation—that's the one I'm fighting. The question was this: now, you see, what's happening out there in the case of the community college is that you've got some bright kids out there, you've got some who aren't too smart, you got—whatever you have —the school kids. Anyway the whole emphasis on the school is on this whole "blackness" thing.

SCHUYLER: The whole *what?*

CANNON: "Blackness." In your days it would have been "race." It's making it very difficult for some of these kids to go to school because they're there to learn how, you know, to learn technique on what they want to do. They're not too interested in learning to be black because they know that already, you see. So, considering that, what do you think is going to happen at those schools? What's going to happen with that generation when they find out that the country isn't really put together that way?

SCHUYLER: I feel sorry for them.

CANNON: In other words they've read Angela Davis, and they have to read George Jackson.

REED: Eldridge Cleaver.

CANNON: Eldridge Cleaver, and things like that instead of . . .

SCHUYLER: That's an ordeal.

REED: Instead of *Black No More;* Al Young, my friend (he's editing the issue in which this interview is going to be), he wrote a novel called *Snakes* and two books of poetry; he's a professor. He taught *Black No More* recently. He said it was real controversial and the kids liked it very much.

SCHUYLER: Well . . .

REED: But that's another point of view he exposed them to.

CANNON: Yeah, completely different point of view from most of the stuff they're getting right now, you know.

SCHUYLER: Oh, yes, they can't conceive of laughing at this situation. They actually take this seriously.

REED: You had a character in *Black No More* who said that the solution for blacks in this country is either to get out, get white, or get along.

SCHUYLER: Yes, that came from Kelly Moore. Kelly Moore was professor of mathematics and later dean at Howard University, and he wrote a lot of sound stuff. And during the war, he wrote an open letter to Woodrow Wilson on the disgrace of democracy. Now, it sounds like some of these people just wrote it yesterday. But that was fifty-odd years ago and another thing Kelly said. His definition of a Negro radical was an over-educated West Indian without a job. Now, another very capable man that came up here during that period was Dean Pickens, who was one of the officials of the NAACP. That man had a tremendous sense of humor and many a Saturday afternoon we sat up in *The Messenger* office and discussed things, what they call rap sessions here now. And then there was another man here, you hardly ever hear his name mentioned, Hubert Harrison. He was what you'd call an over-educated West Indian. But he used to speak on corners here and he had a very brilliant delivery and

all. That's one thing they didn't do during the Renaissance
. . . they didn't attempt to speak any black English.

CANNON: How did Julian fit into all that? Was he just a
showman? Or what? You know who I'm talking about—
Black Eagle.

SCHUYLER: I know . . . Black Eagle. And I been knowing
him since those days. He came here by way of Canada.
He was West Indian of course, claiming to be an aviator.
He wore puttees that you could shave by and fine uniform
but I don't think he got a student's license to fly until he'd
been here about ten or fifteen years. But he got in dutch
with Garvey because Garvey was talking about *sailing*
back to Africa and he was talking about *flying* there. And
so he and Garvey fell out. But I must say that Julian's
been a good hustler.

CANNON: He's still around, isn't he? He doesn't make his
home here, does he?

SCHUYLER: In the islands. See, he got in with these munitions sellers, and that's a very lucrative field. He even sold
munitions to the Finns and to the Guatemalans. He was
trying to sell munitions to the Congo but that didn't make
it. They were getting munitions, but not from Julian.

CANNON: Well, was Jack Johnson a big thing in New York
at that time? Or would he just come through?

SCHUYLER: Part of the time. He lived here for a long time.
He used to live next door to me when I lived up here at
321 Edgecomb Avenue.

CANNON: Bert Williams was living right down the street
from you.

SCHUYLER: I told you Bert Williams lived two doors from
The Messenger office. *The Messenger* office was first at
2305 and then at 2311 Seventh Avenue, and a lot of notable people lived along there as they did along Edgecomb
Avenue, what they called Sugar Hill.

REED: Du Bois lived up there.

SCHUYLER: I think he did. I don't know whether he lived
up there or not. I know Walter White did. Roy Wilkins
did when he got here.

CANNON: The Johnson brothers probably did too.

SCHUYLER: Oh, I got along all right, except in the thirties

—around about '34 or '35, when he came out for segregation, you see, after being for integration all those years. And of course I took exception to that. He said that, in effect, Negroes should cut their communications and associations with whites as much as possible. Of course I said that was ridiculous because Negroes wouldn't have any jobs then. They couldn't live without working and who had all the jobs? And who had all the government? But staying aloof—you can't stay aloof from a thing you're living in the midst of. However, I had high respect for Du Bois but not for some of his opinions, which I think were too far-fetched and which, if adopted, would just have the Negro worrying himself to death. He's got enough worries as it is. No, there are a lot of people that I've crossed their path, among Negroes, I mean, for whom I have great respect and in many instances admiration as individuals. For example, I knew a man in Charleston, West Virginia—Mr. James. Now, this man had a wholesale fruit and vegetable business and he had agents—this was back in the twenties—who went around and bought up crops from the farmers and all and he had a big warehouse, and a spur on the railroad coming in there. And I don't think you could find his name on anything in any of these Negro histories but this was an important thing. It made some Negroes ambitious to do likewise. And if anybody said they couldn't do it they could point to him.

CANNON: They had a model there.

REED: Schuyler, what are you working on now?

SCHUYLER: Well, I work on films and books.

REED: What do you think of the current wave of black films that are out? Have you seen any of them? *Superfly?*

SCHUYLER: Most of them that I've seen are terrible. Of course the boys are hustling and making money and they taught the Jews how to do the same thing, you know. I've seen very few of any merit.

REED: Which ones would you say had merit?

SCHUYLER: That's a tough question.

REED: A lot of people are talking about *Sounder* right now.

SCHUYLER: *Sounder*'s just an ordinary film but it's better

than most of them and I thought it was pretty well done.

REED: What are you working on now?

SCHUYLER: Oh, I just review films, generally. For the *Review of the News,* Belmont, Massachusetts, a weekly news magazine. And then of course books—I've been fooling around with books since 1923. Sometimes I don't want to see any more books. Although I just finished a very good novel last night—but that novel *Augustus* [by John Williams] is very well done in a different way. That is to say, its story is told through a series of diaries and letters and other communications of that kind, one character with another. And it's very effective.

REED: Who are the younger writers you read? You don't have to mention us. Have you read any of James McPherson's work?

SCHUYLER: No.

REED: *Hue and Cry* or Barry Beckham, Ernest Gaines, author of *Bloodline,* and *The Autobiography of Miss Jane Pittman* . . .

SCHUYLER: No.

REED: Cecil Brown? *Life and Loves of Mr. Jiveass Nigger.*

SCHUYLERS No. I didn't read them.

REED: Do you see any plays?

SCHUYLER: Sometimes. When I have the time. You know, I have very little time because in the first place, except for this boy [John, his assistant] here, there's nobody comes here. I do everything myself. Well, I guess my bar's not far. It's around the corner.

CANNON: Do you see any old-timers over there—guys you knew back in the thirities and forties?

SCHUYLER: No.

CANNON: But they all know you over there, though.

SCHUYLER: Oh yes. Frank's is closed, you know, and there are bars where I'm known and if I happen to be in the neighborhood I drop in and take a spot.

CANNON, REED: Thank you, Mr. Schuyler.

Yardbird II
1973

The Great Tenure Battle of 1977

Ishmael Reed has also been teaching off and on in the English department here since 1968. He has just been denied tenure by the department, which has only two black lecturers and no black regular faculty members on a staff of sixty-two. His case is being compared to that of assistant sociology professor Harry Edwards, though the differences between the two are perhaps greater than the similiarities. Reed has not served as a regular full-time professor. This has never apparently been his intention nor that of the English department. He is a practicing writer presumably hired on that basis. Students in Reed's writing course have been enthusiastic about his teaching. His credentials as a recognized writer would seem to be indisputable.

As Reed's tenure denial became known, the controversy was further complicated by an article by University of California journalism lecturer Michael Weiss in the January 17, 1977, New West. The article quoted Reed on the department decision and several department colleagues on Reed. Two colleagues felt that Reed's work was too innovative to win acceptance within the department. One professor, Thomas Parkinson, was quoted at some length: "I don't think this is a racist thing. . . . There would be the same kind of problem with Barthelme or some of the other white experimental writers. . . . Now if Gore Vidal wanted to come, there'd be no question. It's a kind of work we're used to. Vidal writes in a civilized style." Parkinson went on to say, "Ishmael is an artist, but he's also a very . . . he is not a black militant. He is very bourgeois. He's got a white wife. He's an entrepreneur." Other statements were made to the effect that Reed was temperamental, and had canceled classes and a poetry reading.

Though this article, taken as a whole, was favorable to Reed, he was irritated with what he felt were inaccuracies and misstatements. The English department was also quite unhappy with the article. Generally, those in the department seemed to regret attention being drawn to the issue.

I spoke to the chairman of the department, Ralph Rader, who seemed to be favorably inclined toward Reed. He expressed the hope that Reed could be given a job as continuing senior lecturer. Unfortunately, hoping is not the same as voting in a tenure review. Also, whether this senior lectureship would include tenure remains ambiguous. Adhering to the confidentiality of tenure reviews, Rader would not discuss Reed's case. I generally got favorable remarks about Reed from the faculty people I talked to, but the fact remains that someone was doing the voting against him at the tenure meeting. . .

As to whether there was racism or racist aspects to the decision, this is difficult to establish, as no one involved in the decision will violate confidentiality and discuss it. I was told that the only people who know how well the tenure process works are the ones who can't talk about it. Thus one enters the labyrinth.

Last week I interviewed Reed at length. He discussed his view of the tenure dispute and the department, which led to a wide range of other topics. We talked about his career as a writer and publisher. If Ishmael Reed has any opinions that are not controversial, I was unable to discover them. He spoke rapidly, angered by the tenure incident. He is a complex person given to stern assertions and sudden ironies. He can be playful, easily likable, exacting. But he is above all a serious artist, impatient with obstacles to his work. As he has said "Writing is my cult."

JE: An article in the January 17 issue of *New West* likens your case to the Harry Edwards case. How do you feel about that?

IR: My case is not the same. They're trying to make this into some kind of Black Power entertainment. And I'm not into black-confrontation politics.

JE: Then why are they comparing you two?

IR: I don't know. We're both black . . . that's all it is.

JE: But I gather from the article that you felt there was racism in the decision to deny you tenure.

IR: I told the reporter and I told the chairman of the department that I thought that racism was a factor. I didn't say it was a racist decision. Some people might have been against me for other reasons. Because they identified me with the avant-garde or maybe they don't like me wearing jeans and Cardin tops. It could be a number of reasons. I'm not so simplistic as to believe that it was merely racism. But I think if you get forty whites in a room, there's going to be some racism, a racist element. I think you could put that into a computer.

JE: I gather you are unhappy about the remarks of your colleagues in the *New West* piece.

IR: I think Thomas Parkinson of the English department showed very bad manners to call me a savage. Perhaps that means I don't adhere to Judeo-Christian values in my art, but I am acquainted with them, and I don't think they are the only standards of civilization. I think that's a very narrow view. He also got personal about where I live, who I'm married to, what businesses I'm involved in. I don't see how these factors enter into a tenure discussion. I think that for someone who has taught English for twenty-eight years, he showed a lack of precision in language. He called me a bourgeois. I obviously don't own the means of production. I'm not the head of General Motors. He said I am an entrepreneur. I guess I'm to be penalized for participating in the society and trying to build things. Some of his remarks were classic. He mentioned my white wife. My wife is a Semite. She doesn't refer to herself as white. She belongs to the same race as the Arabs. I would never refer to his wife, Ariel Parkinson, as Thomas Parkinson's white wife, Ariel. My wife has a difficult time keeping her career separate from mine—I know I'm controversial. But she's the distinguished American choreographer Carla Blank. Her latest work was performed in Japan. She's well recognized as one of the leading exponents of avant-garde dance in the country. We have independent careers. But to call her my white wife is to dehumanize her, even if it were true. And if I were married to a Northern European or a Southern European, that would be my business.

JE: Why do you think they are saying these kinds of things?

IR: They're embarrassed. I really think they're embarrassed. I'm not going to make a Black Power confrontation out of this. I have my own way of dealing with these issues. I take this philosophically. I am acquainted with American history. I know some of these charges against me are classic, like "temperamental." Any black person who isn't a slave, or any heathen who doesn't want to be a missionary, is considered temperamental. Another word they use is "surly." In *Uncle Tom's Cabin,* Topsy is referred to as "surly," you know impertinent—difficult.

JE: Don't you think some of this is caused by academic scholars reacting to you as a celebrity?

IR: Well, there's also a thing called the tyranny of experience. Ronnie Laing dealt with it. I was listening last night to a broadcast about how the Soviet Union handles its dissidents; it puts them in asylums. That's some kind of arrogant assertion that your view of the world is correct. If I criticize the English department, they say I'm projecting . . . all these Freudian terms. I have to be crazy. This is typical dismissal of non-establishment experience. They say it's crazy or outrageous, or I'm projecting. I think my response has been very mild to some of the things they've said about me.

JE: Parkinson said that you sought out this tenured position. You say you didn't.

IR: They offered it to me. Thomas Flanagan, the former chairman of the department, asked me if I wanted a permanent position here with tenure. I said I would have to hear more details about it. This was in January 1975. He said I'd done such a good job there and was so admired in the department that he felt if he offered this professorship, he could get it through. If he had offered me a senior lectureship, I'd have preferred that. So I asked for more details. A few months went by and he brought it up again, so I said okay put it through. I don't know where Parkinson is coming from on this. I'd always admired him up until now. His participation in the People's Park and Vietnam controversies made me think here is a guy who really stands up. Now I see that when it comes to his own province, where he earns his living, he's not as militant as he is about issues two thousand miles away.

JE: What happened next with Flanagan and the tenure process?

IR: I'd given Flanagan the go-ahead and he'd put it through. It came to the stage where they have to pass some hurdles, and they got over the hurdles. Then about a year ago, Flanagan called me into his office and told me they'd gotten it through, and all they had to do was send it to the affirmative action committee and then there'd be a review. He asked me to submit materials, so I submitted my books. Then he said they didn't have any teacher evaluations. I'd never emphasized teacher evaluations—I'd never made a career of it. But there were highly favorable teacher evaluations submitted from the very beginning. I understand those teaching evaluations were thrown out. Some people in the department claim there never were any evaluations submitted, but I know there were. A couple of people up there told me they had been destroyed. So they asked me to submit ten letters from students, since they had no evidence of my teaching ability. So I submitted ten letters. They're over there.

JE: I find it hard to believe that you had been teaching off and on in the English department since 1968 and there was no evidence of your teaching ability.

IR: Sure, sure. So that's where it stood. I submitted the letters, Flanagan went to Ireland, and Rader took over as chairman shortly before my tenure came up. Rader said they needed more letters, so I got more letters. Obviously, there was evidence of my teaching ability.

JE: Then do you think there was a change in attitude toward you when Rader took over?

IR: There seemed to be a change. For example, he asked me to submit essays. They were acquainted with my fiction and poetry. So I submitted essays. I've had essays published in *Le Monde* and all over the world. I've got a whole big book of essays coming out from Doubleday, which is not exactly a slouch company. So I submitted essays from the Washington *Post* and everywhere else. I had a whole box full of eight or nine books, anthologies I'd edited, prizes received. It's been quite an inconvenience to me to stay up with this tenure review and then be turned down. I'm perfectly happy with the senior lectureship because I don't have to be involved with committees. I can do what I like best, which is teach. I'm trying to do a lot of things and do them well.

JE: Is it true that you canceled several teaching commitments?

IR: Parkinson said that, and he is incorrect. In 1968, during the bombing of the campus with tear gas and antipersonnel weapons, as well as three gases outlawed by the Geneva Convention, I wrote a letter to James Hart, then head of the English department. I said when I signed up to teach a course, I wasn't volunteering to fight in a war. There was a difference. My contract did not say anything about war or being trained for combat, so I canceled one summer course. Not several.

JE: Did you cancel a poetry reading?

IR: That was at the Poetry Center at San Francisco State. The center's director, Lewis MacAdams, had said I "lived and raved" in Berkeley. I took offense, and a lot of other people took offense. I called up MacAdams' friends and colleagues, and they said it was rotten. They said I shouldn't have showed up because it would've seemed like I was hard up for a hundred dollar reading. I just came the night before from a thousand dollar reading in Florida. You might say I'm kind of a matinee idol of the poetry/fiction circuit. I like crowds of people and I get to read my work. Well, finally, MacAdams apologized and later I got a job at the Poetry Center. I have a letter from MacAdams congratulating me on my hard work. I spent the whole summer without pay at the Poetry Center writing grant proposals for the California Arts Council and the National Endowment. Floyd Salas and I got more money for the Poetry Center—$15,000—than they'd ever had before. What we did was open the Poetry Center's poetry-in-the-schools program to chicanos, blacks, women, and other groups. Then some chicanery took place. The program was supposed to be geared to disadvantaged and multicultural groups. The terms of the proposal had been violated. We then wrote a federal proposal with the same wording: multicultural. Well, I think MacAdams went back on his word. He had promised me autonomy and then went back on his word. It's not a multicultural program now, and there was no way for me to implement a multicultural proposal, so I resigned to avoid a black-white power confrontation. That's what they want you to do. They want you to get out there and start screaming to them. But I feel we've been serving too long in this country without serving someone's perverse needs, providing someone's excitment and sensationalism. They can get that off the tube. I won't be a part of that.

JE: Getting back to the tenure question, what specifically do you think caused them to turn you down?

IR: Oh, I found out why I didn't get the position. I found out the reason they didn't do it. A few people would be affected, and I'm not going to say anything about them because I want to protect them. It seems like there's a lot of repression, not only in politics but in cultural areas. I'm really embarrassed. I'm embarrassed for them, because they don't want to give out the real reason I didn't get tenure so they're straining, and in the process they've damaged my reputation.

JE: What is the real reason?

IR: I don't want to go into it. I got the reason from New York . . . from the editor of a powerful magazine. He has contacts here in the city, and he told me.

JE: Is this something that just can't be alluded to?

IR: It's amusing. It's amusing.

JE: Does it have anything to do with your being black?

IR: Well, I think there might have been a few racists in on this decision. There might have been a few conservatives and traditionalists—literary and aesthetic conservatives. I might have been rejected for a number of reasons. But I know the one real reason, the one most important reason.

JE: But you've said you wanted it all out in the open.

IR: I think I want to protect people who have to earn a living there. These people are very . . . well . . . I think the English department needs them. They should be in the English department.

JE: Would this be damaging to friends of yours in the department?

IR: They're not friends. It would be embarrassing to them, so I don't want to go into it. I don't understand why they didn't just offer me a senior lectureship with tenure. I think I've proved my performance as a teacher. I have copies of all the student letters. I think from now on when I send in letters from students, I'll send them in by certified mail like they do in other parts of society. I thought in the cultural areas things were a little less harsh, a little less uptight. Apparently it's not. This whole year has been an experience for me. One thing leads to another. You try to build a program at the Poetry Center for a multicultural poetry-in-the-schools, and you're called temperamental for even trying. It's all part of a national trend. My case is not the same as Harry Edwards' case. I'm not that acquainted with his case. From all I've heard he's apparently a shrewd and intelligent scholar, a family man, not a cut-up. He's a nice straight guy. So if they can do it to him, they can do it to anyone.

JE: When you went to Rader to tell him you thought some racist considerations affected your tenure case, did you confront him with this real reason you've heard?

IR: No, I just learned of it a few days ago from New York. These guys wanted to do an article on me. I don't want an article. I don't want to see people get fired.

JE: Doesn't this show a rather closed, repressive side to the English department if you have to find out what's going on in Berkeley from New York?

IR: Yes. Right.

JE: Isn't the disinterested institution a dangerous myth then?

IR: I told Rader the other day that I don't know many faculty people. Maybe they feel I haven't socialized with them. I don't attend their functions and social gatherings. Over the years I never attended those things. I'm busy. I'm not a party person. I'm up there to teach students. I learn a lot from that—it's mutually benefiical. I learn a lot about craft from teaching it.

JE: It has been my experience that not many of the people in the English department are acquainted with your work, or with anything contemporary. Do you think the department is narrow in its base?

IR: If any English department in the United States or any liberal arts department is so devoted to the experience of one people, like Anglo-Saxon enthusiasm, it should be in the ethnic studies department where all the other super-race programs go on. There should be at least one department that would be neutral and wouldn't take these chauvinistic positions.

JE: You've said that you could make this the best writing department in the country. Have you made any proposals?

IR: I did. I made proposals. But some of these things came off after Flanagan left. Flanagan was the one who had offered me the position, then he left for Ireland. In all fairness to Rader, I don't think he knew all the background on this.

JE: Aren't you typical as an artist in being rejected by academia?

IR: Some writers teach—Barth, Ellison. Some don't. Writing the kind of fiction I'm writing, you have to earn a living from different sources. You have to hustle. I'm not a millionaire novelist, though the *New West* article would make you think I lived in a palatial home. I guess they think I should be in the ghetto, you know, with my own people.

JE: There was some question as to whether the traditionalist professors were equipped to evaluate your innovative kind of work.

IR: I've had scholarly work published. They really sound silly. They raise serious questions about the conservative English department's place in American society. This is not England. We are not Europeans. My black ancestors have been here two thousand years. I don't know of any white people in this country who are really Europeans. Some white scholars like Carl Jung have noticed this. This is not Europe and it is not Africa. It is a new civilization. We've begun a new foundation called "The Before Columbus Foundation." I'm the chairman of the board. We have distinguished poets like Simon Ortiz, artist Bob Onodera, Asian writer Shawn Wong, and Bob Callahan, editor of Turtle Island *Press* as members. We are thinking of a post-provincial America, where you don't have a situation where people are trying to perpetrate the experience of one people, what is beginning to be called the monoculture. This tenure incident shows what happens when a monocultural attitude approaches a multicultural attitude. Most of the Americans I talk to are influenced by variety. It's very interesting because in some areas I'm more sophisticated than some of the people in the English department. Not only do I know Western literature, having been brought up in a quasi-Western society, but I know Afro-American literature. Now I'm being influenced by "native" American writing. This makes for richer writing. I'm into a writing culture. I see it as a cult. I'm influenced by as many cultures as possible and I think that's the way we work here in this society. So I think if we have these liberal arts departments committed to one people's music —where they don't want to play Duke Ellington—and one people's literature, then we're going through the same old stuff. I think it points up the fact that the students were demonstrating against the wrong departments, you know, science and engineering. They should've demonstrated against the liberal arts departments. They're the ones who give you the national mind . . . attitudes about culture. Even Richard Nixon had a teacher.

JE: Then you are saying that English literature as a subject is now reactionary.

IR: It's ethnic studies. They want to create a cavalier

civilized gentleman who'll go around the world bombing people in a civilized way. It's like a stewardship. Someone who will carry on the honor of Western culture, specifically English studies, English culture, and live the good life according to what they consider the good life. I think they are concerned with imparting a culture that is only peripherally concerned with literature. No one in my position, historically, has won. I study a lot about slavery because I think slavery is contemporary; the same institutions that existed in the plantation situation of the eighteenth- and nineteenth-century South exist now.

JE: Is the practicing writer the best teacher of writing?

IR: There is a big difference in a novelist teaching writing and a scholar teaching writing. I see things a scholar can never see because I write every day and have been at it for years and years.

JE: Do these controversies and incidents depress you?

IR: They used to. Not any more. You can't spend all your energies dealing with them. I can be a writer, or I can answer the Washington *Post* where Roger Rosenblatt just spent five columns attacking me. It was a critic who thinks novels by Afro-American writers should be about pain. Fuck pain. I don't think pain is all that great.

JE: Your novel *Mumbo Jumbo* seems to be your most important work as a statement of the coming multiculture. One of its plot lines is "art-napping," in which Third World individuals take their native art from the world's great museumes and repatriate it to their homelands. Would you comment a little on this concept?

IR: *Mumbo Jumbo* has come to be regarded as a manifesto. I wrote it as a novel, but it's taken seriously. Andrew Hope, a hereditary chief of the Tlingit Indians of Alaska, took it seriously and invited me up there to read for The Raven's Bones Foundation. I had recently come up with this hero, Raven Quickskill, in *Flight to Canada,* who was based more or less on a Tlingit legend—a raven myth. A friend of mine, Bob Callahan, had been up to Alaska and knew Andrew Hope. He told me Hope had all my books up there, and I said well that's really a coincidence, and I told about the raven myth I'd just used. I started corresponding with Hope, and all of the sudden these ravens started popping up at my house and he was sending me posters and books about ravens. So Callahan and I did a reading up in Alaska among the totems in the museum up there. Hope told me they were going to bring it all back, that they took this art-napping seriously, and they were going to bring their culture back. That's one of our aims of The Before Columbus Foundation to get this stuff back. We're going to make a test of this before the Soviet Embassy because the Russians, when they settled Alaska, took a lot of Tlingit Indian things back to their museums. So that's a concrete way of implementing some of these things brought up in the novel.

JE: You're going to approach the Soviets to return these things?

IR: Right, because the Tlingits are oppressed without their sacred art. They lose so much from this kind of oppression.

JE: In *Mumbo Jumbo* you seemed to be attacking the Rockefellers and their ilk for art expropriation.

IR: This is a very radical area out here, and we want to educate. We're not going to leave the Rockefellers out, but we want to show in one area—interfering with people's art and cultures, and damaging their psychologies—that certain segments of the Soviet Union and the United States are together on that issue. These are religious objects. Most of them are locked up in museums where the average person can't see them.

JE: For the most part though, it's impossible to return art objects to their original cultures. Aren't you really implying that the artist in creating new forms can repatriate that cultural experience?

IR: That's what the Tlingit Indians are doing. If you listened to the propaganda, you'd think they were a vanishing culture. They're not. They're building new totems. The point to be made is that a lot of stuff has been robbed and pilfered because of certain kinds of attitudes you get in liberal arts departments . . . this idea that everyone else is an infidel. They think there's only one culture that's civilized and all the other people are non-Christian. It comes out of Christianity. I'm sure that all these English studies come out of King Arthur, the feudalistic tradition, the Crusades. But I've never seen Europe as a monolith. That's why I don't get involved in "Black Power" confrontations. I'm a student of heretical movements. The Nazis thought of France and England as the West; so did the Russians. There are all these tribal conflicts that go back centuries. It's not a clear-cut thing. That's why I think the liberal arts institutions in this country need to be reviewed, and that's what we hope to do with The Before Columbus Foundation. We've written in our corporate papers that we hope to generate new multicultural programs. The technology seems to be further advanced than the culture. That's dangerous.

JE: At the Oakland Writer's Conference last fall, you talked about California as the site of a new, emerging culture, a multiculture. And you see quite a future for art here. Why?

IR: There are more different groups here, there's more diversity here. The East is black and white.

JE: You have said that for Californians New York represents our Europe, our Old World.

IR: It's an old world. Jason Epstein of Random House said in a meeting the other day—called to discuss the decline of New York—that publishing would be lost without New York. I don't think anything depends on one city in this country. Most likely things are going to emerge from places like Albuquerque, where there's a strong writing culture, Texas, Seattle, places like that. Washington, Oregon, and California.

JE: Do you really think these places can crack the New-York monopoly?

IR: Sure. It's just a matter of time. There are hundreds of publishers out here. They always say in New York that there's no culture out here. Then why do they pay so much attention to us?

JE: I heard that you asked all the women to leave the room at the Conference for Black Writers at Howard University. Is that true?

265

IR: That's fantasy. I have the tapes of that meeting upstairs. I am sitting here in the flesh. Living here. Going to the co-op everyday to buy groceries. Then there's this image of Ishmael Reed somewhere else doing things. It's like a doppelgänger. I hear stories like that all the time. But I keep all the documents, and lots of files. I'm interested in history. This interview is very good for me in terms of history. That woman called me up and told me that same story. It never happened.

JE: You're always talking about the gay-hippie-cowboy conspiracy in West Coast poetry. What exactly is it?

IR: It's just that when someone's cause receives recognition, they try to keep other causes down. I see that happening in Gay Liberation. I'm having a corporate war right now where I think the gay people involved are taking a reactionary role.

JE: This is within your publishing company?

IR: Yes. And I can think of several other instances where gays have taken a negative approach. I'm not against all gays. Everybody has his own idea of freedom, and I'll be the last person to disagree with that, but it seems certain people on the outs deny everyone else a piece of the action after gaining power. I've found this with gays and feminists.

JE: You've spoken of a publishing Watergate in which the big multinational corporations are buying up all the publishers, such as Fiat owning Bantam Books, and so on. You've said this is destroying the publishing of fiction. What can be done?

IR: Enforce antitrust laws, break up the conglomerates, distribute capital. I'm not against free enterprise, but I'm against these big things. I've written a poem about Pablo Neruda being iced by ITT and Nixon. People said, "You must be a Red." "No," I said, "it's because I'm against conglomerates."

JE: Your publisher, Random House, is part of a conglomerate. How have you fared with them?

IR: I don't think they did a very good job of promoting my book, *Flight to Canada*. There was only one ad, and I've got a box full of terrific reviews.

JE: Why did they underpromote you?

IR: An article came out last month in *Esquire* by Keith Mano saying that the publicity department is controlled by feminists. Extreme feminists are imitating the same institutions they are trying to replace. They practice censorship. Any black or white male writer who disagrees with them is a misogynist. They disapprove of any male who creates a character who doesn't fit into the party line.

JE: Do you mind using a big New York publisher?

IR: They can put out a hardcover book, which I can't do. They give me editorial freedom. My editor is good and she takes chances. But I think more could have been done to push my books.

JE: Much of your work would seem to be potentially good film material. Have you been approached?

IR: I'm talking to Carmen Moore, the composer, about doing *Flight to Canada* for the stage. But I've been through this before. I even went down to Hollywood to do *Yellow Back Radio*.

JE: What about *Mumbo Jumbo*?

IR: Too heady. They couldn't do it. It was written for people who like to read. Currently I'm four months behind on a screen play of my first novel, *The Free Lance Pallbearers*. It took me time to adjust to another medium. I like to do dazzling things for the reader. I'm a book man, not a film man.

JE: Still it seems to me *Mumbo Jumbo* would be a brilliant subject for a film.

IR: They don't want to work with me. They call me "difficult." They pay blacks down there peon wages. I want as much money as anyone else gets. I am interested in this stage thing.

JE: How does *Flight to Canada* size up with the rest of your work?

IR: *Flight to Canada* is the best in that it communicates more to more people. I'm working more with animals now. Since I came back from Alaska, I've been working more with totemic things. Different types of animals. I'll probably do a big children's book.

JE: Your multiculturalism is supposed to break down racial barriers, yet in *Flight to Canada* there are a number of one-dimensional whites. I see that these are satiric, but do you see any contradiction?

IR: I'm not a big man on characterization. I deal in types. I'm interested in sculpture, African, or "heathen."

JE: I'm fascinated with your crazy mixture of the nineteenth and twentieth centuries in *Flight to Canada*.

IR: That's Voodoo. I don't push that anymore because people get so hysterical when you bring up Voodoo. I'm publishing a book by the Haitian Ambassador, Louis Mars, to try to bring in an intelligent discussion of this. Voodoo is the perfect metaphor for the multiculture. Voodoo comes out of the fact that all these different tribes and cultures were brought from Africa to Haiti. All of their mythologies, knowledges, and herbal medicines, their folklores, jelled. It's an amalgamation like this country. Voodoo also teaches that past is present. When I say I use a Voodoo aesthetic I'm not just kidding around. I used to talk about that, but it's not necessary anymore.

JE: What you are actually doing is creating your own culture from past and present.

IR: I went to the University of Buffalo where I was imbued with Western culture, myth, and ideas. I admired Blake and Yeats, people who created their own systems, or revived their own national cultures. So that's what I wanted to do. When these guys call me avant-garde, I'm really only using models I learned about in English departments. I wanted to create a mythology closer to me . . . that's why I got into Egyptology and Voodoo. My experience of these things comes right out of Blake and Yeats. Now, if you look at *The Norton Anthology,* which now goes from Chaucer to me, I'm the only one in there with Egyptian references. Everyone else is into European stuff. It's much easier to work now. You should've read what they used to say when I first came out with these ideas. Now I go to Colorado and read *Mumbo Jumbo* and it's like a cult book. I think some of the most respectable people are now into this Voodoo aesthetic.

JE: In *Flight to Canada,* you make some use of *Our*

American Cousins the play Lincoln was watching when he was shot. Did you go back and read it all?

IR: Yes. It's a weird play. You know there's a subculture in American literature that never makes the institutions like old-country writing, backwoods writing, medicine shows, nineteenth-century speeches. There are tremendous writers there. When I read *Our American Cousins* I thought, this is contemporary. Someone ought to republish it or perform it. Americans don't like themselves. They don't respect their own culture. I understand that the Greek aristocrats preferred Egyptian culture. Americans have been discovered by foreigners. *Our American Cousins* sums it all up. The American goes over to visit his aristocratic British cousin. The Englishman can't understand all his slang, his being rude, drinking whiskey. The English in the play think Americans do nothing but rope elephants and wear coonskin caps. They're called savages.

JE: Critics have compared *Flight to Canada* to *Ragtime*. This seems unfair as you've been at this kind of thing longer than E. L Doctorow. Isn't he more indebted to you?

IR: I got articles from all over the country saying he'd been influenced by me.

JE: How do you feel about Carter and the so-called New South?

IR: I'm gonna wait and see. It might be the Confederacy again, or it might be populist. We've been this way before. Reconstruction in the 1870s with external reforms, and then the planters took over again. In the 1900s there was a populist agrarian movement with blacks, and that went reactionary. So this is the third time around. I don't know whether we have Jeff Davis or Huey Long. We'll soon know . . . from his appointments I can sort of see that in six months people are going to start missing Ford. We'll see.

JE: *Time* recently did a special issue on the South and grouped you with Southern writers. Did you grow up in the South?

IR: I left when I was four years old. I don't know why

Time put me in there. I don't know much about the place. But I have a lot of it in me.

JE: It would seem that most of your readers are white. Does that bother you? Blacks have not seemed interested in your work.

IR: Some identify me with their fathers who "ran away," I guess. It's cultural, but it's changing. Black students had bad leadership in the sixties. They got engaged in a narrow political view about everything. There is a lot of anti-intellectualism among immigrant and ethnic communities. The Irish and Jews went through this. Lots of blacks like my work, a lot don't. It's part anti-intellectualism and it's part politcs that can't handle art. You go to the Caribbean, and artisans are a part of society. I went to Haiti this summer. It's a different black culture. Blacks here were slaves longer than they were free . . . that's one of the problems here. I hope something is being done about it. The Haitians have their own art, statues, fabrics. They've been at it since the 1800s. As for blacks attacking my books, Philip Roth gets his problems from his own people, too. Rabbis attack him all the time.

JE: You've been very critical of Nobel Prize winner Saul Bellow.

IR: I said that in *Mr. Sammler's Planet* Saul Bellow depicts blacks in the same manner that Hitler depicted the Jews, that is as sex molesters. There's also a King Kong image. In John Toland's new Hitler biography, *Adolf Hitler* (Doubleday) he describes how the Nazis depicted ape-like Jewish males making love to Nordic women because that really excited the magazine-buying public. The same thing goes on here. It's quite obvious that King Kong is a metaphor for blacks or Asians. That's my interpretation of it.

JE: King Kong is portrayed much more sympathetically in the new version than in the 1930's version. Does that represent a changing attitude toward blacks?

IR: Well, I think King Kong is probably more civilized than some of these people teaching in the English departments. Gorillas are very fastidious, very aware of hygiene, they're vegetarians. They're all right. *Planet of the Apes* and films like it always make people nervous. It makes the same comment as gorillas—there are always racist overtones.

JE: Getting back to Bellow, I guess you're referring to the scene in *Mr. Sammler's Planet* where a black molests a Jew.

IR: Yeah, just like Hitler. These images would be all right if there were others. Certainly I don't have too-good-to-be-true blacks in my writings. I have a variety of characters.

JE: You're interested in more cultures getting media control. How did you feel about Australian tycoon Rupert Murdoch buying *New York, The Village Voice,* etc.?

IR: They deserved that. That's what Norman Mailer and all these guys, these New York existentialists, have been flirting with, violence and all these bizarre sexual things. The New York intelligentsia brought this on itself. Racism. Smut. It all became very fashionable. They made a hero out of Joey Gallo. Mafia chic. There's always somebody who is better at it than these, basically timid souls.

JE: Are you returning to the Apple Pie virtues?

IR: I'm into that. The older I get the more I see there are virtues in stability and the old-fashioned ideas of good and evil.

JE: In *Mumbo Jumbo* you deal with a conspiratorial view of the Warren Harding administration. You also have pictures of some of Nixon's people in the book. You wrote this before Watergate. Wasn't that a sort of prophecy?

IR: I think prophecy is an important part of writing, at least as important as technique or form. I think there are magical processes going on in writing. Like this raven thing. I'd been writing using the raven myth, and when I went up to Sitka in Alaska the ravens disappeared. It was very unusual. Then the day before I left they all returned and flew around the totems. It was a strange experience.

Jon Ewing
January 1977

Jon Ewing is a free lance writer who lives in Berkeley, California.

ACKNOWLEDGMENT:

Portions of this interview originally appeared in *The Daily Californian,* January 18, 1977.

JON EWING

Crushing the Mutiny

Often, political movements originate in cultural movements and so ones which threaten your humanity should be challenged in a rational way before you have to fight it out in the streets, irrationally. It's been said that I oppose reason; that's not true. What I'm against is too much reason.

Passages supporting slavery appearing in the Bible and the Koran have provided the justification for slavery, and have been quoted by slave masters all over the world.

"Black Power" might have begun from talk circulating at cocktail parties in Paris of the 1940s. Bryin Gysin wrote a book about it called *The Process.*

People tend to forget that Hitler came from Bohemia, not Main Street, and was in contact with the leading experimental artists, film makers, and writers of the day, so much so that, according to Albert Speer, a deputy, "He took his Bohemian habits to the Chancellery."

An influential political organ in the nineteen-sixties, *The New York Review of Books,* began at a party during a newspaper strike.

One hundred years ago, after black and white common people fought a war against the southern Master Race, which dreamed of a worldwide Ivanhoe type empire built upon the backs of "inferior" people, Master Race theories have again begun to rear their viperous heads like the rattlesnakes in eighteenth-century American cartoons.

Their spokesmen are people like Dr. Shockley, the Colonel Blimp of genetic theory, who, during a local program in San Francisco, had to be told that the graph he was pointing to for "evidence" was upside down.

Dr. Shockley, a Californian, is primitive with his racism; others conceal their Master Race theories in language you have to look up in the *Glossary of Literary Terms*.

Such was the case with Mr. Robert Moss in *Saturday Review*, November 15, 1975, in an article with the ambitious title of "The Arts in Black America."

Mr. Moss's first and most serious error occurred when he described Imamu Baraka as leader of a "new breed of black artists" for whom "art was chiefly useful in the cartridge belt in the coming race war."

He repeated the error when he wrote of Baraka as the "founder of a new school of black poetry." Studying the way Baraka, then LeRoi Jones, became the reluctant hand-picked "Emperor" of the "new black poetry" might reveal the literary politics operating in America today, where aesthetic brokers in their smoke-filled rooms (of not only literature, but dance, theater, and painting) use words like "quality" and "standards" the same way John Dean used the word "inoperative."

Baraka was no "founder" of a "new breed" of "black artists"; the "new breed" founded itself, and Baraka has said as much in an article he wrote for the now defunct *Diplomat* magazine. Baraka wrote, "There were others before me." His collaborator on the anthology *Black Fire*, Larry Neal, said the same thing in a Washington *Post* interview conducted by Hollis West.

Who were the others? They were David Henderson, Calvin Hernton, Lennox Raphael, Charles Patterson (whose role in conceptualizing the new black theater is never discussed, though alluded to in Harold Cruse's *The Crisis of the Negro Intellectual*), William Patterson, Steve Cannon, Tom Dent, Joe Johnson, Askia Muhammad Toure, N. H. Pritchard, boys from Chattanooga, Harlem, Brooklyn, New Orleans, and Trinidad, boys who were experimenting with black urban and rural forms before the publication of *The Dead Lecturer* and the publicity accompanying the production of *Dutchman*. Many of these writers were anthologized in Walter Lowenfels's landmark book *Poets of Today*.

Mr. Moss accuses the Afro-American avant-garde of lacking workmanship when his research is as faulty as a skyscraper whose foundation consists of toothpicks and whose architects omitted the elevators.

Why would critics, black and white, ignore these writers and deny to these writers the credit for forging one of the most influential, and independent, movements in American writing of this century?

Baraka was made founder of the "new breed" of black poetry so that Mr. Moss, and people like Richard Ellman, in *The Norton Anthology of Modern Poetry,* could say that the black poets took their techniques from "Ginsberg and Co. . . ." because of Baraka's close ties to this group. In other words, Ginsberg founded the "new black poetry." Nothing niggers never did could they do for themselves. Black English.

Allen Ginsberg, who in his "puerto-rican mugger" poem, printed in the *New York Times Magazine,* bemoaned the loss of his credit cards when we all thought that a Zen Buddhist was supposed to go from door to door begging rice for his orange bowl. Allen Ginsberg, who in his *Planet News* didn't see fit to credit Scott Joplin with the quote: "Go way, man, I can hypnotize this nation. I can shake the earth's foundation with 'The Maple Leaf Rag.' " Allen Ginsberg, whom Baraka once described as "Frank Sinatra to my Sammy Davis, Jr." Next thing you know they'll be saying that Sinatra invented tap dancing.

In his *Mein Kampf,* published in 1927, Adolf Hitler wrote: "Since the Jew—for reasons which will at once become apparent—was never in possession of a culture of his own, the foundation of his intellectual work was always provided by others."

In 1975, Mr. Robert Moss makes the same accusation against the Afro-American avant-garde when he accuses them of "furtively pilfering" from "white masters," as if Doctorow invented *Ragtime;* Al Jolson and Eddie Cantor, blacking up; and the Marx Brothers, minstrel cross fires and conundrums. Critics like Morris Dickstein and Irving

Howe have made comments similar to those made by Moss concerning the Afro-American avant-garde.

I can't vouch for the other "profiles" Mr. Moss included in his article, but mine contained major errors, the most glaring of which was a description of a group called "The Red Menace" which Mr. Moss claims appeared in my last novel, *The Last Days of Louisiana Red*, as a, lowercase, "red menace"; how can Mr. Moss cover as broad and as difficult a topic as "The Arts in Black America" when he can't even read *Time* right?

Mr. Moss says that my ideas are "silly" and that the "Afro-American" past I draw upon is "primitive" as though the cosmopolitan Greeks, who indulged in cultural exchange with Africa, meant blacks when their writers referred to a "backwoods" people who were roaming the countryside, smashing the creations of other people, because they considered them "graven images."

For Mr. Moss, my master is William Burroughs, of whom, according to Mr. Moss, I am a "devout follower"; well, at least they gave me a Wasp, fellows. When your "virtues" outweigh your "failures" maybe they'll give you one too. Something to write my mom in Buffalo about. Finally made it, Mom.

This particular fiction was begun by critics like Mr. Moss who somehow prefer to read the reviews than to go to the works. In February of 1968, in *The Nation* Ms. Sara Blackburn wrote in a review of my first novel, *The Freelance Pallbearers,* "If comparisons are to be made, they should be to Burroughs, *but this novel is all Mr. Reed's own!*" Over the years this statement has been misinterpreted by people who, unlike Ms. Blackburn, didn't read the book and so, now, in 1975, I've become known as a "devout follower" of William Burroughs.

Throughout Mr. Moss's article, Mr. Moss felt compelled to provide Afro-American artists with masters, a sophisticated version of the old inferiority arguments which used to hold that the slaves, being subhuman, couldn't possibly have invented "spirituals," the mistress in the Big House must have composed them.

William Burroughs and his collaborator Bryin Gysin

have written extensively about their use of the "cut-up" method including an essay in *The Evergreen Review*. The "cut-up" technique, not "comic surrealism," whatever that is, is what distinguishes Burroughs from other "Super-fiction" writers, as Jerome Klinkowitz has described them. I don't use the "cut-up" method, so how can I be a "de-vout follower" of William Burroughs? How can Mr. Moss trace the influences of white masters upon the Afro-American avant-garde when he seems incapable of pre-cisely identifying the techniques employed by what Mr. Moss refers to as "white masters"?

In his article, Mr. Moss included a box in which he listed the "Chronology of Black Cultural Achievement" beginning with the publication of *Poems on Various Sub-jects: Religion and Morals* by Phillis Wheatley, which Mr. Moss dates as 1775, when the book was actually published in 1773; his chronology ends with Lorriane Hansberry's *A Raisin in the Sun,* 1959.

Since then, Mr. Moss argues, most of the movies, drama, and literature written by blacks have contained the same plot. Just think of the probability of most of the movies, drama, and literature written by blacks since 1959 bearing the same plot. A slave was a slave to his master because he had no individuality. Not only is Mr. Moss's statement untrue but the plot Mr. Moss says most of us write tells us more about Mr. Moss than the subject matter this "workman" is writing about.

In his review of novelists there are so many important omissions as to render his conclusions invalid. Ignoring the work of Toni Morrison, Gayl Jones, Al Young, Kristin Hunter, William Demby, Charles Wright, Clarence Major, Cecil Brown, Ron Fair, Barry Beckham, Henry Van Dyke, Alice Walker, and Robert Boles is like writing an article called "The Arts in White America" and neglecting to mention Pynchon, Barth, Roth, Mailer, Brautigan, Bellow, Michaels, Hawkes.

In his review of painters, dramatists, musicians, the same is true. Mr. Moss's inadequate sampling of artists is similar to a man asserting that the world is flat and then pointing to the horizon as proof.

To Mr. Moss, the Afro-American avant-garde indulges in "polemics" and are "parochial," the same kind of charge Philip Roth leveled against Jewish writers in his article "Imagining Jews," published in *The New York Review of Books,* in which he accused prominent Jewish novelists of making all of the villains in their novels goyim. "Polemics" in the literary world that Richard Kostelanetz writes about usually means that you don't agree with the point of view expressed by the narrative or by some of the characters.

At the end of his article, Mr. Moss submitted some recommendations to the Afro-American avant-garde—recommendations which sound like high-handed scolding. Since we haven't produced a "Hindemith" (whose *Kammermusik No. 1* and *Suite for Piano* include movements called "Ragtime," and "Shimmy"), and since we've made no cultural achievement since 1959, Mr. Moss recommends a "rigorous workmanlike dedication be valued over emotionalism, and self-indulgence." After the poor scholarship and hysteria contained in Mr. Moss's article this sounds like Martha Raye telling everybody to calm down.

Sneak attacks such as these have come from white liberal critics against Afro-American culture before but none as blatant and as strident as Mr. Moss's. But with his stridency Mr. Moss may have done Afro-American culture a favor. By his unpleasant tone, and his errors, Mr. Moss might have just revealed to fair-minded observers the kind of aesthetic bigotry Afro-American artists have been up against all these years which now, like Captain Queeg in the *Caine Mutiny,* snaps pencils, bites its fingernails, cracks its knuckles, and begins to stutter under the baleful stare of the prosecutor.

I say this because the strongest protests I've heard so far about this article have been from whites. This shouldn't come as a surprise, either. While blacks and whites have been wrangling over the legitimacy of ethnic studies, a whole generation of black and white students has become acquainted with Afro-American culture. Even if all of the black studies programs are eliminated, their impact upon American culture will remain unshaken.

Admittedly, some of them were of dubious value and corrupted by those who wished to turn them into street corner rallies, or sensitivity sessions, as often happens in something as "unscientific" as liberal studies, black or white, but many are solidly conceived and taught by first-rate scholars using first-rate materials. Whites were there learning and growing along with the rest; indeed, those Afro-American instructors who aren't timid will tell you that some of the best work came from whites, the blacks, often, feeling that being black was enough and that a black professor ought to give a truant black student an "A" because "you gave that honkie one."

I remember a scene at a party given me by Jeff Richards of *The Carolina Quarterly* at Chapel Hill, North Carolina, where a young white student who looked like Stonewall Jackson began reciting passages from Jean Toomer's *Cane,* from memory. Another white student, during the same visit, supplied me with a couple of fugitive slave narratives I didn't own; their passages were well used and key passages underlined. Other instructors and writers can tell you of the dedication and earnestness white students and a new breed of white critics have brought to Afro-American literature.

It's only right and fair, because what clearer sign of an Afro-American willingness to communicate than the fact that we've grown up exposed to the great achievements of European-American civilization, so much so that many of us know more about them and can appreciate them more than European-Americans. The first black Prix de Rome, Phillip Wooby, translated Lucretius at the age of nineteen at Harvard. How's that for devotion?

A new generation of whites is meeting us halfway, learning about the great achievements of our cultures, and even though incorrigible cultural Whigs like William Buckley still say that Bach's worth more than all of the black studies programs in the world, this development may be more far-reaching towards the goal of racial understanding than anything in this century. And it came through cultural revolution, the way most profound revolutions occur; a man enters the city on the back of an ass; his autobiography becomes the Empire's bestseller.

The most touching example I've seen of the new trend is a project called *The Diary of an Escaped Slave,* a handmade book with table of contents and bibliography by Lisa Herbert, Carolyn Samiere, and Brita Dorst, three sixteen-year-olds, two white and one black, who are juniors at San Francisco's Convent of the Sacred Heart High School. It's the fictional account of a character they've named "Ruth Gibson" and her escape from slavery.

Shortly after the *Saturday Review* article appeared I received a letter from Paul Desruisseaux, an editor of *The California Monthly,* an alumni magazine of the University of California. Mr. Desruisseaux is certainly no fire-bomber and he wrote: Mr. Moss ". . . didn't read far enough." Another white writer, Paul Buhle, editor of *Cultural Correspondence,* had written a rebuttal to Mr. Moss's article in his forthcoming book, *The Recognition of American Darkness,* almost as soon as the *Saturday Review* reached the streets. Young Ray Riegert, a reporter for the *Berkeley Barb,* wrote: "Moss's work names good reading as a study in cultural stupidity and has occasioned an outcry from both white and third world community." Greil Marcus, a critic for the *Rolling Stone,* and the *Village Voice,* referred to the article as "a disgrace."

And former *City* magazine critic, Bob Fox, wrote: ". . . I was so worked up over the thing that I sat down to write a scathing letter to the editor, then realized that I was boiling over to the extent that I couldn't confine myself to only a few choice diatribes—I wound up with a 20 page critical reply, entitled 'The Logic of the White Castle: Western Critical Standards and the Dilemma of Black Art.' "

Regal Kay Boyle made all of us appear conservative when, commenting on the interest in third world writing among her white students, she said, "White writing is dead," shocking a San Francisco June meeting of the Coordinating Council of Literary Magazines. I don't think the two events are related, but now the CCLM, founded by William Phillips of the *Partisan Review,* has Native Americans, Chicanos, blacks, and Asian-Americans on its boards and in its membership, which, in my mind, makes it an organization exemplary of the peaceful cultural and political change possible in the Unites States.

This year's National Poetry Festival held at Thomas Jefferson College in Allendale, Michigan, included an Afro-American, Asian-American and Native American contingent, a fact which went unnoticed by American cultural media which seem bent upon remaining "provincial," and out of touch, like the recent issue of *Commentary* which viewed the new American fiction as all white, and Ms. Helen Vendler, the closet book-burner from Boston, warning in the New York *Times* about the dire consequences of American children reading literature by Native Americans and Afro-Americans. And they call us "ethnic," and "ghettoized." They, who scold politicians, yet cover up just as politicians do. *Saturday Review* hasn't, of this date, seen fit to print any of the avalanche of letters I know they've received from those protesting their latest venture into cultural racism. The same magazine which gave us "The Myth of Negro Literature," and described Al Young's book *Snakes* as "Uncle Tom" because it didn't sound like Eldridge Cleaver.

These pleas from the Vendlers, and from *Saturday Review,* come too late.

Third World cultures, who are in reality First World, will eventually take their place in the American cultural establishment, and Mr. Moss's article will then appear as quaint as the arguments opposing the steam engine, and Charlie Parker.

Afro-American culture has always been the establishment, though only white Ragtimers have benefited from the profits. As the establishment we say to white intellectuals and artists the same thing a former establishment used to say to us: Raise your voices of "moderation" and "responsibility" against the "extremists" in your midst, especially those among you who in a former despicable period saw the works of your people gutted and your "ethnic studies"—your cultures—expelled from the German universities, and your geniuses hastened into exile.

As for those of us they call "crazy" because we find that to be normal in a slave master's society is to be a slave, we will learn from our brave Jewish friends; we will hunt and expose the cultural Nazis and their black Vichy regime, the desecrators of our arts, relentlessly, whether they nestle in Rutgers University in New Brunswick, New Jersey, or keep their ratholes within the column inches of the *Saturday Review*. We are humanists and we are for mankind. We view an attack upon our people's cultures and expressions of beauty as an attack upon all peoples' cultures and expressions of beauty. Millions upon millions of Third World people, many times the numbers killed by Hitler's Germany, have suffered and have died because of Master Race theories. We also say: Never again.

Yardbird V
1976

You Can't Be a Literary
Magazine and Hate Writers

We made it to *Yardbird* V, and our brains didn't "bust" like they said they would.

As in most things, you don't know how hard it is to put out a magazine until you've tried. That's why we are unhappy to learn that *Black World*, the country's largest literary magazine, has ceased publication. *Black World*, edited by Hoyt Fuller, was a model of efficient operation. Mr. Fuller was among the first to acknowledge the explosion of poetry by Afro-Americans, in the 1960s. His magazine served as a bulletin board for an international community of writers.

It seemed, however, the more Mr. Fuller began to devote his time to organizing a literary festival in Nigeria, *Black World* came under the influence of a local Royal Family replete with Queen Mother and Jr. Prince.

Black World's managing editor dutifully chastised those writers Jr. Prince disapproved of, and rewarded those he liked. His likes and dislikes were fickle, mostly concerning matters other than the literary merit of the writers under question.

The Royal Family, which swore up and down about its devotion to freedom, liberation—its love for black people —maintained a literary enemies list.

During *Black World*'s last strident year there was much talk in its pages about "fools," "traitors," and "enemies." Scream! Now I understand what was meant. Dynamite tantrums like Jr. Prince's remarkable and disturbing piece in *Black World*'s March 1976 issue, a kind of graffito

"Checkers" speech, which accused blacks of "a low level of original thinking," placing Jr. Prince to the right of the late Senator George Murphy, a tap dancer from California. Yet they're always calling us "reactionaries" and "right-wingers."

We were wondering how Mr. Fuller, usually a fair editor, would permit these frenzied attacks on Afro-American writers.

When the managing editor wasn't subjecting them to witless acerbic signifying, she handed their books over to convoluted "Victorian" black academics who dismissed them with a couple of remarks and sneers or would print gossip about them—not even quality gossip but old mangy grungy smut which would make the *National Enquirer* seem dignified.

Hoyt Fuller once suggested that if a "brother" mugs you you shouldn't punish the "brother" but give him an image to go by. He was answering Chicago "middle class" blacks for advocating strong measures against criminals who rob millions of dollars from Third World communities every year.

Fuller's is a quaint Christian notion, no matter how stylish its ideological front, which most Afro-Americans would rightly regard as dopey. The way to stop a mugger is to mug back. Houston Baker, Jr., a slithering critical mugger, based an entire review of my book *The Last Days of Louisiana Red* upon where he thought I lived in Berkeley. Not only was the review illiterate, but he was too lazy even to check the telephone directory.

I tried to make a citizen's arrest on this mugging review, sending three letters to *Black World*.

Mr. Fuller replied that he didn't have room to print my reply to his critic's slander of my book! In other words, *Black World* could stomp you any time they wished or say that you were in "conspiracy" to "suppress the black revolution," or that you were responsible for getting Marcus Garvey deported, or that you shot Jesse James in the back and you had no recourse to set the matter right!

John A. Williams said he was "sandbagged" by *Black World* because John A. Williams is a gentleman who likes his old-fashioned just right. "Sandbagging" isn't anything new at Johnson Publishing. Richard Wright was "sandbagged." Ralph Ellison, James McPherson, Robert Boles, Al Young have been taunted. Ernest Gaines relentlessly excoriated. Amiri Baraka libeled.

The star *Black World* critic ended a book suggesting that those who didn't agree with his arguments should be done in by "machine gunners." A bloodthirsty town, Chicago.

A man can't even have ribs and links without being called a "decadent." (Decadent? How come it's the puritans who're always machine-gunning people?)

Addison Gayle said there was too much "hedonism" going on. (Here comes the Witchfinder General, hide the carrot juice!) *Black World* thought it was a simple matter of white faces being white racists. It should be so easy. Like Pogo said: "We have met the enemy and they are us." Pogo should be mayor of Chicago.

Like they jumped on Robert Moss, "a white racist," but let Clyde Taylor slide. Moss said black writers hadn't matured since 1959. Taylor said it hadn't matured since the 1920s! Which one is the "white racist"? Do "white racists" come in "white faces"? The fallacy of literal-mindedness as someone said.

John A. Williams said they "sandbagged." Baraka accuses them of inconsistency. After reading O. O. Gabugah you feel maybe it's a good idea that *Black World* quit. I mean, when the parody is better than the original a mutation occurs which renders the original obsolete. Reed's Law. Then you think of all of the good things that Mr. Fuller, a former model, tried to do. From this we may derive a lesson. You can't be a literary magazine and hate writers!! It's kind of like what I think Nathan Hare is saying. Sure, there's a lot of slavery outside, but there's a lot of slavery in us, too!! Seems that we would have had enough slavery for us to go through another four hundred years of slavery, or has slavery gotten good to us?

Yardbird V
1976

The Children of Ham

In case you haven't heard, scag is another name for heroin. Substitute the word devil for scag and *The Children of Ham* (Stein & Day), Claude Brown's new book, becomes a medieval mystery in which scag had supernatural power over people. They come under its influence because of bad homes, society, and one fellow says he became addicted because he was from the country instead of the city.

A few years ago, a burglary ring of clever Miami teenagers was ready with all of the sociological jargon concerning the responsibility for their actions when they were captured. That jargon is in this book of narratives by anti-junkies who've formed a "family" and live together in "spots" (apartments) of abandoned Harlem buildings.

No one seems to have ever been drawn to scag, "a monster," because it made them feel good and powerful, and gave the kind of confidence which led them to steal, and indulge in other risky adventures.

Scag is a turn-on for those who can't afford to import a California swami. The book goes on like that, all about scag and the evil it makes people do.

The children of Ham don't use it and hold views about junkies which lend credibility to a recent New York *Times* article reporting a shift in attitudes among blacks regarding black criminals. One Hamite, Herbo, proposes a Judgment Day for junkies. "You have countdown signs every day, just like the newspapers show for Christmas that you got twenty-one more shoppin' days to Christmas." If this doesn't deter addicts, Herbo proposes that when Judgment

Day arrives prisoners, armed with baseball bats, be encouraged to commit mayhem upon the incorrigible junkies. Each prisoner would have a kill quota.

When I met Claude Brown at Notre Dame, I expected to meet Mr. Ghetto coming at me like a swaggering ostrich handing out all kinds of jive, you dig? Instead, I found someone who talked like the host for "Masterpiece Theatre," and who ordered in French. The author of *Manchild in the Promised Land* had gone to etiquette school. "You're the first black Wasp, Claude," I remarked.

Occasionally, the black Wasp comes through in lines like: "The old feisty dowager surely would have expired sooner had she not been too concerned about her family to relinquish life, despite the agony of its extension."

Claude Brown means well. His conclusion is that if you care for each other as the children of Ham care for each other you won't need heroin. *All you need is love!*

I wonder how the mothers and fathers of those suburban junkies who've received more care and love than any generation in history with the exception, perhaps, of some child emperors, would say about that. All you need is love. Claude means it.

But even Claude Brown can't breathe life into an image like "the rats were as big as cats." Claude had returned to his old stomping grounds, only this time he's a tourist. His predictable glossary, "cops . . . blow . . . dudes," are from an old rock record which provides background music at a suburban bar-b-cue. From time to time the tourist abandons his subjects and addresses the liberal audience this book is intended for: "The common tragedy among these youngsters is that by the time they reach the age of nineteen or twenty they are thoroughly and irreversibly demoralized."

I wanted to say, they know that already, Claude. They've been told that for twenty years through reports, fiction, non-fiction, poetry, motion pictures, documentaries, etc. Through every conceivable media and from every point of view, yet the heroin problem is worse, claiming four hundred thousand victims. There are more white addicts than black and the addict population of Los Angeles exceeds that of New York.

The liberal of ten years ago is now indifferent to these problems and with a new phony Zen Buddhism entering national politics indifference will now seem aesthetic. The liberal can't do anything about his own addicts much less about the condition of an addict in Harlem. Heroin is big business, and in the present United States big business is above the law and often owns it.

In the midst of Mr. Brown's eloquent, futile pleas, and interesting, often poetical, testifying from his subjects concerning politics (colorful), and their values (flashy cars and clothes), there's a considerable amount of homosexual rape, lesbianism, thievery, murder, and whoring, and shooting gallery material.

Mr. Brown meant for his book to be an earnest illustrated sermon directed at arousing the American conscience, but the book will be read as a peep show.

For four hundred years Americans have made entertainment from blacks squirming, biting each other's ears off, roasting, and hanging. Crowds used to witness these affairs in a picnic atmosphere. Placing blacks in lurid situations, despising them, dehumanizing them, has always been a national sport.

The standard hack busing speech is probably descended from the barker's pitch in some hideous ancient American medicine show.

Claude Brown had the best intentions, and some of the children of Ham might be touched by the magic wand of publicity and rescued from their plight. But for every bright and ambitious Hamite there are thousands who won't be rescued. The book will be liked for the wrong reasons. A peep show under the guise of sociology, just as Public Television's shoddy "Harlem Voices" was presented under the guise of freedom of information, or freedom of the right to know, etc. Of course, if the media were so interested in the public's right to know, they'd show the whole range of black life as they do with white life; from the Bowery to the White House. Only the Bowery parts of black life are portrayed.

The author of *The Children of Ham* meant for the book to be about some extraordinary people of ambivalent morality who transcended the situation in which they were thrust. But the book will become popular because of the Bowery parts. Claude Brown is best at writing about himself in the first person. That book will be a classic and it will be post-Harlem.

You can't go home again.

Washington *Post*
April 11, 1976

The Multi-Cultural Artist: A New Phase in American Writing

In recent years, far-reaching and profound changes have occurred in American writing—changes which have, for the most part, been ignored by the American Writing Establishment.

No longer is American writing a country club for eastern white men over forty, but more and more is likely to be done by men and women of different regions, classes, and ethnic groups. (According to Webster's Dictionary, "ethnic" means "heathen.")

As the larger publishers abandon fiction and poetry as unprofitable their duties have been taken over by an expanding small press movement which has discovered that you don't have to sell over 10,000 hardcover copies of a book to stay in the black.

New York, long the capital of American writing, has been supplanted by Regional Writing with centers in cities like Chapel Hill, Austin, Grand Forks, Seattle, Albuquerque, Des Moines, Berkeley, San Francisco, and Boulder, Colorado.

Richard Kostelanetz, in his *The End of Intelligent Writing*, caused an uproar in American writing circles when he charged that middlemen were preventing "intelligent" writing from reaching "intelligent" readers. Kostelanetz named leading American critics, editors, and publishers in his indictment.

Among his list of neglected writers, Kostelanetz included those who have been called "multi-cultural" writers or

"Third World" writers although some who've been listed as belonging to these groups would rather be judged on the basis of individual talent.

These are American writers of Asian, African, Latino, or Hispanic descent who were either born in America, or whose families have dwelled in the United States for many generations.

The fervor created by these writers reminds one of the excitement surrounding what has become known as the "Second Renaissance," a term used to describe the resurgence of Afro-American writing which began in the early sixties, and which now constitutes a segment of the American Writing Establishment—some of its key members have been nominated for National Book Awards and have had other symbols of national recognition bestowed upon them.

Nikki Giovanni, a leading poet of Dudley Randall's Black Broadside writers, appeared on CBS television to accept an award from the daughter of the United States President she'd ridiculed in her early militant poetry: "President Johnson, your unfriendly uncandidate, has declared war on Black people."

Some of the multi-cultural writers have been inspired by Amiri Baraka, Sonia Sanchez, Ms. Giovanni, and Haki Madubuti (formerly, Don L. Lee). In the words of Alberta Alurista, a young Chicano poet, "We preferred to write in the language of the slave and not that of the slavemaster."

Through racist literary criticism, Walt Whitman has been characterized as the first American poet. New evidence indicates that Whitman was influenced by Native American poets just as were the American transcendentalists of the nineteenth century.

Up to now, translations of the Native American oral literature was left to anthropologists and tourists; a new generation of Native American writers has changed all that. Prominent among them are James Welch, Leslie Silko, Roberta Hill, Simon Ortiz, and Phil George.

The Chicano writers, Americans of Mexican descent, are engaged in writing actively in the Southwest and California. Chicano writers Rodolfo "Corky" Gonzales, Kris Gutierrez, Jesus Luna, Arturo Rodriguez, and Rudolfo Anaya, recently participated in a panel discussion during a meeting of the Coordinating Council of Literary Magazines, held at Boulder, Colorado. The discussion, chaired by Anaya, dealt with the typical question confronting "multi-cultural" writers: Whether the writer should be politically engaged. "Positive literature" was the phase which dominated the discussion.

Although ignored by the mainly eastern, and white reviewing media, Anaya's novel *Bless Me, Ultima* is viewed as a classic of Chicano literature.

Puerto Rican-American writers are centered in New York City, and some of them were anthologized in *Nuyorican Poetry,* edited by Miguel Algarin and Miguel Piñero, published by William Morrow Paperback.

In his middle twenties, Victor Cruz, who resides in San Francisco and New York, is the elder of the Puerto Rican-American poetry movement; two of his books, *Mainland* and *Snaps,* were published by Random House and a third book of poetry, *Tropicalization,* will be published by Reed, Cannon & Johnson Co.

Another group neglected by the American Writing Establishment are the Asian-Americans, descendants of the Chinese who came to the West to build the railroads. They are mainly based in San Francisco and are producing novels, poetry, plays, television shows, and oral histories of Asian-America.

Frank Chin, Lawson Inada, Jessica Hagedorn, Cyn Zarco, Shawn Wong, and Mei Mei Berssenbrugge are leading writers of this group.

Mr. Chin's *Chickencoop Chinaman* was the first play written by an American born Chinese to be produced in the New York theater. Mr. Chin, Shawn Wong, and Lawson Inada are engaged in a project to reprint *No No Boy,* a novel by the late John Okada, a Japanese-American writer whose wife burned his papers in a fit of grief when the University of California at Los Angeles refused to accept them.

Some of the individuals within these groups are influenced by each other, producing a new and fresh American writing and language, and an exchange of forms and techniques. Multi-cultural poetry might even relax and warm the typical brittle, austere, clinical proselike line of so much of standard American poetry people in the United States and other countries cite when they refer to American poetry.

This is not the fault of the domestic and foreign reader; multicultural writing doesn't get published that much and when it does it's not reviewed, thus depriving not only foreign readers but readers in the United States of an intelligent view of the tremendous range of writing now being produced in this country.

Le Monde
June 11, 1976

Harlem Renaissance Day

The following is based upon a speech delivered on May 4, 1976, at Washington Irving High School. The occasion was the sixth anniversary awards day of the New York City High School Poetry Contest. At the conclusion of the speech I read some poetry by Claude McKay, Langston Hughes, and Countee Cullen. The selections were greeted with applause and warm enthusiasm from the audience of high school writers, their parents, and teachers. Afterwards, students who weren't familiar with the writers came up and requested a reading list. Later that day, I participated in the "American Retrospectives" reading sponsored by the Academy of American Poets, and held at the Donnell Library Center. I was joined by Quincy Troupe, the poet, and anthologist of Giant Talk, a compilation of Third World writing. I read the same selections; Mr. Troupe read works by James Weldon Johnson, Helene Johnson, Jean Toomer, and Sterling Brown. Again, the audience, this time mostly adults, was extremely receptive to the poets' works. You might call it the first annual Harlem Renaissance Day.

As a tribute to the Afro-American influence on the arts of the 1920s, this period has come down to us known as "The Jazz Age."

The whole country seems to have been swept away by a black tidal wave of art.

George S. Schuyler, that irrepressible wit, in his essay "Our Greatest Gift to America," observed of the period, "It has become not unusual, in the past few years, for the Tired Society Women's Club of Koekuk, Iowa, or the Delicatessen Proprietors' Chamber of Commerce, or the Hot Dog Vendors' Social Club to have literary Afternoons devoted, exclusively, to the subject of the lowly smoke." He was speaking of an important literary appendage to "The Jazz Age," a "movement" of writers known as the Harlem Renaissance.

It was called the Harlem Renaissance because Harlem was where the action was. Some of the writers belonging to the Harlem Renaissance didn't even live in Harlem. That didn't matter. Harlem became the symbol for the international black city. It was home of "The New Negro" (Uncle Tom and Sambo have passed on . . .) from a title of a book, compiled by Alain Locke, the brilliant Harlem Renaissance philosopher.

Harlem was where Madame Walker, the cosmetics queen, and other patrons threw parties, and where the cabarets were. It was the scene of considerable political activity. A young congressman named Adam Clayton Powell, Jr., was leading boycotts against Harlem merchants.

Shuffle Along, Running Wild, and the Charleston got the Harlem Renaissance going, according to Langston Hughes. He described "Shuffle Along," starring Florence Mills, as "swift, bright, funny, rollicking, and gay." That's how the period was. They did things in a grand way. When Florence Mills died, suddenly, in 1927, a flock of bluebirds was released above the funeral procession.

I still remember Langston Hughes, witty, such enormous sophistication behind that cigarette holder, inviting me for a drink at Max's Kansas City. He encouraged young writers even though, shortly before his death, he told Arlene Frances, on a radio show, that we were all downtown writing poems even we didn't understand. That was Langston Hughes, who wrote all day, breaking only for cocktails and dinner. The walls of his Harlem town house were covered with Afro-American cultural memorabilia, particularly from the Harlem Renaissance.

Rudolph Fisher, Claude McKay, Langston Hughes, and Wallace Thurman weren't slouches; you can't look at their work without being impressed with their outstanding writing skills.

With the Depression, the Renaissance came to an end, critics say. The whites stopped going uptown. The speakeasies closed; the publishers were no longer interested in books written by "New Negroes."

Recently, the Harlem Renaissance has come under fire. Some say the writers weren't militant enough. That they were writing for white people. That they drank too much gin. Wallace Thurman was a novelist, playwright, screenwriter, editor, and publisher of a magazine called *Fire*, but some contemporary critics seem only interested in the quantity of gin he drank. There was that extraordinary statement printed in *Black World*, formerly the country's largest literary magazine, and the organ of Black Aesthetic criticism, which said that the Harlem Renaissance was part of a conspiracy to divert attention from the more militant figures of the time.

In other words, every time Cullen, McKay, and Hughes wrote a poem they thought, "How can I make this poem divert attention from the more militant spokesmen of these times?"

Some sullen, humorless critics of the Black Aesthetic movement seem to have long since abandoned rational argument and take their lead from Addison Gayle, Jr., who at the conclusion of his careless new book, *The Way of the New World*, recommends the machine-gunning of those who disagree with him, surely a sign of intellectual insecurity.

A literary Banana Republic approach to things by those who've forgotten that the mainstream aspiration of Afro-America is for more freedom, and not slavery—including freedom of artistic expression.

Perhaps the civil rights movement lost its steam because people noticed that blacks weren't practicing civil rights among themselves. Apostles of the Black Aesthetic held "writers' conferences," which served as tribunals where those writers who didn't hew the line were ridiculed, scorned, mocked, and threatened. The ringleader, Addison Gayle, Jr., a professor at Bernard Baruch College, argues that the aim of black writing should be to make "black men feel better," as if we didn't have enough Disneylands.

Others, usually critics safely tenured at heavily endowed colleges, have charged the Renaissance writers with having patrons, as though a patron wrote something as beautiful and as meaningful as Hughes's *The Negro Speaks of Rivers*.

Hughes, Cullen, McKay, Thurman, and the others aren't here to defend themselves, but I'm sure that they would agree: That just as with airline pilots, teachers, students, advertising men, actors, carpenters, editors, publishers, and cat burglars you judge workers by the quality of their work, not by how much gin they drink, or how many men or women they kiss, or who their friends are, or which parties they attend, or whether they've successfully created a plan to end the world's evils, or have prevented the universe from collapsing.

With that in mind I'd like to share with you a selection of poetry by Langston Hughes, Claude McKay, and Countee Cullen, members of the Harlem Renaissance, one of the classiest, noblest, artiest, brightest, most terrifically spiflicated, smartest, shook-up, and elegant moments of our Century.

New York *Times*
August 29, 1976

I Hear You, Doc

Shortly before his death, Dr. François Duvalier, the late Haitian President, appeared on United States' television. In answer to the question "Why do you receive such a bad press in the United States?" Duvalier responded, with an owlish glint in his scholarly eyes, "They're afraid of twenty million blacks wanting to know what I know." During those last days, his enemies reported him to be acting "erratically" and imagining himself to be in communication with dead Haitian heroes, Toussaint L' Ouverture, Henri Christophe, and Dessalines. There was the photo, finally, of a dying Duvalier resting his hands on his seated son's shoulders, the traditional pose of the Houngan choosing his successor.

A mile from his entombment, the women broke into "inexplicable panic," according to the New York *Times*. I was reminded of the time Vodoun drummer Marcus Gordon had finished a concert during which a woman convulsed and fainted. He smiled and said, "One of them came down." The spirit had hit her like a born again Christian.

Jean-Claude Duvalier, the heir and son, speaks in terms of Antenna Systems, Terrestrial Microwave Links, Coaxial Cable Systems. He's into telecommunications, which is what Vodoun has always been about. The central figure in the Vodoun spirit altar is Legba, who has to be "fed" first; Legba is the spirit of the "Crossroads" and the medium between two worlds. The "inexplicable panic" the *Times* referred to was possession, the phenomenon, scientifically verified, in which a host becomes a human radio for cosmic forces. There's little room for the "unknown" in the vocabulary of a "pragmatic" society, but in Haiti articles concerning telecommunications and Vodoun are only a few columns apart on the *front page!*

I saw Duvalier's resting place. Duvalier has received the rare tribute of becoming a loa; his photo is placed alongside the other loas at Vodoun observances. The monument consists of conical shapes, resting on a flat geometric concrete surface, lying at what appears to be the four cardinal points. It could be a modern abstract interpretation of the Houngan's temple, the *humfo,* with its circles, straight lines, and triangles.

Vodoun is always contemporary. It's appropriate that his tomb be an abstract rendering of a *humfo.* They called him Papa because he was number one Houngan. His favorite number was twenty-two. It appeared on the license plates of his black Mercedes limousine, which used to roll through the gates of the National Palace, the shape of his slight figure in the back passing out bills, with his photo on them, to the peasants. As a young man, he belonged to a cultural circle which produced the magazine *Les Griots,* whose aim, according to a youthful manifesto, was to "put back in honor the *assortor* and the *asson,"* the drum and the gourd of the Vodoun observance. The Catholic Church couldn't figure out whether the young intellectuals were studying Vodoun scientifically, as they claimed, or *practicing* it.

I had heard so many horror stories about Haiti, that before I left I made out a will. From the Miami airport on Friday, I told Dancer, "Now I begin my descent into hell." After five days of intensive traveling alongside the coast and into the mountains, of speaking with artists, hustlers, scholars, and peasants, I came home with a hint of what Duvalier was talking about.

There's a big difference between the national psychology of a people who've been independent since 1804, and that of North American blacks who've been slaves longer than they've been free. There's more confidence. There don't seem to be the miserable self-destructive tendencies which occur in a society where there are few statues of your heroes downtown, and where Duke Ellington wasn't deemed good enough to receive a Pulitzer.

The difference in attitude is a difference in aesthetic freedom. I mean, you don't see blacks up and down southern highways selling statues of African gods, do you?—well, the exception might be Oba Oseijeman in North Carolina. The "objective correlatives" of the Haitian African psychology are visible in everyday life, while here, where suppression of Afro-American cultures has been mean, they are invisible and abstract: jazz.

I remember sitting on the steps of the National Institute of Arts and Letters on West 155th Street after a literary ceremony in which I received an award for my fourth novel. I was talking to a famous liberal intellectual and his son. And when I asked why someone like Miles Davis didn't receive an award, I heard the kind of answer that Hitler might have given had someone asked his opinion of Schoenberg's twelve-tone system. (Even though Schoenberg said he was trying to create a "New German Music.") And these were intellectuals who marched against the war. Who is worse? An all-white American Arts establishment, which does not consider the arts of Afro-Americans art? Or Richard Nixon, who invited Duke Ellington and Lionel Hampton to the White House?

And so, in Haiti, the people are not searching for identity; they know who they are. The strength of their culture is not demeaned.

In downtown Port-au-Prince, there is a statue called "Le Marron Inconnu." It shows a peasant naked except for some skimpy cloth about his waist. He is blowing a conch shell, head lifted toward the sky, another Vodoun position. In his right fist he holds a machete.

Boukman, the Houngan, was supposed to have made just such a gesture the night of August 14, 1791, when a secret society met at a place called Alligator Woods. Afterwards, he sacrificed a black boar. It was the beginning of the struggle against the Europeans which would lead to independence. This scene is frequently seen in the art, both common and high, of Haiti. Even on the murals of the Episcopalian Church, but cropped out of postcards sold in the church's gift shop.

Maybe the reason the Haitians became free before North American blacks is because their work tool was also a weapon of war. We were picking cotton with our bare hands.

The machetes and rifles are everywhere. The kind of civilian military force you used to see in the Lower East Side in the 1960s, is conspicuous. There's hardly any crime in Haiti. I left a Toyota with goods inside, unlocked, all over Port-au-Prince. Poverty doesn't seem to compel people to commit crime there. It is said that the government has put out a contract on felons. But there are low crime rates in African countries, too.

American journalists who spend their time at the bar at Habitation Leclerc (named for Napoleon's brother-in-law), where for $250.00 per night you can get a double room, often refer to the Haitians as "paranoid." They describe Haitian religious and cultural leaders as "witch doctors," in such usually sober and intelligent magazines as *Harper's*.

I think this comes under Laing's "Politics of Experience." Having been threatened, even invaded, by a number of groups, including the Mafia, the CIA, the right, Santo Domingo, and the left, Cuba (black independence is often opposed by both the right and left!), perhaps the Haitians feel they have every right to be on guard.

Before I left, a black feminist poet warned me about traveling to Haiti. "They're killing black Americans down there." Apparently, some of those involved in the CIA excursions were black Americans. A few days before I left, there appeared, in the San Francisco *Chronicle,* an article about "Haitian government crack-down on dissent." People also speak of "repression" and "dictatorship" when referring to Haiti, as if United States' allies were led by school crossing guards, or leaders of the community sing.

Americans see Haiti as a pretty grisly place. Herb Gold, the novelist, said something about Haitians selling cadavers to North American doctors for money. I wonder, do they use forms similar to the ones poor people sign in America for "experimentation"?

I had read a lot about the "distended bellies," and the "ribs showing," but if I wanted to see poverty all I had to do was remain in my office in one of Berkeley's slums. In the United States, forty million people don't get enough to eat. If the richest, most powerful country, second to none, as Texans brag, with all of its wealth and resources can't feed almost a fourth of its population, does one expect a country which has little, whose soil can't grow much, to feed its citizens adequately? The Haitians are poor, but make ingenious use of what they have. One of the most amazing institutions I witnessed was the Iron Market, the economy's lifeblood, where recycling is the most important aspect of the economy.

They talk about Haitian illiteracy, when at a major university located in California, 60 per cent of the entering freshmen must take remedial or "bonehead" English.

I spent the last evening, Friday, at Miami's Aztecan Hotel, which reminded me of the Lower East Side's Second Avenue, if it had a view of the Atlantic. The next morning, when I ordered bagels, lox, and sturgeon for breakfast, the waitress smiled and the cashier struck up a conversation. We tried to place each other's "talk." She was from the Bronx.

Going to Haiti had always been an ambition of mine. In 1969, I was listed among the secretariat on the letterhead of AFNA (American Association of the Festival of the New World), which was headed by Dr. Robert Pritchard, a concert pianist, who was recently ejected from the Klan meeting he was attempting to cover for a magazine. It was carried by the networks.

We held a conference in Buffalo, New York, which was marred by the bahavior of an ambitious "spade" poet who yearns so much for attention that he's not above accusing his colleagues of criminal acts in books of "literary criticism." He once killed an article a major magazine was going to do on my work, by going to the naïve liberal editor and telling him that since they had already covered him, and since he and I were in the "same school," they didn't need to cover me. He even went to the writer and ridiculed the article. Liberals love being abused by this character, so they've given him generous grant money for a magazine that hasn't been published in years. He was an opportunist who wanted a bigger role and so he set out to wreck the conference.

He spread the rumor that we were a CIA front, and caused dissension among the conferees, struggling American and Haitian artists, who had been asked to pay their own way, by suggesting that for some others, who were "stars," the conference was picking up the tab. During the sessions, he sat to the rear of the auditorium drinking from a wine bottle and making offensive comments. When, at the end of the conference, we made plans to travel to Haiti, the word got around that we were attempting to begin a "voodoo cult" in North America. I was threatened in Pee Wee's bar, on Avenue A near Twelfth Street. "Someone like you ought to be dead," the man said. I went home and burned his name. When I saw him again, he begged: "Take it off me! Take it off me!" My first and last textbook attempt at "black magic."

Behind this, I dropped out of the organizing thing, and traveled to California to live, permanently. I had been dividing the year between California and New York. I spent three years in a kind of exile, in an apartment of a gothic house of stone, often sulking in its Zen garden with bridge and waterfall. It was here that I wrote my second novel, *Mumbo Jumbo,* which involved a considerable amount of research on Haitian history, Vodoun and North American Vodoun, HooDoo.

A few months before the trip, I read of Dr. Pritchard's vindication in a Jack Anderson column. It seems vindication that Pritchard hadn't belonged to the CIA at all. He was the one who warned François Duvalier of the CIA's attempts to kill him. There was even a bomb dropped on the palace! It didn't go off. "Supernatural intervention?" Who knows? There was that strange rumor concerning the feud which occurred between John F. Kennedy and Duvalier when the United States discontinued aid to Haiti. They still whisper about that feud between the two strong-willed men. There was that photo in Dr. Mars's study of the ambassador shaking hands with the young U.S. President. It all seemed correct, and formal. Dr. Mars's smile was correct and formal. Kennedy was tight-lipped. The photo was taken during the feud. They said that Duvalier sent the Houngans to Arlington Cemetery, where they gathered some goofer (graveyard dust) so as to perform telepathic malice on the President. Kennedy was killed on November 22. Twenty-two, the Vodoun mystery number. Duvalier's favorite lucky number.

Dr. François Duvalier, former head of the Haitian Bureau of Ethnology, was more than a scholar of Vodoun. He acted out his personal loa, Baron Samedi, lord of the cemetery, "Gangster, Statesman, Clown, Diplomat, Artist." He had a reputation for being both malevolent and benevolent, just as loas are. They will laugh with you, heal you, reward you—but they can also murder.

During the AFNA conference, Pritchard, after reporting to me a conversation he had with François Duvalier, smiled and said, "He said he's very interested in Reed coming down." We never met. He died. I went on to other things. I don't know about politics, but I've heard some pretty awful things from American journalists about the Doctor's career.

Once, when the American ambassador's plane attempted to take off, without the government's permission, from Duvalier airport, the Haitian air force hemmed it in. When Duvalier regarded another American ambassador as insolent, he ordered him to the palace, and berated him in foul backwoods Creole. The Haitians might have enjoyed that.

The Haitians see Duvalier differently. There are icons to the late President everywhere. It wouldn't have been Haiti's first Vodoun government.

Haitians admire courage. The state provides television for recreation and so they stand in the park, near the National Palace, watching Muhammad Ali pulverize people on television. Jean-Claude Duvalier, according to

Encore magazine, is working to supply them with more television. Twentieth-century Vodoun. He's spent fifteen million dollars since 1973 on telecommunications. Satellites will aid in overseas telephone service.

Muhammad Ali's name will get you all over the island. Or say Joe Frazier and you'll become involved in a friendly conversation. There are photos of American celebrities like Aretha Franklin and James Brown on the walls of the nightclub of El Rrancho Villa in Pétionville, where the Rolls-Royces and the celebrities hang out. They play Barry White in the perfume shops. In Port-au-Prince, there is a discotheque called The Brooklyn.

And so with a view of Baie de Port-au-Prince, which I'd call "swimmable," the plane landed at the heavily guarded Duvalier airport. One wonders what the fate of commandos who would storm this airport unannounced. I'd heard of exiles who had returned because of reports of the liberalizing tendencies of the new regime, taken from the plane to jail. Amnesty International had said that Haitian jails were the worst in the world. I hadn't read their report of United States jails, which are only country clubs for those who steal big, or steal intangibles.

There was a huge painting of a "voodoo ceremony" on one of the airport walls. I couldn't make out the vé-vé, the geometric design which accompanies the energy of any particular loa; it appeared to be Ogun, a male loa, a kind of Mars figure. I didn't see many male loas in Haiti; however, the goddess of the sea, Erzulie, seems to be omnipresent, sometimes represented as a mermaid done in wood, iron, painting on pictures found in restaurants, shops, churches, and as a wood carving in the courtyard of the Villa Creole, where I lived.

A *National Geographic* article referred to Haiti as the West Africa of the Caribbean. Indeed, some have argued that, having expelled Europeans very early, Haiti is more genuinely African than the actual place, invaded and occupied to this day, in some parts, by Europeans. On Tuesday, I drove up the coast towards a place called Iboe beach through villages whose architectural styles were

African, primarily consisting of "mudhuts," as the Americans refer to them, whose stability, and quality, despite inexpensive materials, have been vouched for by new Afro-American architects like Carl Anthony. If the American journalists had looked inside one of these "mudhuts" they might have found a freezer with a fresh supply of Coca-Colas inside, as I did in a small village five miles from Arcahie.

Dr. Louis Mars, ambassador from Haiti, greeted me at the entrance to the airport. I was glad to see him. He was a man, as a nineteenth-century writer would say, "of aristocratic bearing." In Haiti, people know their place, and you don't find much democratic familiarity. When I tried to act democratic and Yankee with the waiters at the Villa Creole, they put me in my place by insisting that they fetch my coffee instead of me getting it myself. The black desk clerk referred to another black as "boy." The "boy" will get your luggage, he said.

Dr. Mars is a member of the elite, just as was his father, Haiti's intellectual giant, Dr. Price Mars. Members of the elite refer to lower-class Haitians as "peasants."

Duvalier waged war against what he referred to as mulattoes, persons of mixed ancestry. He made it possible for a dark-skinned person to rise and own a villa.

Dr. Price Mars defied the dictator on this color caste theory and though a book was burned, he lived until his nineties. Dr. Mars had been out of the country for fifteen years, serving in various diplomatic capacities. He is a trained psychiatrist and author of a number of books and articles about Vodoun, just as his father was. The publishing company of which I am director, Reed, Cannon & Johnson, will be publishing his major work, *The Possession Crisis in Voodoo*, translated from the French for us by Ms. Kathleen Collins, a film maker and short story writer. It is one of the books we plan to publish which, we hope, will introduce an intelligent discussion of the subject. In the United States, Vodoun has been ignorantly associated with terror and "black magic," which is European, by the way.

There are no "devils" in Vodoun either, and accusations of "devil worship" have no basis in fact, and are most likely part of the hysteria whipped up by those who would maintain an unconstitutional Established Church in the United States. Certainly, Vodoun has been exploited here, just as Buddhism has. There are more Buddhists in California and Nevada than in China. Imagine that. The Chinese hate Buddhism and see it as another Christian cult.

It has been my experience that certain people walking about with bad loas in their heads (psychotics) are unable to be healed using traditional European techniques. Maybe that's why Pope Paul VI issued that curious document *Africae Terrarum,* in 1967, in which he urged priests and bishops to "look anew at the non-European mentality," suggesting that the Church could learn from other traditions and rites. It is a tenuous truce the Catholic Church has made with the non-Western African dieties and rites in the Americas. Even the most sophisticated Creole Catholic has a Houngan tucked away somewhere in the background.

With a few snaps of his fingers, Dr. Mars got me through customs in about three minutes. I could feel the glare of some of the well-heeled tourists at my neck. They had to wait, sometimes for an hour and a half, and here I was in my polyester jacket, blue jeans, earth shoes, heading with Dr. Mars to an awaiting black Mercedes, inspectors smiling all along. His chauffeur was a little late in bringing up the black Mercedes and Dr. Mars, in his smooth style and his manner, like that of a cultured detective in a gothic mystery, commented, "In Haiti, things are leisurely; no stomach ulcers."

Many of us, in the States, have bad posture, I guess from getting whipped down, or having seen too many lynch scenes of niggers who held their heads too high. I have it too. The Haitians walk erect, maybe from the manner of using the head as a vehicle for conveying goods. It may also be due to a proud tradition. Dr. Mars spoke of his ancestors. Rarely does one run into an American black who can trace his before the 1800s. One of the central tenets of Vodoun is ancestorism. In his study

there is a picture of Jean Baptiste Mars, in period French
officer's outfit; he fought with Henri Christophe and
other Haitian volunteers with George Washington in
1778 at the Siege of Savannah.

We drove up Route Delmas Avenue to Pétionville,
to the Villa Creole, two thousand feet above Port-au-
Prince, and laid out like one of those jigsaw buildings by
M. C. Escher, with columns, courtyards, labyrinthine en-
trances and exits; lizards darting about. While checking in,
I asked Dr. Mars and the hotel clerk about some of the
"loa feedings" which were to take place that weekend:
the M'Sieu Guimeh Sauveur; for Maitresse Tenaise, and
Maitresses Mambo. The two conversed in Creole. (Dr.
Mars's English was quite good, as in a letter to me which
goes ". . . you had an enjoyable time in Haiti. So much
for the better.")

They told me that these were private family affairs and
off limits to outsiders. "It's family! It's family!" they said.
I got the message. I decided that I didn't want to see an
anthropologist's or tourist "voodoo ceremony" and that
when Haiti wanted to invite me to one Haiti would let
me know. The night before I left I had won their confidence, but refused to press the matter. The fate of anthropologists who've lost their grant money to the rum
purchases of hustlers wouldn't befall me. Haitians are
players but the North American black is the player's
player.

In 1791, as the revolt against the French began, there
were 36,000 whites and one-half million black slaves.
They were colonials who knew how to hold a fork. We
were up against Europe's jail and asylum inmates, who
have been referred to as savages by Europeans up until
modern times. I remember talking to a distinguished Polish professor, in the faculty club of the University of
Buffalo, and the way he spoke of the Poles who immi-
grated to America and were the ancestors of Buffalo's
present Polish population—he could have been Archie
Bunker discussing "spades."

So when the hustlers tried to tourist me with "soul
brother," etc., while trying to sell me something, I'd say,

"I'm as broke as you are, you see me walking, don't you?"
Dr. Mars departed for his Pétionville home of the handsome tiles and furniture which featured redwood burls,
glowingly sheened.

The Americans sit about the Villa's pool, which is con-
veniently near a bar, drinking daiquiris and snoring with
books like *The Final Days* resting above their swimming
trunk waistlines. While dining on rich Creole food, vin-
tage wine, and other delicacies, one could see the peasants on the hills, walking in and out of the homes of what
appeared to be a clean shanty town, a goat here and there
chewing on whatever goats eat.

Betye Saar, a painter who's hung in the Whitney and
the Museum of Modern Art, hipped me about Haiti. She
loved it. She described the poverty as "clean" poverty.
People say it isn't depressing filth like one views in other
Third World countries.

The original Villa Creole was planned as a hospital.
It's run by a man named Dr. Reindall Assad. It's surrounded by a sea of bougainvillea. The waitresses wore
white, like Mambos, and one could feel their smolder-
ing hatred for the guests behind the polite smiles and
service. I thought of the popular scenes, accompanying
the expulsion of the French from Haiti. Men, women,
and children being hacked to pieces by angry peasants.
The Haitian revolt gave the southern planters the willies.
They thought it would move North.

There was sculpture in the garden near the front entrance, including one of Erzulie, in her mermaid aspect,
her vé-vé etched in the wood. A kind of checkered heart
pierced by a dagger. The Villa was under Erzulie's protection.

Haitians seem to be geometry crazed. The symbols appear on restaurant mats as well as quilts and traffic signs.
I was never good at math and was stopped by Haitian
police twice for going the wrong way down one-way
streets.

Haiti is a nation of artists. Artist societies are everywhere. Instead of brazen, ugly neon signs, hand-painted walls and signs abound. There is a wall of a building on Forty-second Street at about Eighth Avenue, in New York, which an arts council commissioned artist Al Loving to cover with abstract art. Such walls are common in Haiti. Even the jitneys are painted with scenes. The women's fashions are supremely colorful, with creative and original patterns. No two are alike. I've never seen such fashions—some are rumored to be made with secret fabrics. The Vodoun observances make use of sacred original fabric designs. The men wear similarly interesting shirts often with marine designs so that the Island seems one with the water which surrounds it.

The typical Haitian style of art is abstract, which came as a surprise to me. The other dominant style resembles what Western modern art refers to as "surrealism," a style based on Vodoun philosophy of time and space, and employing Vodoun symbology. Having never visited a truly "black" country, and having listened for ten years to American black aestheticians who spend their vacations in Paris, I expected to see Moscow Museum type portraits; perhaps the portraits of Workers singing revolutionary songs while harvesting the five year plan, or something close to the middle camp Peking People's ballet.

Black American intellectuals have conferences in which they complain about those artists among them who "distort" reality. Haitian art "distorts" reality just as a good deal of the African variety does. It appears that a black aesthetic criticism had little to do with the traditions of art in black countries, as it consisted merely of old discredited theories of Marxist art given a black veneer.

Guinean novelist Camara Laye (*The Radiance of the King*), in an interview with William Lawson, which appeared in *Yardbird Reader*, Volume IV, spoke of an experience his father, a sculptor, had when portraying a "sensual" European man. He sculpted his penis because, as the sculptor explained to the complaining subject, "Listen, this is the way I saw you." "Expressive beauty is more important than ideal beauty," was the lesson Laye drew from the anecdote. By this definition, Haitian art is expressive.

Just as in Vodoun, artistic expression varies from village to village and individual to individual so much that some rites are celebrated on different calendar dates, depending on the area in Haiti. In Haitian art, based on Vodoun principles, the artist uses certain universal forms, to which he brings his own individual aesthetic sense. This approach is what I have attempted to use in my novels. Though my characters are often called "stereotypes," their forms fall solidly within the Vodoun tradition.

For example, I bought three statues of Legba, the African loa known for his protruding penis, from agents who represent Haitian artists. Each one was different. A wide variety of cultures is represented in Vodoun. I even saw a Vodoun Krishna, in the Naders Art Gallery.

They take their art seriously here. One President discovered this too late. When President Nord executed a poet, the people rose and caused his downfall. It was considered unpatriotic to kill a poet.

The United States Marines occupied Haiti from 1915 to 1930, an occupation remembered with much bitterness and during which much Haitian art was destroyed, Vodoun observances were interrupted and the participants gunned down. The Haitian warriors who surrounded the Marines at Port-au-Prince, described as "bandits" by the New York *Times,* were said to have been possessed by Ogun, the war loa.

That evening, I drove with a guide named Bernard, and his friend, to a nightclub on the Bay one reached by driving along Harry Truman Boulevard. The nightclub was a boat. There was a mambo band performing and above them was a cage in which the papier-mâché serpent god Damballah was held. Couples were doing the mambo, said to be Legba's dance, since Legba is a cripple who shuffles on one foot.

In Africa, Legba was a young man. In the new world, he is a wise old man. They were doing that mambo, too, left hip to left hip, right hip to right hip. There were some New England librarian types dancing with some Haitian men. The guides and I sat chatting, drinking Heinekens. I was taking this all in. I was dressed in my three-piece North American white Houngan suit I bought at Grodin's on Telegraph Avenue in Berkeley, especially for the trip. I pulled out my jet black Watson cross, said to have been popularized by a HooDoo man named Watson in the 1930s. I had it made by a sculptor —one of the few sculptors in the Bay Area who works with jet. It's supposed to melt when it comes in contact with the evil eye. Bernard and his friend examined it. They looked at each other. They offered to show me a "voodoo ceremony." "You have to have reservations," Bernard said. I declined.

After midnight that Saturday, I heard considerable yipping, drumming, and the sounds of an instrument which made the noise of crickets. This is what the tourist books must mean when they said "hear voodoo ceremonies after midnight." It goes on like that until the rooster crows at about five-thirty. A culture which still rises with the rooster can teach us a thing or two.

I'm not the kind of guy who would loll about a swimming pool eating burnt lobster while in the hills those who aren't as fortunate are visible, so on Sunday I set out, on foot, to Port-au-Prince, five miles from Pétionville. It's a very fabulous walk down Avenue Panamericaine . . . quilts, ironwork, and wood sculpture are sold along the way. Guards holding rifles could be seen, protecting the villas of foreign embassies which lay behind gravel pathways leading upward. Americans are easy to spot. The children would stop and say, "Hey, what's happening, man," or "Say, brother."

There was this guy named Johnny Caesar who was dressed in pink shirt, snug-fitting black trousers, and a dark blue velvet Apple Cap. Like many Haitians I'd talked to, he had a strong rap. He walked alongside me asking questions, making small talk. I became interested when he pointed out the American ambassador's villa. It looked like a facade in a 1920s movie about Babylon. Shangri-la came to mind. "Suzy," a columnist, described it as "a beautiful white house with red-tiled roof, green shutters, patio and porches everywhere—swimming pool and palm-lined driveway. The grounds drip with tropical trees and flowers—frangipani, bougainvillea, hibiscus, oleander, flamboyants, mahogany, a giant fig tree, at the end of the drive were two mudilla trees flanking the front lawn." Heyward Isham's wife, Sheila, has furnished the house with Asian objets d'art. They weren't exactly going native. I read that the multilingual ambassador was "assiduously studying voodoo." During the week, I went to the United States Embassy, left my card, requesting an interview with the ambassador concerning "his interest in Haitian art and culture, for the *Rolling Stone* magazine." The ambassador never called.

Winding down the hills towards Port-au-Prince, I saw colonial modern, I guess you'd call the architecture, movie houses. Charles Bronson seemed to be playing at all of the theaters. There were more images of Charles Bronson than of Jean-Claude Duvalier. I walked until I reached the National Palace, built by a Haitian architect, stopping only to have a drink in one of those cool tropical restaurants with ancient fans whirling above your head like in *Casablanca*. In this particular one, there was a portrait of Jean Duvalier behind the bar, replete with decorated chest, ribbons, and formal tux. Up in the mountain villages, it's Mamma, Simone, said by some to be the real power, whose portraits are in abundance.

Arriving at the National Palace, I walked to the fence and took a photo of the soldiers. In its yard were tanks and anti-aircraft guns. A bayonet-toting soldier approached me. Johnny Caesar hurried from my side. Give me a dollar for a Coca-Cola he said. Later, I learned that people were warned to keep five feet away from the fence. There was a statue of General Jean Jacques Dessalines, who led the fight for Haitian independence after the death of Toussaint L'Ouverture, in a park nearby. He was mounted on a horse.

The assignment was to observe Vodoun as a part of

national life, which meant focusing upon items less obvious than the tourists' "voodoo ceremonies." I spotted a gem! There was another monument, in this general area, consisting of Assons done in wrought iron. Assons are the sumbols of the Houngan's power. They resemble abstract human figures with arms but no legs.

I took a jitney back to Pétionville and the Villa Creole. Johnny Caesar took me into an alley to get some change for a twenty-dollar bill. It was pretty crowded in there with dilapidated houses and flies buzzing about, and there seemed to be a lot of people crouched in doorways. I said hi to everybody and they said Creole for hi back. Most Americans would call these miserable conditions but they were no different from the standard of living found in many neighborhoods in the Usited States.

In the midst of all this poverty, actually in the center of it, surrounded by huts in which the sanitation wasn't exactly the kind you'd find in the Plaza, was a neat little store, well stocked even with a supply of imported beer. A saleslady was standing inside, with her husband, wearing those pompadours Haitian women like to wear. Her husband changed the twenty and charged me a dollar for the service. She put her hand over her mouth and said something to the other women. They laughed. Then she looked me up and down with a stare of ridicule. That's me, "the Holy Fool," I thought.

I returned to the Villa. I was becoming homesick. Downstairs there was a slick-looking, fashionably dressed European, sitting in a chair, head thrown back, smoking a cigarette. A little band danced, "tommed," and drummed for him while he threw them twenty-cent pieces. I went upstairs and played my tapes of "Alfonzo's House Party," a high-class disco show they run on KRE radio in San Francisco. I made a lot of friends among the Villa staff with those tapes.

I spent most of the next day hunting down a rent-a-car, which in Haiti is quite a ritual, which reveals the complex system of log-rolling, back-scratching, shrewd negotiating, probably harking back to a pre-Marxist, pre-Adam Smith, pre-Keynesian time when trade was closer to gambling.

Lotteries, and "numbers," and "lucky" phenomena are constant features of black cultures. Life and death decided by the roll of the dice or the throwing of cowrie shells. The Mafia wanted Duvalier out because there was a lot of gambling going on in Haiti. Vincent Teresa's *My Life in the Mafia* contains some interesting information. It seems that some crime bosses negotiated with François Duvalier to make the Villa El Rancho into a top mob casino which would subsist upon junkets brought in from the United States. In exchange Duvalier would receive 10 per cent of the take. Teresa admits that it was hard to chisel Duvalier out of his bread. "His people watched the books like hawks." The book also contains an interesting portrait of the late dictator. "Papa Doc just listened. He didn't say much. Once in a while he'd nod or speak soft in that broken French-English of his. You could see he was a very smart guy. He had a good education—you could tell when he talked. He was very short, on the slim side, with tan, not dark black, skin, and he wore glasses. Behind those glasses were piercing brown eyes—eyes that made you feel like he was looking right through you, like he had X-ray eyes. We called them snake eyes. He'd never take those eyes off you."

First, they brought a stick-shift up to the Villa which didn't operate very well. People lined the streets watching me futilely attempting to stop and start the thing. Haitians are very curious about foreigners. From the time you land at the airport or your ship docks in the harbor everybody knows your business. They wear a sly smile to let you know they know. During the second time I was stopped for driving down the one-way street, a mob scene occurred. Not really a mob scene. The people just stared, quietly. All of these quiet people staring at you like in a science fiction movie.

I finally got a dark blue Toyota which easily handled the roads along the coast and the mountain paths. There seems to be much road building going on in Haiti; the country takes on the appearance of Marxist-Leninist

China with trucks bringing workers into the city, drilling, and industrial activity. It seems to be a country on the move. "My father brought you the social and political revolution, I will bring you the economic revolution," Jean-Claude had promised. It's difficult to judge the standards of living in other countries by using the United States as a yardstick. There were slums in Port-au-Prince which occur in many nations where the people move from the country to the city, mostly because they are bored and that's where the action is. As Jimmy Reed sang, "Bright lights, Big city." But the slums reminded me very much of photos I'd seen of 1840s California gold bars, and homesteader tents. I wondered what a modern industrial nation would think of the United States if the period of covered-wagoned pioneering was contemporary. Would they say America is so primitive that people have to get about in covered wagons? In many pre-industrial societies, the past and the present might be a block apart. And so the road building goes on. The triumph of the regime will occur when the road to Jacmel, where, I understand, the really heavy Vodoun goes on, is built. The present one has been described by one Haitian wit as "a riverbed." I didn't see a road, however, that was as bad as Market Street in San Francisco, or Main Street in Buffalo, New York, which looks like a World War II combat scene set in Italy.

Actually, Haitian transportation might be superior to the American style. It's intimate, and prompt, and more reliable than the New York subway. People are zipped about the land in brand-new Peugeots and Renault station wagons which arrive every few minutes to pick up passengers, and drop them off, wherever they find them on the road. (San Francisco Muni drivers complain about the nineteenth-century equipment they have to use; one out of five trolley cars breaks down each day.) The drivers exhibit better manners than in the rude American services, where you might get your head snapped off if you mistakenly supply an operator with a wrong number, or have a heart attack because you tried to catch a bus whose driver saw you coming, yet fiendishly waited until you're just about there, sometimes dragging you for a few miles if you get your coat caught in a closing door.

Since I couldn't use the stick-shift, the driver drove me about Port-au-Prince and attempted to strike up bargains with his employer's competitors, apparently without his employer's knowledge. The driver gets a discount, or percentage of the take for every customer he introduces to the employer's rivals.

There exists a whole system of industrial spies and counterspies, involving an intrigue more complex than that in a Hitchcock movie.

An interlocking interdependent machine works from the lowliest peasant level all the way up to the high government officials who live in the hills of Pétionville, in villas of such modern design that they seem like spaceships about to take off. Haitian architecture is diverse, and fantastic! In the mountains there are solidly built ornate structures policed by men with rifles. On Panamerica a barber had built himself a little half-globe scooped-out number, where he held shop, which seemed to be held up by a pole. He didn't want me taking pictures of it. It's this system that makes the country go. As soon as a man sold me a piece of luggage another man rushed up to sell me a lock for it.

Not once did I see the depressing idleness that one sees in North American cities, where people stand on the corners waiting for government or big business to give them jobs instead of creating them for themselves. A miserable slave master's Christian psychology which preaches that everybody should own things, but you, because it's a "sin" to own things. Only white people should have plantations. God meant for it to be this way. North American blacks live with this unreal legacy. Their leaders are often unemployed but colorful intellectuals who demand metaphysical things on "Face the Nation." Freedom. Dreadful freedom. It never occurred to them that in a capitalist country the primary demand should be equal access to the capital. Welfare is the bribe they hand out to keep blacks out of the free enterprise system, they pretend they want so much to endure. You know how "lucky" niggers is. I've gotten more hassles—mostly from white radicals who resent niggers who aren't dependent on them—from heading a corporation than when I was writing poems praising Che Guevara. If you don't believe it's subversive you should have seen me and my fellow officers go into a California bank to withdraw a modest sum of money. The bank dick came over and glared at us. People gathered about, as this bank officer, a black woman with blond dyed hair, stalled us. Our lawyer had to threaten to challenge the bank's certification before they'd give us our own money. Maybe making your own jobs is more subversive in a system which runs on restricted "free enterprise." Like the famous couple—they had to be Haitians, they are—who run two outlaw carpeted limousines from JFK to Manhattan, challenging the white-ruled New York cab monopoly which is so powerful they choose their customers instead of the other way around.

Every summer we hear about unemployed ghetto youth as the black leadership servilely appeals to the conscience of the white businessmen who've put the economy in trouble because their bad industrial ideas default. It never occurs to the black leadership that the racist banking system denies black businessmen loans, therefore depriving them of providing jobs for their own. If this is a true enterprise system where each man has a chance to succeed or fail, then perhaps the government should be the financier of the last resort. There are so many beautiful, creative industries to be formed, like Cristo's eighteen-foot-high, twenty-four-mile-long nylon fence out here in California, which spawned a payroll in the millions of dollars. Here thousands of people stand on the corner because of people with metaphysical goals telling them that because of "technology" they are obsolete when there's such a rush back to the pre-Ford handmade object, it ain't funny. The handmade object has become a work of art in everyday life which one man begins, and finishes. Yes, many Haitians may have distended bellies and may be suffering from malnutrition, and granted that man does not live by mangoes alone, but they are busy. Busy as ants, plowing, sowing, making things, creating beauty from wastes like the symbol of their ancestors, the scarab.

They take pride in their work. If somebody is selling you tomatoes they're the best damned tomatoes you ever seen. Big luscious juicy tomatoes. And if somebody is selling you flowers they are freshly picked beautiful flowers. There are no fixed prices. People can negotiate the price according to quality. A built-in protection against consumer fraud.

There was this little kid in the mountain village of Kenscoff. I've seen thousands of little kids like this in the United States. But this kid was earning a living as a guide. He spoke three languages. "I'm Peter Jackson," he said, as I sat in the mountain cafe drinking absinthe. "Permit me to show you the brandy factory, very good, very good, very good." He had become infatuated with the English expression "very good." His detractors, the other kids, came up and said, "His name ain't no Peter Jackson," and I said, "It is, and he is a gentleman and a scholar." And it did me a lot of good when Peter Jackson beamed.

The Haitians are poor but it's their country. They live under a "dictatorship," but as someone said, "It's their dictatorship."

That evening, after going over the copy editor's questions regarding his manuscript, with Dr. Mars, I drove down to Ollofson's, the famous gingerbread house where Graham Greene, Truman Capote, and Irving Wallace hang out when they come here. It was once used as headquarters by the Marines. It was also, at one time, the presidential palace. I struck up a conversation with a white American named Bradshaw. He had attended Harvard, and done a thesis about the exploitation of labor in underdeveloped countries. He now employs laborers to make baskets for him, which he imports to the United States. "They exploit me, I exploit them," he said. He put it succinctly, in a way as to sum up my experiences of that day. "You go to Puerto Rico, and the Marines run it. You go to Jamaica and the British run it. But here in Haiti, the Haitians run it. You can't take it away from them. It belongs to them."

The next morning I drove up the coast towards Arcahie, a place where once lived Ti Bouton, a Houngan so powerful he was said to have "conversed with the streams and could produce rain in the dry season, and make lightning strike." The Villa Creole's proprietor, a Creole gentleman, had heard of my questions to Dr. Mars and the desk clerk which took place when I checked in. He had approached me the previous day, and asked me, "Voodoo man, can you make rain?" He was placing his hands on my shoulder, affectionately. I was fuming, frustrated because they had promised to bring up the car the day before, and it was twelve hours late. "Make it rain?" I said. "I can't even get a rent-a-car."

Haiti is hot, muggy. The translator described it as a tropical country yet one which hungers for rain. Jean-Claude Duvalier may be progressive, entertaining the Chinese ambassador the week I was there; talking about telecommunications, etc. But somebody ought to hip him to chemical toilets, though, of course, there's something to be said about pissing when you have to. Americans probably have gastrointestinal illnesses, bladder problems, etc., because they're always holding things in, due to custom, and maybe psychology. Somebody ought to suggest desalinization, as is being tested in Bolinas (one of America's private fiefdoms of Bohemian Texans who probably, as children, laughed when they hear that Kennedy got shot). That's what's wrong with one-man rule. No matter how "progressive" the dictator may be he doesn't always get the best information which occurs during a free exchange of ideas.

I lost my way and was stopped near the border of Santo Domingo, which is heavily armed. The late President Trujillo was an enemy of Haiti. Thousands of Haitains were said to have been exterminated during his rule. It was a nervous border with people swinging rifles about. That's one thing that makes me shaky. All those guns being waved about, being played with, it seems, at times. An innocent dictatorship which hasn't reached the stage of high-class lawyers, subtly sitting around creating things like the Houston Plan. I was determined to get to Kyona

Beach but the roads made it impossible. It was as jammed and untraversable as Queens Highway into La Guardia Airport. The caste system determines who passes on the left, in Haiti, who is first in line. I, being a democrat, drove sixty miles an hour down some pretty rough mountain curves in order to prevent honking Creoles from asserting their skin privileges until I realized that in Haiti, I was the Creole! I passed through some rather monotonous-looking villages and Duvalierville, a showcase with the late dictator's picture everywhere and some modern Parisian-styled buildings.

Returning, I came into a little village to attend a Texaco station. It rained! The sky was like an ocean, upside down. People ran out of their houses for water. All the way back to Port-au-Prince the scene was repeated. People were sharing troughs and sewers, washing their clothes, as the rain came.

That night I had dinner with the Ambassador and Madame Mars. He gave me the impression that the Haitian Vodoun scholars knew little of the varieties of Vodoun outside of their country, the Brazilian Umbanda, the Cuban Santería (slowly creeping into Miami), and the North American HooDoo. He spoke of the late Maya Deren, the American film maker, whose interest in Haitian dance brought her to the island. She claimed to be a "voodoo priestess." Too much amphetamine brought her to tragedy; it was supposed to have been given to her by a doctor whose clients included celebrities, and a former President of the United States. Dr. Mars thought it curious that Deren, a white woman, would see herself as a "voodoo priestess." Not so curious at all. There are white loas in the Vodoun pantheon. Some are beautiful, sophisticated, and mysterious; others are clowns who have bad tempers and drink a lot of gin. I asked Dr. Mars how many Houngans he thought were present in Haiti. Thousands he said. "Too many, maybe."

The ambassador told me to inspect the Cathedral of the Holy Trinity, an Episcopalian church which boasts murals done by some of Haiti's finest "naïve" painters. They ain't all that "naïve" because, perhaps unknown to the Church, the "Christian" stuff has Vodoun written all over it. The works are by Philome Obin, Wilson Bigaud, and Rigaud Benoit. Bigaud's "Marriage Feast at Cana" is a Creole wedding (Creoles and their haughty manners are the subjects of many of the "naïve" painters' barbs), but near the bottom you see somebody about to cut a cock with a machete or sacrifice a boar, Boukman's revolutionary act. There are also conchs. "The Last Supper" consists of black apostles sharing a table with a white Christ (Judas is also white). In the front of Christ is the Erzulie dagger through the heart, and a squiggly design I found a short time later at the Haitian Bureau of Ethnology (a disappointing exhibit) on a vase created by one of the indigenous Indian tribes—the Arawaks, who gave the island its name Ayti—the name restored when the blacks took power. The Haitians have kept the traditions of those Indians, who were wiped out by the Europeans, alive. Perhaps this vé-vé is a tribute to the Arawaks whose fireplaces, tools, and pottery are on display at the Bureau, for their help in adapting the newly arrived Africans to the New World, and for teaching them to survive under harsh European rule. The Africans came from stable kingdoms, a fact that even the most biased European explorers verified. Usually, there was adequate food and shelter for members of a society. Native Americans influenced Vodoun and in some places, such as Brazil, where the old African gods were forgotten, Native American gods were substituted. The fierce Petro group of loas are said to have been influenced by the Arawaks. During the Haitain Mardi Gras the Haitians observe the Arawak traditions and dress up like Indians, a custom which was transported to New Orleans, possibly when Haitian slaves were sent there. Black Indians still participate in the Mardi Gras pageant.

There is an expression, "Haiti is 95 per cent Christian, and 100 per cent Vodoun"; I didn't know the truth of this until I discovered that Vodoun material was not only hidden in the murals of Christian themes but was being hustled right out of the church's gift shop! Not only were there vé-vés, and other Vodoun paraphernalia for sale, but stationery with Vodoun symbols on it, Grand Bois, Agew (Erzulie's husband, a sea loa), and Ghedes, the cemetery loas. Drawings of caskets and crosses accompany these. The Ghedes are gluttonously ghoulish loas of satire. Amused by my startled reaction to this discovery, the black clerks made an expression which must be the Haitian equivalent of a wink.

The Naders Art Gallery featured an exhibit saluting the United States' Bicentennial, a kind of Freedom Train tableau whose only blacks were slaves appearing in crowd scenes. One would think that curator would know better. Blacks in South America have a condescending attitude towards North American blacks; we were slaves longer than they were, a fact which they attribute to our passive nature. Curious then, that many black movements in the rest of the world find their impetus in the United States' militant movement. Presently, the white regimes of Southern Africa are blaming their problems on Black Power agitators from the United States.

There were the usual pictures of Thomas Jefferson, and other rich planters striking dandyish poses with important documents in their hands. It was weird to hear the Naders Gallery workers humming American revolutionary songs like Yankee Doodle, along with the exhibit's sound track. Some of the guards were dressed in Bicentennial uniforms, I guess you'd call them. They look like black minutemen with their white pants, black coats, and Napoleon hats. On July Fourth, 1976, the New York *Times Magazine* section carried a full-page ad paid for by the Haitian National Office of Tourism. It refered to the battle of Savannah, where Dr. Mars's ancestor had fought, and boasted of eight hundred and sixty-one Haitians having lost their lives in this gallant effort, which goes uncited by the established American historians, who devote, often, about three paragraphs to blacks within their books, usually arguing that everybody had a good time. The ad ended, "Come to Haiti where Americans have been loved for more than two-hundred years." Marines, too?

Most of the gallery paintings held Vodoun themes. Enguerrand Jean-Gourgue's work was the most impressive. In one, people with bodies with the shape of vases eat lobster and cockroaches. In one called "The Magic Table" there occurs the mating of a bull and a snake among Vodoun objects. The text accompanying the exhibit explained "Haitian naïve painting is full of allusions to the ceremonies and symbols of the voodoo religion. With more than two hundred variations of the loas or spirit forces, the voodoo pantheon is a rich source of artistic imagination. The images one finds in paintings are based on the living characterizations of divinities Damballah, Aida Wedo, Agoue (Agwe), Ogun, Erzulie Freda Dahomey (the good Erzulie, Mother, protector of the home) and the Guedes (also Ghede), among others, appear again and again." Some painters like Hector Hyppolite were actually Houngans. He was obsessed with the theme of black womanhood. He not only idealized black women, as does one painting of a nude amidst flowers and birds, but also portrayed them as treacherous and unfaithful. He claimed a "mystical marriage" with the Vodoun goddess of La Sirene.

There were painted wooden statues of devils all over the museum: devils with French faces. The French still go about Haiti, arrogantly, as if they owned the place, and God made it especially for them. There were red devils, purple devils. Some of the devils had green heads and black horns. One devil had a black penis with orange testicles.

I left the gallery and headed towards the National Museum. It was closed down the entire week.

Thursday I went to the famous Iron Market. This institution with its bustling con artist bargainers, serves as a metaphor for the energy and drive of the Haitian people. The energy and drive which incurred the eternal wrath of the Western nations when Haiti defeated Napoleon's armies. Haiti is a kind of Sonny Liston-Bad-Nigger island of the Caribbean. Perhaps its problems would be eased if that eighteenth-century war would be played back as a computer war, this time with the French emerging victorious. Then, perhaps, all trade barriers against the island would be lifted and people would stop maligning its honor. But I don't think the proud Haitian people would go for such an arrangement. Their Iron Market was built in 1889 during the administration of President Florvil Hyppolite. It is two block-long wings built of sheet iron, featuring some remarkable and ancient-looking arabesque towers. It's the ultimate flea market; reminding one of those food co-operatives on the Lower East Side of Manhattan. Everything in the world seems to be on sale here, and in variety. The reason that Communism has failed so miserably among North American blacks is that they crave variety—Marx demonizes variety as much as he does the middle class, which he accuses of "conjuring up" things, and as much as he demonizes the discovery of America.

I'm wondering why American journalists who sit on their fannies in plush interiors, million-dollar Haitian drinking clubs, haven't filed copy about this amazing insitution along with the gossip about people eating their children, whatever.

Everybody and his brother was trying to hustle me in this place of flies, food, clothing, scultpure, etc. There were people who were obviously "crazy" wandering about the stalls. In Haiti, I understand, crazy people are left alone; they are believed to be possessed. I bought a handbag whose base was cardboard, a comb made of animal bone, a woven towel with a Japanese theme on it, and three yards of a fabric decorated with red and yellow flowers and hearts. I bought a cane which a guide got for me for one dollar instead of the five the salesman was asking. They cussed each other over the deal in Creole. I bought some "voodoo dolls" made from scraps of cloth. So much of the stuff was made from recycled materials one gained the impression that Haitians rarely throw anything away. The "voodoo dolls" had apparently been brought in from the countryside; although "black magic" is frowned upon by self-respecting Houngans, there exists a class of sub-priests who will take someone "out" for a small fee. Bokors, they are called.

I put all of the goods, including some bottles of Barbancourt rum I bought in a modern supermarket, which had American magazines on sale, into my Toyota and headed back to the Villa. My head was throbbing from myriad images, and ideas about Haiti, which someone has called "the magic island." I found it to be more than a Hollywood "voodoo" island of zombies and teeth gnashing witch doctors, though there is evidence that zombies exist; Zora Neale Hurston, whose name is being invoked in a black literary power stunt by those who have little understanding of what she was all about, took a photo of one which appears in her book *The Voodoo Gods of Haiti*.

I was a little uneasy in the Villa, and was really glad to be going home the next day. It wasn't the Villa's fault —the staff and the guests were courteous to me. I wanted to get back. I never thought I'd be glad to see the Miami *Herald*, even though I had to pay a buck-fifty for it.

Next morning I headed for the airport, and did it again. Headed down a one-way street. The cop gave me one of those stony-faced stares that Haitians are famous for. The evil eye which brought down President Joseph Nemurs Pierre-Louis (the people just stood and glared at the presidential palace). I thought of myself spending the rest of my life in one of those prisons Amnesty International was talking about. The Haitians are pretty strict. The young American girls from New York colleges were warned in Ollofson's that the penalty for pot smoking was life. As the cop got into the car, I thought, This is it. He ordered me to drive it about a bit. Then he directed me to the airport. I shook his hand and he smiled. He just wanted to see what the Toyota could do.

Before I knew it I was in the bar at the Miami airport, waiting for the Cuban bartender to bring me a red rosé. He ignored me. I just sat there, reading the New York *Times,* anticipating what would happen next. He kept waiting on the white customers and when none of them wanted anything he stood in front of the cash register. A white customer came in. He sat next to me. The Cuban came down, waited on the white man, and then contemptuously asked for my order. I was home. Next, some fat white man, reminding me of those caricatures I saw at the Naders Gallery, tried to prevent me from taking a painting depicting a ceremony to the loa Simba, on the plane. I was so exhausted I just walked right past him, and asked the stewardess who was standing at the plane's entrance for permission to take it aboard, which was granted.

I didn't bring the suitcase of interwoven hemp and wooden strips aboard. I'd paid seven dollars for it. I wanted to see whether these products, made of such inexpensive items by Haitian peasants, were durable. Standing in the baggage area at San Francisco, I found out. It made all the top-shelf luggage look like Cinderella's sisters as they witnessed the lowly maid's entrance into the ball. Some well-dressed people said, "Look at that one!"

Somebody in *Life* magazine called me the meanest man in America, but there are times when even the meanest man puts up a few corny tears of pride. Like Pappa Doc said, he got a bad press in the United States because they were afraid that twenty million black people would want to know what he knew. I think they call it *connaissance*. I hear you, Doc.

Remembering Josephine Baker

There was the joke making the rounds recently about someone having witnessed God and remarking, "She's black." If she is black she is probably Josephine Baker. God sits on an Art Deco throne of silver and black satin surrounded by a chorus line of Jazzy Jassimines, Bandanaland Girls, Bamville Vamps, and Syncopated Sunflowers. By the leash, she holds a black panther wearing a diamond bracelet around its neck. Heaven has a banana yellow sun and looks like Hawaii.

Occasionally, archeological diggings in white Mediterranean countries turn up figurines of black goddesses, and black madonnas. When jazz and Josephine Baker entered Europe, Europe went out of its mind: "The blue spotlight turned Josephine's tan body into a true café au lait. Her slicked-down hair looked as though it were painted with tar, and the bananas took on the brilliant yellows of a Cézanne painting."

Attending one of her performances were De Gaulle, Hemingway, Piaf, the Fitzgeralds, René Clair, and Stravinsky. She made love to His Royal Highness Gustav VI, Crown Prince of Sweden, on a bed "shaped like a swan," with satin sheets. Champagne icing in a silver cooler. The King of the North promised the Black Goddess that he would be her "Knight in shining armor," and gave her a diamond-and-emerald pin; ". . . a knight in shining armor astride a white charger, his sword of tiny pearls held; the horse's eye, a flashing red ruby."

"Never fall in love with royalty, they'll break your heart," warned Nellie Melba, the long reigning queen of the Covent Garden Opera in London, the wise woman who had a dessert named after her—*pêche Melba*. Josephine follows her foolish heart—the heart of a beautiful innocent from Boxcar Town in St. Louis, from where she was carried off by Bessie Smith.

A plain ghetto girl, unimpressed by the Krupps, the Rothschilds, by royalty, by Hemingway, she called Picasso, an admirer, a "funny little fat man." She took a simple step she learned from Benny, of Bert and Benny, a vaudeville team, and polished it into an art form: "My favorite position is to put my hands on my hips and spread my feet apart and throw back my shoulders."

She landed herself the Château des Milandes, where Louis XIV, the Sun King, spent the night; not bad for a kid from Boxcar Town. But by this time the country girl knew the difference between Tahiti and Haiti; spoke four languages, and dated shieks from Araby. But it's not all a fairy tale life of champagne, colored wolfhounds, big limousines, Vuitton luggage, and clothes designed especially for her by Dior, Worth, and Chanel; "Old Man Trouble" can't be put off. This woman with the hooker's heart was a millionaire in 1929, when American bankers were trembling on window ledges many stories above the street. When her luck ran out, the hookers she befriended wore her jewelry on the streets of Paris.

There's an amazing scene in which she is Hermann Goering's guest in the town house the Nazis confiscated from her. She had been passing Nazi secrets to the French Resistance—the Maquis—and Goering, the decadent, who favored her onyx green bathtub, and spent the supper sniffing coke, and scratching from heroin, forced her by gunpoint to eat poisoned fish. She escaped down the laundry chute and spent months lingering near death until a triumphant recovery. She sends a cable to Mistinguette in Paris: "Darling. Please keep the stage hot for me until I get back. Love. Josephine."

At the end of the war she received the Legion of Honor and the Rosette of the Resistance, and entered a liberated Paris in the company of Charles De Gaulle.

Gallant, courageous, and good-hearted people without

shrewd accountants end up broke. She was just too much for some people. Ziegfeld's wife, Billie Burke, hated her. Bob Hope snubbed her. Trashmouthed Walter Winchell, a colunmist addicted to bad alliteration, set out to ruin her. He called her pro-Communist, pro-Fascist, anti-American, anti-Semitic, and anti-Negro. Senator Joe McCarthy cleared her.

So good-hearted was she that she allowed herself to be taken by some "civil rights" hustlers who made demands upon her to "open Las Vegas to blacks." And what did it get her? She required of the management that the best tables be made available to blacks at her performances; she ordered them expensive food and drink free of charge. The blacks couldn't handle it, all of this generosity, and didn't show up to enjoy the results of their "demands."

Special people who are soft touches come to the world and get creamed. Are taken to the cleaners. Poor Josephine. Sweetheart. She never forgot who she was, though, and held her head high and if she wasn't a goddess she was certainly a Queen, which is almost like being a goddess. And there's that magnificent scene which almost made up for the Nazis, the club owner who had her arrested, and the civil rights hustlers who believed that they owned black celebrities and could extort and intimidate them at will. In 1963 in the midst of a spontaneous and stirring speech during the March on Washington—a speech that brought her a rousing ovation, a note was handed to her. John F. Kennedy, who with his brother Robert intervened when the immigration authorities denied her entrance to the United States, had invited her to the White House. When she arrived he was waiting at the entrance to greet her. The Black Goddess meets the Knight of the American Camelot. In *Parsifal,* the German Camelot, African royalty visit the knights of Europe. This and other scenes make Stephen Papich's book *Remembering Josephine* (Bobbs-Merrill) often read like an old, old tale.

I saw her a year before she died. She was greeting people at the Rainbow Sign in Berkeley, California. Ntozake Shange, a poet and playwright, coaxed me into the receiving line because I was shy. And when it came my turn I presented her with a copy of the novel on whose cover I had used an old photo of her to represent two sides of the Vodoun goddess Erzulie. And she flashed that famous smile and squinted those famous eyes and she said, "Do you know the young man who wrote this book?" I was so awestruck, I said, "Yes, ma'am, I knows him," forgetting that that young man was me. That was Josephine Baker. Such a divine presence she made you forget yourself.

New York *Times Book Review*
December 12, 1976

The World Needs More Guys
Like Pee Wee

We were sitting in the Only Child Restaurant on Broadway and Seventy-second Street. It was difficult to manage the dry eyes. Quincy, Deborah, Walter Cotton and me, and Walter, a playwright and screen star, said, "The world needs more guys like Pee Wee."

"That's it," I said. "That's what we'll put on the wreath." I ordered another rosé.

For ten years, lots of characters, actors, writers, painters, sports buffs, reporters from TV networks, political, screen, and stage celebrities, good listeners, simple pimps, second-story men, and "the family" of regulars, players—just about every poet who ever moved west of Avenue D, and east of First Avenue—had gone into Pee Wee's, at 203 Avenue A between Eleventh and Twelfth streets, on the lower East Side.

In the heat of the sixties, Malcolm's poster was on the wall, and I'd seen my publicity there too when I'd come in from the West Coast from time to time. When Winnie Stowers left for the Coast he received a rare tribute: a photo in the window.

It had the best black jukebox below Fourteenth Street. I used to see Ed Sanders, on one of his periodic vacations from the West, nudging against it. Pee Wee's was where the alienated went to have their community. And there was Pee Wee, Emmit C. Watthall, whom you might term a "lovable" guy, chomping on that ever present cigar, kidding you, or shooting the bull. You knew when he was mad—he'd be awful quiet. And he had his wife, Millicent, a real fine lady. She'd be in there too, at his side, helping him. He worked as a fireman, and had three daughters and two sons he was devoted to. I used to see them in the bar sometimes, dressed up in little kid finery. Years later there was one tending the bar. I knew I was getting old.

I used to kid him about being a "capitalist," and he used to kid back. That was before I found out that an independent black businessman or worker threatens the status quo more than those who spend a lot of time saying that they do. That's all. Saying it. That's why Pee Wee had to struggle to stay in business. He had to fight white ethnics, those inhabitants of the little Miserables all over the country, who are often as desperate and poor as the blacks they're pitted against. Pitted against each other by the New Feudalists, who spend their time on the loveliest beaches studying tax loopholes and taking pills.

He had to do battle with cops and "inspectors" who pulled every technicality in an attempt to close him down. He was a black man, standing erect, and tough, making space for himself in a world hostile to black men. He had to take it from his own people, who'd pull stunts in his bar they'd never attempt in the Plaza Hotel, like this pile of mildewed drek who went into Pee Wee's that night and shotgunned Pee Wee because he insisted that they pay for their drinks. "I don't give beer away, I sell it," Pee Wee said. I can just see Pee Wee now, saying those words, inhaling from one of those cigars, smiling squint-eyed. That robust frame, that big neck filling out his collar. The greatest stutterer downtown.

"Man, them niggers put it on today—they put it on. They had two big Cadillac hearses trimmed with silver. And there was a whole bunch of big Lincolns, and some Bentleys and Rolls-Royces. And the casket was gold. And everybody was dressed up—the men in silk suits and the women wearing all their *Essence* fashions. The preacher interrupted the sermon and said, 'I never seen this many people attend a funeral before in my life.' And then they came from St. Albans all the way downtown past the bar, and at the grave site, among all of the fancy wreaths and flowers there was our little one. Chrysanthemums, and red and white roses: 'THE WORLD NEEDS MORE GUYS LIKE PEE WEE.' " Steve Cannon gave me a detailed description of the day's event; the funeral. But it wasn't all sad. "Then they all went back and partied. Pee Wee would have wanted it that way."

The sociologists will say that it was environment that made these hoodlums kill Pee Wee. *Ebony* magazine will say that. I can hear them now. "Of course, it's terrible what happened to Pee Wee, but one must consider the economic and social forces that went into play. . . ." The creeps who did it probably won't serve a year. Pee Wee got life. All the black Pee Wees we keep losing. They get life in a pool of blood. The Pee Wees of this world, the spine of black manhood.

They're always calling me "conservative" and "right wing" but all I know is when you lose your spine, you can't walk.

Daddy

My daddy was sweet
My daddy was kind
My daddy he sure was fine
I'll always remember the day he died
It was enough to make the whole world cry
There are so many questions left in my head
That can never be answered now that he's dead
Why that man shot him I'll never know
But to his wife and kids it was one big blow
If only there was just one way
To bring my father back today
There was so many things we had done
Just being together we could have fun
My daddy he had lots of friends
Who helped him along the hard rough bends
Everyone loved him very dearly
Why did daddy die so early?
There is nothing anyone can do or say
That will take the place of my father today
I know one day my father and I will meet
Everything I wanted will then be complete
Well right now I'm glad we have each other
My brothers, my sisters and my mother

Gayle Watthall
New York *Times*
December 16, 1976

● DISCUS BOOKS
DISTINGUISHED NON-FICTION

THEATER, FILM AND TELEVISION

ACTORS TALK ABOUT ACTING Lewis Funke and John Booth, Eds.	15062	1.95
ACTION FOR CHILDREN'S TELEVISION	10090	1.25
ANTONIN ARTAUD Bettina L. Knapp	12062	1.65
A BOOK ON THE OPEN THEATER Robert Pasoli	12047	1.65
THE CONCISE ENCYCLOPEDIC GUIDE TO SHAKESPEARE Michael Martin and Richard Harrier, Eds.	16832	2.65
THE DISNEY VERSION Richard Schnickel	08953	1.25
EDWARD ALBEE: A PLAYWRIGHT IN PROTEST Michael E. Rutenberg	11916	1.65
THE EMPTY SPACE Peter Brook	32763	1.95
EXPERIMENTAL THEATER James Roose-Evans	11981	1.65
FOUR CENTURIES OF SHAKESPEARIAN CRITICISM Frank Kermode, Ed.	20131	1.95
GUERILLA STREET THEATRE Henry Lesnick, Ed.	15198	2.45
THE HOLLYWOOD SCREENWRITERS Richard Corliss	12450	1.95
IN SEARCH OF LIGHT: THE BROADCASTS OF EDWARD R. MURROW Edward Bliss, Ed.	19372	1.95
INTERVIEWS WITH FILM DIRECTORS Andrew Sarris	21568	1.95
MOVIES FOR KIDS Edith Zornow and Ruth Goldstein	17012	1.65
PICTURE Lillian Ross	08839	1.25
THE LIVING THEATRE Pierre Biner	17640	1.65
PUBLIC DOMAIN Richard Schechner	12104	1.65
RADICAL THEATRE NOTEBOOK Arthur Sainer	22442	2.65
SOMETHING WONDERFUL RIGHT AWAY Jeffrey Sweet	37119	2.95

GENERAL NON-FICTION

ADDING A DIMENSION Isaac Asimov	36871	1.50
A TESTAMENT Frank Lloyd Wright	12039	1.65
AMBIGUOUS AFRICA Georges Balandier	25288	2.25
THE AMERICAN CHALLENGE J. J. Servan Schreiber	11965	1.65
AMERICA THE RAPED Gene Marine	09373	1.25
ARE YOU RUNNING WITH ME, JESUS? Malcolm Boyd	09993	1.25
THE AWAKENING OF INTELLIGENCE J. Krishnamurti	35923	2.75
THE BIOGRAPHY OF ALICE B. TOKLAS Linda Simon	39073	2.95
THE BOOK OF IMAGINARY BEINGS Jorge Luis Borges	11080	1.45
BUILDING THE EARTH Pierre de Chardin	08938	1.25
CHEYENNE AUTUMN Mari Sandoz	39255	2.25
THE CHILD IN THE FAMILY Maria Montessori	28118	1.50
THE CHILDREN'S REPUBLIC Edward Mobius	21337	1.50
CHINA: SCIENCE WALKS ON TWO LEGS Science for the People	20123	1.75
CLASSICS REVISITED Kenneth Rexroth	08920	1.25

(1) DDB 6-78

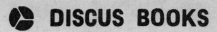

DISCUS BOOKS

DISTINGUISHED NON-FICTION

DISCUS BOOKS
DISTINGUISHED NON-FICTION